MW01244082

Hope you enjoy
This book.

Joe
- 2013 -

THE DAUGHTER ALSO RISES

THE DAUGHTER ALSO RISES

How Women Advance
in Family Business

ANNE E. FRANCIS, PH.D.

B&A BOOKS

B&A Books
2040 West 31st Street, Suite G #127
Lawrence, Kansas 66046-5164

2012 Revised Edition

ISBN 978-0-615-67934-1

Book and cover design by Matthew T. Stallbaumer

Printed in the United States of America

Contents

PART ONE:
THE FAMILY BEHIND THE FAMILY BUSINESS

PART THREE:
THE DAUGHTER ALSO RISES

Illustrations

Foreword

It is always surprising to read a book that so seriously and articulately questions the validity of the many cultural assumptions, myths, traditions, and practices that seem to underlie the structure of family-owned businesses in the United States. In *The Daughter Also Rises*, Anne Francis makes it clear that there are other ways to think about how a family business should be run, and about who is best qualified to run it. Leadership succession in a business, for example, may always have been decided by primogeniture, but the existence of such as tradition does not mean this is necessarily the best—or the only way today or in the future. Dr. Francis argues strongly that daughters of business owners are as capable as sons to be groomed as successors, and she backs this up with examples drawn from her years of consulting experience. With her keen insight, she challenges many traditional concepts, offers practical alternatives that have been ignored for too long, and forces us all to rethink our concern for the future of family businesses in new and exciting ways.

There is no question that leadership demands commitment from the best of us, and this is no time to limit participation to half of the population, especially when within this long-ignored half there are so many who are motivated, deeply committed, well educated, and well prepared. Dr. Francis is especially well qualified to speak to these issues. As a family therapist and business consultant with over thirty years of hands-on experience dealing with the most complex and intimate issues in the lives of business owners, their families, their managers, and their other professional advisors, she has truly "seen it all." Her insights can give us hope that the skills and dedication of all our children will be encouraged and accepted, hope that our sons and daughters can combine their gifts to the benefit of each other, and hope that the dream of America's business-owning families--that their company continue after them--will truly come to pass.

This book deserves to be read over and over.

Leon A. Danco, Ph.D.
Center for Family Business

Preface

I have a confession to make. I hadn't initially wanted to write *The Daughter Also Rises*. I thought it would take too much time away from my work. I worried that someone would publish another book, exactly like mine, at exactly the same time. I worried that my book wouldn't be received well. But mostly I worried about whether I had anything new to say. Hundreds of good, and some great, books about leadership and family-owned businesses already existed. As a business consultant and marital and family therapist, I had kept up on the professional literature, the ever-growing number of popular books on women and work, and trade books on family-owned businesses. I thought that perhaps enough already had been written about the subject. I am pleased to say that I was wrong. When *The Daughter Also Rises* was first published in 1999, both business families and professionals working with business families received it enthusiastically.

The world of business has changed since then. A 2007 survey indicated that nearly 60 percent of family-owned businesses now have women in management positions[1] and as many as 30 percent of family businesses will now consider a daughter for the top job, up from just 10 percent in the 1990s.[2] Today, some family businesses have taken the "no women allowed" sign down from their doors, and daughters are increasingly deciding to join their families' businesses. Family businesses appreciate their daughters more as a valuable and needed resource, and these women have a better chance of playing a key role in the continuity of the family business.

Yet most women are *not* headed for the CEO's office. The reasons for this are many, including the lack of formal and sequential training, time taken off for child-rearing, and primogeniture, the traditional practice of transferring leadership from father to first-born son. Fathers still expect a son to join the business but give a daughter a choice; fathers still consider a son the CEO-in-waiting while seeing a daughter as a mother-in-waiting.

Women continue to seek my counsel to learn how to get their father or uncle or whoever is in charge of the business to take them seriously, notice the contributions they make, and invest in their leadership potential. Skeptical fathers still challenge daughters who are fortunate enough to get noticed and demand that they, more so than sons, repeatedly demonstrate their intent and readiness for more responsibility in the family business.[3] Finally, the hostility of some workers who are reluctant to work under a female boss can present an obstacle for daughters.

While many obstacles confronting women in family businesses are the same today as ten years ago, scholars and consultants know more about how to overcome those obstacles. We know more about the opportunities and challenges that influence daughters' entrance into the business and contribute to their success or failure; more about the different pathways daughters take to positions of leadership; and more about the trademarks of families that successfully transition their business to the next generation.

The past decade has shed additional light on mothers' leadership role in preparing daughters to join the business. The mother, invisible as she may be in the actual running of the business, often is the one to impart the values of both the family and the family business to her children, a fact not surprising to me as a family business consultant.

Family businesses continue to need the underutilized talent that young women can bring, and this is great news for daughters who have the ability and the interest to do so. *The Daughter Also Rises* incorporates the most recent research about business families and the businesses they operate to help women — and the people they work with — achieve the success they want and be part of the team that makes the family business thrive.

The second edition of *The Daughter Also Rises* is a statement about where I am now in understanding the relationships, problems, and possibilities business families face. In *The Daughter Also Rises* you will meet Karen, who almost left a position she loved in the family business because she didn't recognize that the special relationship she shared with her father created a difficult problem between them at work. You will witness Harry, who knew his daughter was the better choice to succeed him but who felt obligated to hand the baton to his son because his father had handed it to him. You will read about Anita, who felt guilty for having opportunities her mother never had in the family business. You will meet Emily, who felt selfish for leaving her husband at home with their children while she traveled for work. You may identify with Helen, who downplayed her business savvy so as not to upstage her uncle. Perhaps some of their stories will resonate with issues you contend with today.

Gloria Steinem once said, "Perhaps we share stories in much the same spirit that explorers share maps, hoping to speed each other's journey, but knowing the journey we make will be our own." *The Daughter Also Rises* is a book of stories shared by women — and men — who work with members of their family. My goal is to speed you on your journey, knowing the journey you make will be your own.

THE DAUGHTER ALSO RISES

PART I

THE FAMILY BEHIND
THE FAMILY BUSINESS

CHAPTER ONE

Roadblocks to Women in Family Business

Organizations want quality people, well educated, well skilled and adaptable. They also want people who can juggle several tasks and assignments at one time, who are more interested in making things happen than in what title or office they hold, more concerned with power and influence than status. They want people who value instinct and intuition as well as analysis and rationality, who can be tough but also tender, focused but friendly, people who can cope with these necessary contradictions. They want, therefore, as many women as they can get.

— Charles Handy

Change of the kind that will allow you, as a family business daughter, to succeed in family business cannot happen without tremendous effort and determination by everyone who works and lives together. Family members, but especially you, must be willing to ask the difficult questions that are not being asked, articulate the problems no one wants to hear, design solutions for the problems everyone denies, and manage the change those solutions create.

Throughout this book, you will hear from women who are where you want to be and from others who are in places you want to avoid. In addition to daughters, you will hear from founding fathers, because in all but a small, albeit growing, number of cases, it is still men who start a family business, shape its culture, and determine its informal policies toward women. You will hear from mothers, who often are the silent partners in the business. You will meet siblings, friends, and spouses of women who grew up in business families. Their voices will teach you a great deal about the realities for women working in family enterprises and what you will need to succeed.

WOMEN AS THE UNDERUTILIZED RESOURCE

Family businesses *must* maximize all of the human resources available to them: women as well as men, daughters as well as sons. Family-business owners no longer can afford to select only the most qualified men available to lead their company because smart businesses know the most qualified man for the position may be a woman. Women not only bring whatever intellectual ability they possess to a business but also can contribute in ways that are different from those of their male counterparts. If you aspire to a career in your family's business, you cannot wait for time, good fortune, or someone else to make it happen. You must accept the responsibility to do whatever needs to be done to maximize your potential for success.

I remember a conversation with my mother shortly after my freshman year in college. My grades were nothing to brag about, and I had no idea what major I wanted to pursue as I continued my education. I knew I was supposed to be in college, but I wasn't sure why. My mother responded to my confusion with no uncertainty. "You need to stay at school," she said. "That's where you'll find the boys who are going to be someone." In that moment,

I realized what I think I had always suspected: In our culture at that time men must *be* somebody; women must *find* somebody. I wasn't in school to find a major and study for a career. I was in school to find a man who would provide a future for me.

A woman's attachment to a man or her ability to parent children no longer exclusively defines her. In 1999, an article appeared in the *New York Times*[1] that reflected the widespread acceptance of the change. It described the family-owned and operated company, Zildjian (pronounced zild-gin), the oldest, largest, and leading cymbal maker in the world. Ever since the business began in 1623, Zildjian father has passed the business to Zildjian son, generation after generation after generation. In 1999, a Zildjian father was about to pass leadership on again, but for the first time in almost four hundred years, the father passed it to a Zildjian daughter. The company named Craigie Zildjian, then forty-eight, as her father's successor. The Zildjian succession plan represented a dramatic bow to gender equality, particularly in family-owned businesses, which were notorious for excluding women from their executive ranks.

Given that less than one third of family businesses survive into a second generation, barely 10 percent succeed to a third generation, and only about 4 percent to a fourth, you can bet a family-owned business that had thrived for almost four centuries did not name a daughter as successor because the choice was politically correct. It was because Craigie Zildjian's selection was the right move for the business. Armand Zildjian, president and chairman of the board of the privately held company, explaining how he chose one of his four children to succeed him, said Craigie, "has been in the business longer than anyone. She has the most serious intent of anyone. She shows very good logic and she has very good business sense. You always pick the best. I am very satisfied with her."

Although the Zildjians and some other families put gender aside in selecting their business leaders, they are still the minority. The Zildjian family made the *New York Times* not because it represented the typical family business but because of its extraordinarily unusual succession plan. As of 2011, almost 15 years after Craigie was named CEO, she is the only female CEO of the 100 oldest family-run businesses in America.

HAND-ME-DOWN BELIEFS

Today's businesswomen are better trained and more experienced, and they wield greater influence and power than ever before. Many of them are attracted to smaller, family-held businesses that can offer greater flexibility and more leadership opportunities than larger, publicly held companies. It would seem that business families would do everything in their power to tap this talent. Why then are families still overlooking or discouraging women from joining the family business? Why did the *New York Times* recognize Craigie Zildjian as such an anomaly that she merited being the subject of an article? Why do families expect sons to work in the family business but give daughters a choice? Why do so many daughters who make it into the business feel that their families undermine their professional capabilities and ignore their contributions? Why do families pass over daughters as potential successors?

Personal and professional development starts early and often without a conscious plan. If, as a daughter, the family views you as a temporary employee — until you marry or have children — you will not receive the same development opportunities in the business as will your brothers. The family will not expect you to work in the business during summer and holiday breaks, will not include you in shop talk around the dinner table, and will not encourage you to get a business degree. As a result, half of the potential heirs to the family business—you and your sisters—will lose out on crucial early training. While the eventual reason for advancing your brother over you may be experience and readiness, the experience and readiness will have resulted from an unconscious gender bias that limited your access to important developmental experiences.

When I consult to a family business, I often find a daughter or a daughter-in-law in a position far below her capabilities. Likewise, I often talk with a mother who directly participates in the operations of the business but who essentially is invisible. Occasionally, this situation results from a woman's well-thought-out choice, but more often it reflects the unconscious gender biases of the family.

My friend, Nan, a college-degreed, full-time mother of three and one of three children who inherited money from the sale of her father's business, understands how this can happen.

"It never occurred to me," she told me. "I mean it never crossed my mind to think I might apprentice with my father or someday take over his nursery and garden business. Both my brothers used the business as their summer job. I never asked to work there nor was I ever invited. My brothers showed no interest in working with Dad after college, and they each went into different lines of work. Then my mother got sick. Dad couldn't take care of Mom and keep the business going, so he sold it. Again, he didn't ask me if I had an interest in it nor did it occur to me to consider it. Years later, my husband casually asked why I had not pursued a career in the family business. Only then did I consciously question my decision. That's how powerful the unconscious messages were in my family."

Just as family genes for hair color, height, body shape, or gender pass from one generation to the next, so do family beliefs and attitudes. Your family is no different. The stories that are passed down about such matters as money, loyalty, trust, and betrayal become intricately woven in the fiber of your family and eventually become the filter through which your family views the world. The attitudes become the reality by which your family judges other people, makes decisions, tolerates change, expresses feelings, and treats people within and outside of the family. What once were stories become the facts, the absolute Truths, of your family.

Every family's idiosyncratic beliefs at times nourish and at other times starve it in its quest for meaning, purpose, and survival. One family's story may revolve around pain and suffering, overcoming—or being overcome by—adversity; optimism and courage may characterize another family and its stories; fear and pessimism may mark yet another family. Before you read further, take a moment to think about the beliefs that most characterize your family.

I recall one successful business owner, Gus, who was convinced that his construction company was headed for failure. He wasn't sure when or how or why, but he couldn't shake a vague and ever-present feeling that the company was operating on borrowed time. His feeling persisted, even in the face of reality to the contrary.

No one at work knew of Gus's worry because he hadn't shared it with his wife or his father, who still worked part-time in the company's administrative office. I learned of his worry only because I was the consultant invited in to help with succession, and I had been asking questions both about the business and the family behind it. I learned that Gus descended from two generations of men who owned companies associated with construction. His grandfather had owned a brick factory and also a bricklaying business in the early 1900s. The business had generated a healthy profit, and the family had enjoyed financial and social status in their rural community. Then the Depression hit, and new construction stopped. Gus's grandfather had to close the bricklaying company and lost the factory because he couldn't pay the mortgage, but the family continued to live as if it had the financial means of the past. The children went to private schools, the parents vacationed in Europe, and the large dinner parties continued. Gus's grandfather never mentioned the family's financial hardships, and no one in the family asked where the money was coming from — until after the grandfather drowned in an apparent suicide.

A generation later, Gus's uncle, Simon, owned a cement company. It was successful for about fifteen years, then it closed. Gus didn't know much about what happened to the business except that his uncle "had a mid-life crisis," abandoned his family, and moved away with a young woman. Gus's father wouldn't talk about it.

Without realizing it, Gus had incorporated the family's belief in the destructive powers of success and money. With fifteen years of business success, he was waiting for calamity. Gus's family is not unlike each of our families. Over time, deeply ingrained beliefs, events both positive and negative, superstitions, and fears all combine to create the family story. Family legacies then become both the gifts and the burdens we pass on to unsuspecting future generations.

To help you think about your family stories and the roadblocks they construct for you in the family business, I have outlined four of the most common gender biased beliefs American families hold.

Belief One: Motherhood Is Womanhood

Despite the opportunities now available to women, many still see work as the second-best option to being a stay-at-home mom. It is socially acceptable and necessary for most women to hold jobs: Today, women represent almost 60% of the work force, they head 25 percent of households, and families increasingly depend on working wives' incomes to make ends meet.[2] Still, statistics don't alter the unconscious attitude that *ideally* women who are mothers shouldn't work. A recent study by Cambridge University found that increasing numbers of men *and* women believe moms' work comes at the expense of family life. In 1998, 51 percent of women and almost 46 percent of men believed family life would not suffer if a woman went to work. By 2002, this number had fallen to 46 percent and 42 percent respectively.[3] This isn't evidence of a full scale gender-role backlash, but certainly it represents growing sympathy for the view that a woman's place is in the home rather than the office.

The fact that women hold a greater number of bachelor's and master's degrees than men, hold political offices, run for President, and own eight million businesses in America still has not altered these beliefs. Many business owners who also are fathers sincerely believe their daughters cannot direct as effectively, analyze as decisively, or negotiate as definitively as their sons. They believe this regardless of its accuracy. One father and business owner explained it to me this way, "Nothing personal, Anne, but it's just not in a girl's genes." What the…? Was gender equality just a pipe dream?

Most women today think of motherhood as a relationship and a responsibility, rather than an all-encompassing identity, but many men, especially older fathers, still find it difficult to embrace a more expansive view of their daughter's potential, particularly as it pertains to the family business. For them, motherhood equals womanhood, and to think anything else denies a daughter her birthright. Unfortunately, this thinking keeps daughters out of the family business and leads many managers to assume it is not important to move women up the organizational ladder. They believe that women are ill-suited for management because their tenure is temporary and their advancement robs a man of a needed advancement.

And fathers are not alone in this belief. Daughters often don't think about joining their family's enterprise when considering their career options, and when they do, their reasons for joining support the belief that they see themselves as temporary employees: they want to help the family out; they are willing to fill a position no other family member wanted; they are dissatisfied with another job.[4]

The reality is that while some women may share common interests and face common enemies, it does not mean all women are the same. This is especially true as it pertains to having children. Some women find motherhood their primary source of fulfillment; others are not at all attracted to the role; still others want to experience motherhood and also want a career. Challenging hand-me-down beliefs about gender roles can prove daunting.

Ellen, a thirty-six-year-old employee of a family business, spoke with me about the frustration she felt while working for an owner who believed that men were workers and women were mothers. Ellen's boss wasn't literally her father, but he considered her the daughter he never had and treated her as such. This proved to be both an asset and a liability for Ellen.

"I've never been domestically inclined," Ellen told me. "I live with a man, but I'm not married because I see it as interfering with my career. I'm ambitious and competitive, and I love my work. My boss, George, knows this about me, and we've talked about it many times; but he still doesn't understand it. It just doesn't compute for him. Last week I scheduled a meeting with him to discuss my future with the company. I've worked for George for ten years; he knows I'd like to run the business some day, and I think we both know I'd be a damn good choice to succeed him. His one son is an owner, but he is more your academic type and has nothing to do with operations. When I raised the subject of succession with George, the first thing he said was that he knew I'd be ready to take over in a few years. The second thing he said, which shouldn't have surprised me but absolutely did, was that he didn't want me burdened with the business. Burdened? Who is he kidding? I know he means well, but with his kind of protectiveness I'm going to be back on the street looking for a job, and he's going to be without a successor."

Ellen's struggle emphasizes the powerful force the unconscious exercises in decision-making situations. If you are not respectful of this dynamic, it will be difficult for you to understand how and why those who promote others in a family business make their choices, and what you can do to alter the decision-making process. Promotions to mid- and upper-management positions are inherently subjective, and they come within the context of complex relationship and interdependent tasks.

Everyone holds limiting assumptions about the world, the motivation of others, and self-understanding. Freud called them defenses; friends call them blind spots. Most people don't recognize these assumptions without assistance from others—perhaps a spouse or sibling, a friend, counselor, or advisor—yet they infrequently ask for help in clarifying those assumptions, instead resting content with the known truths. Remember this in dealing with your father, husband, sister, brother, mother, or boss.

Ellen needed to understand the beliefs about women that prompted George to protect her, even while those same beliefs built a roadblock to her advancement. He thought that women should have to work only until a man was supporting her, and he didn't want to prevent Ellen from having the marriage, home, and children he believed she really wanted. During conversations with George, Ellen's defensiveness had invited further protectiveness. His world didn't include a place for women driven by their ambitions and achievements, for whom motherhood did not fulfill all their desires. Ellen was an oddity in George's world, but he respected her, and he appreciated what she brought to the family business. Ellen knew this and heeded my advice not to despair, not to quit, and to keep having conversations with George about work and her ambitions.

I advised George that he needed to make his decision about succession based on ability rather than gender. We talked for hours about the family he grew up in and the values he held. As George grew in his self-understanding, he better understood how his truths negatively affected his decision-making. Over many months, both Ellen and George came to accept different truths about each other. George realized that Ellen could not be the daughter he had in his head, but she could be the best person to succeed him. Ellen realized that while George would never understand her lifestyle choices, he respected her work, and he was capable of separating the two.

Belief Two: You Can Have It All

Even today, a primary reason most successful male family-business owners appear to have it all—a business, a marriage, and a family—is that they have a wife at home who takes care of everything *but* their work. By many standards, these men have attained the American dream. But they often pay an enormous price for their success in terms of not knowing their children, not being part of the everyday life of their family, not having time for their marriage, and not getting to enjoy the things their success brings. By the time they realize what they have lost, it is too late to recapture it.

Some who argue that you can have it all use corporate businessmen and successful family-business entrepreneurs as examples. Men in high-powered careers point to the fact that no special privileges or policies allow them to succeed at work and have good home lives. The difference between men and women at work, they maintain, is that men accept that business is incompatible with attendance at every school assembly, basketball game, and piano recital. This argument appears solid enough, but it is flawed by its dependence on the assumption that someone else is around who *will* attend the assemblies, bus the children to lessons, and sit through recitals. The someone who most often is responsible for these things is the woman pictured in the frame on the businessman's desk—his wife. Even though having it all is unrealistic, many young men still believe it an entitlement, and they are disappointed when their marriage and lifestyle fail to live up to their image of the American Dream. Some of these men leave their marriage for a woman willing to take on a more traditional role that allows him to have it all.

Historically, society did not entitle women to have it all, but as they gained more rights and education, they began to think they were entitled to have it all. This is where the problem got complicated for women. The strength of gender roles is impressive and fights against women having both a family and career. Giving is the chief activity that has defined femininity: giving to children, and parents, and friends, and a husband. While women may *think* they are entitled to have a family and a career, they don't always *feel* entitled to both. They often feel selfish and unfeminine for wanting a career, fearing a career will interfere with their primary role of caretaker.

In many business families, the belief that one can have it all translates into the following two messages for their children: sons can work *and* have a family; daughters can work *or* have a family. No parent (or very few of them) would be concerned about how a son plans to juggle the responsibilities of business and family; very few parents would *not* be concerned about how their daughter would do this. Gender stereotypes exist, and family firms are not immune to such discriminations. If you are highly ambitious and aspire one day to follow your father as CEO, for example, but your family believes that your foremost responsibility is to satisfy the needs of your family, then you have little chance of satisfying your career ambition.

The strength of traditional gender roles is what eventually led to the Superwoman complex. Women, recognizing that people might call their ambitions as well as their femininity into question if they did not fulfill their primary role responsibility—caretaking—came up with what seemed like a perfect solution. They could have it all if they could *do* it all, and Superwoman was born. Suffice it to say that the Superwoman solution had many flaws. No man or woman can do it all, and women needed to find a more reasonable solution. A more reasonable solution, however, meant that men and women would have to work together to find a solution, and rigid gender roles would have to change.

Today, some women and men are addressing the immensely complicated problem of balancing work and family, and together they are finding workable solutions. But stereotyping still makes it difficult for daughters—and sometimes sons—to find their own best version of having it all. Consider Sandra, an ambitious woman who was working her way to the top of her family's furniture-making business. She was on track to be the next CEO, succeeding her uncle, who had run the business with Sandra's father until he retired early for health reasons. Sandra was married to Pat, a college professor who was working toward tenure, and they had two young children.

Sandra came to see me because she wanted advice on how to tell her uncle she had decided to stop working and stay at home. I couldn't have been more surprised. I had known the family for years, had helped them craft a shareholders agreement, and set up a family council. Sandra was both capable and ambitious and had seemed the most likely next CEO.

My first question was the most obvious: why? Sandra explained that neither she nor Pat was home enough, and that if she left work "at least the kids grow up knowing one of their parents." With further questioning I learned that Sandra had made the decision unilaterally and presented it to Pat. He was surprised but agreed that it would make life simpler, and he supported her decision.

Sandra had solved a problem, but I was concerned she might be creating some even bigger ones. She loved her work: would she miss it? Would she resent Pat for his getting to continue his work? Would the business suffer as a result of her absence? I suggested that she might have acted too swiftly in trying to solve a complicated problem with a simple solution. She didn't disagree and acknowledged that she hadn't talked to her uncle because she really didn't want to leave the business, but she couldn't think of an alternative.

I met with Sandra and Pat together and suggested they approach the problem differently. Instead of thinking that some *one* had to stay home, I instructed them to think of ways they both could change so the kids had more time with each of them and neither had to give up their career. Pat thought it was a great idea and sheepishly admitted he had gone along with Sandra's plan because, "I didn't want to quit, and I thought it was either

her or me." Since Sandra had made her decision, Pat had been feeling guilty about protecting his self-interest, which was making his work less enjoyable.

Over the course of several months Sandra and Pat crafted a plan. She worked out an arrangement with her uncle that allowed her to be out of the office on Fridays. As a college professor, Pat had more flexibility than Sandra. He rearranged his office hours so he had two half-days a week at home during the school year and two full days a week during the summer. Blocks of time with the kids made each of them feel more connected to them in a consistent way.

Reality is that men *and* women who are parents and have careers can only have it all if they are both pitching in. It's called collaboration. Sandra and Pat found a way to make it work, but only after they worked *together* on finding a solution that would work for *both* of them.

Belief Three: Women Are Not Technically Minded

I belong to a generation of women raised to believe that only boys could master math. The first time a girl outscored a boy on a math test was cute; the second time she was labeled an egghead. The girl who didn't fit her prescribed role made everyone uncomfortable.

Calling a smart girl an egghead is no longer politically correct, but the belief that they can't think technically, or even on their own remains fixed in the unconscious of many families and persists in the cultures of the businesses they own. A family business that operates on the assumption that women don't do technical tasks runs the risk of overlooking women for positions for which they are well-qualified, keeping women in positions for which they are overqualified, advancing men who are less-qualified, and recruiting with a bias against women.

Belief Four: Society Needs Women at Home

Many men and women today believe that the problems children in our nation face are a function of women's absence from the home. Delinquency, drug use, poor scholastic performance, and teen pregnancy have all risen in the past few decades thanks to a number of interrelated sociological, psychological, and economic causes. American culture is becoming increasingly polarized between rich and poor, educated and illiterate, upwardly mobile and minimally employable. In an effort to simplify the complex problems families face, society seems to target working women as the source of their children's problems.

Solving the work and family dilemma requires new ways of thinking and new behavior by all of us, and still solutions will be difficult to achieve. A client recently told me a chilling story about a senior management meeting he attended. One vice president was unable to attend because he was picking up his sick child from school. Unfortunately, the CEO needed information from him about a merchandise distribution issue. The CEO could have called the vice president on his car phone or at home, but instead he expressed a deep-seated prejudice. He questioned the vice president's virility and his commitment to his career, and he criticized the vice president's wife for not being more available to her children (no matter that the children belonged to both of them or that she was out of state on a business trip). The CEO ended his tantrum by making it absolutely clear that men who left the office to care for their children or for any other reason having to do with family risked their advancement.

If you want to learn more about the family history that may block your entrance into the family business or stall your advancement, take the time to answer the set of questions titled "Underlying Rules in Your Family." You will find similar question sets throughout the first six chapters of this book. Each set

Underlying Rules in Your Family

Answer the following questions, perhaps in concert with other family members, and then discuss your answers.

1. What are the basic rules in your family? (Examples might be never trust money to a woman; children should be seen and not heard; some are created more equal than others; a man is the king of his castle; knock on wood because only luck will save you.)

2. What stories do family members repeat at family gatherings, reunions, funerals, or weddings? What can you figure out from the stories about your family's underlying beliefs?

3. What secrets surround your family? How does the family maintain those secrets? How does it pass them along?

4. What stories does the family have about the family business? What legacies endure about success? Failure? Betrayal? Money? The founder's character?

5. Who gets the credit or blame for the success or failure of the business? Why?

6. Which members does the family allow in the business? Whom does it exclude? What rationale justifies those decisions?

7. Are the rules in your family the same for women and men? In the business? How does the family convey the rules? Has anyone in the family ever broken the rules? What happened?

8. How do family members express their interest in the business? Does the family expect some but not others to be part of the business? How does the family convey these expectations?

THE DAUGHTER ALSO RISES

prompts you to explore how the ideas in the text exist in your life or in your family-business situation. If you spend some time contemplating your answers and the ideas and emotions they generate, you will stimulate your thinking about your role—or potential role—in the family business and identify some topics to pursue in conversations with family members and others.

The Road to Change

As I said at the outset of this chapter, if you want change of the kind that will allow your greatest success in the family business, the change has to begin with you. It is normal to want things to change without having to do anything different. It is normal to want others to make changes before you do. It is normal *and* it doesn't work. If you're like me and most people, when you complain about a relationship, you usually know exactly what the other person needs to change, but you probably know little about what you need to change.

If you want a relationship to change, the first step is to take responsibility for your contribution to the problem. If you blame your overly demanding, guilt-inducing mother for causing your anger and guilt, you will feel helpless because you cannot change her. But if you identify the problem as yours—your inability to clarify limits with your mother—you now have the power to make a change.

To say that you have a problem does not imply that you are wrong or at fault. It has nothing to do with culpability. It simply means that you are the one most troubled by a particular situation and that you are the one most interested in changing it.

I designed *The Daughter Also Rises* to be useful and practical, but be forewarned that it does not lay out rules for the one best way to live and work with your family. My goal is to give you a deeper understanding about yourself, your family, your family's business, and, should you choose, how to combine the two. When you have finished reading this book, you will know what you contribute to the problems, the possibilities, and the successes you are experiencing in your family and in the business it operates, and you will know what you need to change for things to be different.

This book will be most useful if you read it all. Do not skip the chapter on joining the family business because you already work there. By reading it you will learn what you and your family did well, and perhaps not so well, to prepare you for working in or advancing in the business; you will gain insight into missteps you've taken; you will find out how good the match is between you and the business. Each chapter contains information relevant to you and your relationship to your family and the family business.

Having read and completed the set of questions in this chapter, you understand the roadblocks that can derail your success in the family business. The next step is to examine the individual personality of the founder as well as the family behind the founder, for in their characters lie the heart and soul of the business.

CHAPTER TWO

Daughters and Their Entrepreneur Fathers

It doesn't matter who my father was; it matters who I remember he was.

—*Anne Sexton*

We must understand the nature of an entrepreneur to address adequately the unique problems facing daughters who work in a family business. Organizations reflect their leaders, and only by knowing the founder can we understand the company culture, clarify the family myths that permeate it, identify the values that influence policy-making, and appreciate why and how decisions are made. Who is the entrepreneur? What prompted him to start a business? How does he think? Is he as self-confident as he appears? How does he make decisions? These are the kinds of questions any employee might ask.

Most likely, your father or grandfather founded your family's business. Those who are relatives of the founder, especially children, will consider more personal questions about him as well. Why does he seem so distant emotionally? Does he run the business or does it run him? What does he worry about? Why does he have trouble relying on me? Why is it difficult to talk with him? Why does he seem so driven?

Certainly, not all entrepreneurial men are the same in personality or disposition. At this point, however, a study of the general characteristics that describe this kind of man provides a starting place toward understanding the person who founded the family business. Enough similarities exist to warrant some generalizations. My intention is to offer a profile of entrepreneurial men that can serve as the backdrop for a critical review of the father-daughter relationship as well as the special challenges and opportunities that await daughters and entrepreneur fathers who work together.

On the following pages, you may run into your father or your grandfather. You, your mother, or your brother may appear in some of the examples. You may at times think I've peeked into your house and recorded some of your family conversations. I haven't, of course, but I have spent hundreds of hours talking to family-business executives and their families. From them I have learned about the kind of person who turns an entrepreneurial dream into a reality, and creates both opportunities and challenges for his children. With this in mind let's begin our journey into the mind and world of the entrepreneur.

THE MAN BEHIND THE ENTREPRENEUR

A man who becomes an entrepreneur is the world's best example of an individualist. He is what he is in part because of his self-reliance and his need to be in charge. He does not easily work with or for others. In fact, most successful entrepreneurs cite rugged self-reliance and singleness of purpose as the characteristics that enabled them to survive the early days of the business. I may be describing the man who founded your family's business.

Like most dreamers, the entrepreneur is a visionary. He sees something he thinks he can do and hopes he can make money at, and he pursues it with passion. A vision and a healthy dose of unfounded self-confidence often carry the entrepreneur through the turbulent early years of the business, when only he and perhaps his wife believe in his dream. There's no room for doubt when he has committed everything—money, time, security—to the dream of a successful business. Only later, after he succeeds, might he be able to admit the uncertainty that accompanied his dream. As Leon Danco suggested, "Genius, especially in the case of the entrepreneur, is 90 percent dumb luck or accident."[1]

Assets And Liabilities

Everyone goes through life with a mixed bag of personality assets and liabilities, and how individuals view these can differ widely. How a person uses or exploits personal assets and hides or overcomes liabilities shapes character. Let's examine some of the more common assets and liabilities.

Self-Reliance

The very characteristics that contribute to successful entrepreneurship can also limit a man's ability to work with and have relationships with others. An overabundance of self-reliance, for example, can make it difficult for him to use advisors, either the professional or the family type. Having to ask for advice or needing to share a worry seems to be a weakness, so he keeps his anxieties to himself. He mistakenly believes self-reliance is only an asset, not also a liability. The success of the business, he tells himself, is proof enough that his way is the right way. After all, over one third of family-owned businesses fail in the first generation—and his hasn't. Why should he depend on others or change his way of operating? Why should he risk doing things differently when his way works? Why should he open himself up to other people's criticism by revealing some of his insecurities?

It's not that the tenaciously self-reliant man doesn't have feelings; he has plenty. But in his pursuit of self-sufficiency, he never learned how to identify and express those feelings. Perhaps he didn't avail himself of opportunities to talk about them with others. Maybe he was always too busy to think about his feelings, or thinking about them made him feel uncomfortable. However, keeping such things close to the chest eventually prevents him from getting what he really may need — someone to talk to, someone to support him, someone who can appreciate his victories and understand the nature of his fears. As one fifty-something man poignantly explained during a seminar I ran for executives and their spouses, "My wife accuses me of refusing to share my feelings with her. It's not that. I want to talk to her about things more now than ever in my life. But I can't share what I don't know. I have to know my feelings before I can give them away. That's why I'm here." I'll never forget this man's honesty or his candid plea for help. The CEO of a multimillion-dollar company, he summoned considerable courage to admit this in the presence of peers.

Contrary to what many women think, biology does not wire men to be relationship Neanderthals, but social mores certainly discourage men from learning the art of relationships. Our culture gives little praise to men who pay attention to relationships or who value time with their family at the expense of staying at the office to close one more deal.

The unfortunate truth is that fame and glory do not often come to men who are unwilling to sacrifice a personal life for professional advancement and financial gain. Striking a balance between work and family is never easy, but entrepreneurial men are especially ill-suited to the task. Their self-reliance makes it particularly difficult for them to maintain connections to those they most love and need. Family life, after all, has little to do with personal accomplishment and much to do with being involved in other people's lives.

The entrepreneur's wife is usually his most loyal ally, yet too often his unrealistic expectations of himself, his lack of experience expressing feelings, and his fear of her response keep him from talking with her about his doubts or his worries. Although it may be on his mind, he won't tell his wife that the demands of the industry frighten him, or that he doesn't know how much longer the business can succeed, or that he is lonely. Take a minute and reflect about whether this may describe the relationship your father has with your mother.

He likely is lonely, however, trapped in a self-defined role that the culture also encourages. He cannot ask aloud, "What will I be able to do if the business fails? Will my wife still love me if I'm not able to provide the same lifestyle next year?" He convinces himself that his silence protects his wife from worry, when in fact it prevents him from sharing an intimacy with her. And he is avoiding the feelings he has run from his whole life—dependency, loneliness, sadness, doubt.

Every adult, male and female, needs to possess self-reliance, but when a person practices reliance on self to the exclusion of reliance on others, it becomes problematic. Everyone needs other people, and the ability to form attachments is a sign of emotional health. The entrepreneur who insists on total self-reliance will find it difficult not only to enjoy intimacy with his spouse but also to develop meaningful friendships with other men and women. Close relationships demand a certain amount of self-disclosure, trust, and dependence, all of which are unfamiliar to the defensively self-reliant man.

The overly self-reliant man defensively shuns other people's attempts to be close, and in doing so he may avoid the discomfort in being vulnerable, but he also denies himself the intimacy that relationships offer. He never experiences the relief of saying, "I need help," "I don't know," or "I can't solve this problem," and knowing someone is there and wants to help.

It is easier for the overly self-reliant man to think that his wife "just won't understand" than it is to risk rejection should he articulate his insecurities to her. It is easier to refuse her support than for him to acknowledge his need for it. The loneliness that his wall of secrecy creates for him may be painful at times, but it is familiar, and far less threatening to him than acknowledging the need for companionship. He is unsure he can achieve intimacy, and he doesn't want to risk failure. Fear of failure and relationship inexperience lie at the heart of the emotional distancing act this type of man performs with his wife, yet he does it with such skill that he convinces both of them that he doesn't want what he probably most needs.

Within the business itself, too much self-reliance may prevent this same man from hiring and promoting others. He is convinced that no one can ever know the business as well as he, and no one can be trusted with his business. At the least, this attitude will prevent him from expanding the business beyond what he can absolutely control. The business will die with him because he will have no one who can take over. If he has children, his need for control will prevent him from adequately preparing them to run the business or from appointing a successor early enough to ensure a smooth transition when it is time for him to retire.

Self-Confidence

Self-confidence is a huge asset that contributes to the initial success of an entrepreneur's business, but it can be a crippling disadvantage when it prevents him from noticing the world beyond himself. Overabundant self-confidence will interfere with the entrepreneur's ability to acknowledge other important variables that made him successful, including such things as good fortune, timing, and sheer luck. He may dismiss important market shifts because he thinks his business is immune to them. Convinced that his formula for success is the right formula, he may postpone needed changes—until it is too late. Once a business is behind the market trend, instead of in front of it, catching up is very difficult, even for the very self-confident.

The overly self-confident entrepreneur may convince himself that he always knew things would work out because he had the right formula. Confidently thinking his way is always the best way, he may not learn from others' successes and failures, he may be unable to acknowledge his mistakes, or implement needed changes.

Persistence

An entrepreneur is persistent in part because he has chosen what to be persistent about. He selected the dream to pursue, and since it is his alone, he can persist long after others have given up. I have never known a successful entrepreneur who was not persistent, even obstinate, but I have met plenty who didn't know when to surrender. Persistence is an asset, but it becomes a liability when it forces the entrepreneur to stay with an idea or project well beyond its usefulness; when it turns useful criticism into relentless criticism; when resolve morphs into obstinate control.

An entrepreneur who also is a father may fail in his effort to create in his children the same passion he has for the business. He will try too hard, and his persistence will drive his children away from, rather than toward, the business. He forgets that he cannot make his dream their dream any more than someone could have forced their dream onto him thirty years earlier.

Paola Barilla, whose grandfather founded the European pasta empire Barilla, S.P.A., once described his father as a man who understood that dreams had to develop over time. "My father always believed that whatever comes naturally and is not forced puts down the deepest roots. He wanted us to develop a kind of affection for the business. His fear was that if he pushed us and pushed us, in the end we'd reject it."[2] Paola Barilla's father was justified in his fear. The entrepreneur who is stubbornly persistent about his children being part of the family business runs a high risk of alienating them from it.

The founder of a business feels great pride in his creation and experiences it as an extension of himself. If his children do not share his same passion, he may experience it as a rejection of him rather than as an expression of their individuality. This can make it difficult for his children to pursue their own dreams or to even express their dreams, for fear of upsetting the father they love.

Paternalism

A man who is an entrepreneur tends to have a paternalistic outlook on life. For him, the financial rewards of his hard work are the means by which he cares for both his employees and his family. He bestows father-like benevolence to both; in return, he expects childlike appreciation from both, most particularly his family. As the patriarch, he also assumes that he is in charge. He may listen to those dependent on him, but in the end he has the final word in all important matters.

Paternalism is not inherently negative, but the entrepreneur who is overly paternalistic may run into problems, especially in his personal life. For example, he may make decisions that affect his family without first consulting them because "I know what is best." Unfortunately, others in the family might not always agree with him.

One such family-business owner confided to me his anger and disappointment when his wife and teenage son declined his surprise invitation for a weekend in Chicago. He had found some precious free time in his schedule and wanted to spend it with them, and they had rejected his generosity. He failed to see the controlling context of his offer. He had assumed that when he was free his family would make themselves free. He had expected them to drop what they were doing and leave with him the next day, but his son had a school activity to attend, and his wife had agreed to take an elderly neighbor to a doctor's appointment. He had failed to consider their needs and their schedules but nonetheless, their rejection hurt.

This business owner did not intend to be selfish — he thought he was being generous — but he was used to others accommodating his needs. He assumed his family ran like his business where he was in charge, he made the decisions, and they carried out his decisions. In return for their loyalty, he would reward them with a generous gift. But a business is not the same as a marriage or a family, and in this family, power and control were out of balance. Too much control by one family member inevitably breeds defiance by other family members. Spouses must share power in order to respect and trust each other, and while children need to know that parents are in charge, they also must know that decisions consider their needs.

An entrepreneur's paternalistic character may impede his ability to view his children — even as adults — as potential, capable employees who can add value to the business. He may find it especially difficult to view his grown daughter — his little girl — as an asset to the business. If he allows her to work in the business, she may not get the necessary training to be successful; he may find it impossible to think of her as a leader in the business. He may be unable to take criticism from her or consider that she might teach him something. At worst, he may experience her competence as a threat to their relationship—she no longer needs him—and unintentionally encourage her failure, preferring instead to keep her dependent on him.

Dangerous Combinations

Too much of an asset will inevitably turn it into a liability. Exaggerated dose of self-confidence, paternalism, and persistence, for example, can combine to produce an entrepreneur who is intolerant of others' failures to live up to his expectations, however unrealistic those expectations may be. This intolerance for error, both in himself and in others, prevents him from being able to question his decisions, ask for feedback from others, or seek counsel from those he works with. At home, it prevents him from asking for support, talking over issues with his wife, admitting his mistakes, or saying "I'm sorry."

This same combination of overdeveloped characteristics can produce a father who gives the impression that he is the best authority on any given subject and who seems immune to arguments that do not support his conclusions. This attitude can devastate his children. His need to be right and to be the best and the smartest will prevent his children from developing the capacity to think for themselves; at the worst, it will leave them with a crippling dependency on him. Even though every asset is its own liability, most liabilities can also turn into assets. Unless you understand the man behind the entrepreneur, keeping in mind that men who become entrepreneurs are not supermen, you won't understand the complicated relationships between him and other family members, particularly those who work with him in the family business; you won't appreciate the problems inherent in combining family and business relationships; and you won't be able to formulate solutions to the problems.

ENTREPRENEURS AS FATHERS

One night when I was ten, the doorbell rang and my mother answered it. The man at the door pushed her aside and said, "I know your husband isn't here, lady, so just give me whatever money is in the house and your kids won't get hurt." My father—a tall, fairly large man—was at home, but that particular day he had switched cars with my grandfather and his car wasn't in the driveway. Upon hearing the threats, my father rose and slowly walked to the door, gently nudged my mother aside and, in a soft voice, said to the man, "Get the hell out of here and *you* won't get hurt." Startled, the man ran from the house. To this day, I remember how proud I felt of my father. He was my hero, someone who would protect me from danger.

Daughters frequently see their fathers as heroes they idealize and adore. My own father, for example, delighted me with his antics and could humor me out of almost any bad mood. He could turn a swim in a creek into a magical adventure. Suddenly I'd be surrounded by the sound and touch of tropical fish, giant waves, and a sea monster that he would tame before my very eyes. I would giggle as my father rescued me from the underworld demons and dream of the day I would marry a man like him.

My father, like most fathers of his time, was strong, silent, and distant, and he expected my mother to handle the parenting while he concentrated on work. He was often gone, trying to make a success of his business and to meet the financial demands of a family of nine. He left early in the morning and came home for a late dinner and a quick play with his children before bedtime. Then he went back to work. I knew my father as the holiday, the Sunday afternoon, the break from Mom, the bedtime storyteller.

The very qualities that made my father my hero—his strength, his size, his silence, and perhaps especially his absence—also kept me from knowing him as a person. His absence was natural, and his presence conspicuous. In the absence of an involved relationship with him, my father fascinated and intimidated me.

Distance Manages Discomfort

Men in general, and in particular the men who become entrepreneurs, tend to manage stress and intense feelings by denying the discomfort of their feelings. They provide well for their family financially, but they wall themselves off from the emotional aspects of family life. They do not necessarily love their wife or children less than other men, but they are unable to connect to their family emotionally. Accustomed to being viewed as a hero of sorts, these men avoid situations where they might disappoint someone. They spend most of their time in the world of work, where they feel in control and accomplished. Work is familiar and has clear expectations and goals; at work, success is measurable. An emotionally distant father behaves in ways that others mistakenly interpret as his preference. Since he seldom discusses his feelings, others learn not to discuss feelings with him; they do not inquire about his worries, for example, even when it is evident he is worried about something. While this behavior may have its base in others' respect for his privacy, the entrepreneur interprets this failure to ask about him as indifference, and he distances himself further, thinking that others don't really care about him. In his mind, their deference is evidence that he can rely only on himself, which reinforces the negative feedback loop.

Cheryl and David

Let me tell you a story about Cheryl and her father, David. When he was in his early thirties, David started a machinery repair business. It did well and today is very successful. Cheryl, now a thirty-year-old woman, is the accountant for the business; David is still the boss. One of his outside directors, with whom I had worked over the past decade, referred David to me.

David is a man's man. He is tall, athletic, intense, and well-spoken. He is not the kind of man who seeks advice from others easily, but he wanted help in responding to his daughter's criticism that he is "cold, deprecating, and impossible to talk with." David respects the man who referred him, so by default he respected me. Cheryl was angry with David following a monthly planning meeting where he criticized her work. This was the third time in the past year David had criticized Cheryl in public without initially or subsequently addressing his concerns directly to her. This time she confronted him, accusing him of discounting her use of a consultant to upgrade the company's financial planning procedures. According to David, "All I said was that the company didn't need some egghead to tell us how to do our work." David didn't understand what the "big toot" was all about, and he also didn't remember most of what he had said in the meeting. He didn't remember, as I learned later, that he had said that Cheryl ran to outsiders whenever she had a problem instead of using internal resources.

After the meeting, Cheryl told David that he had humiliated her and that his insults were inappropriate and uncalled for. David reacted with puzzlement and asked what she meant. She explained that since he had never directly addressed his concern to her, she assumed his silence was approval for her use of consultants. His public criticism shocked her, and she was angry that he made her look incompetent. He said he didn't understand how it made any difference whether he criticized her use of consultants in a group meeting or to her alone because the issue was the same. She disagreed with him, and he disagreed with her.

This confrontation did not occur in a vacuum or without an historical context; in fact, it repeated a longstanding pattern of David's. He had grown up with parents who fought incessantly, and often he had been the target of their anger. Over time he learned to avoid disagreements as a way to avoid criticism. This was wishful thinking, of course, as we all know that disagreements are impossible to avoid when you live and work with other people. But by adulthood David's avoidant behavior was ingrained; he criticized employees only in meetings because he knew they were unlikely to respond. At home he criticized his wife only when the kids were around and he knew she wouldn't return his criticism.

I met with David and Cheryl over the course of a few months. The first step was to help them both understand how David used coldness and distance to protect himself. The next step was to help them communicate more productively. They loved each other, there was no question about that, and each of them wanted to have a better relationship. David was able to tell Cheryl that he never wanted her angry at him but realized his wish was unrealistic, and he now knew that his way of avoiding her anger only made her angrier at him. Cheryl admitted that storming away in a huff was also unproductive.

At my urging, they agreed to meet weekly, in private, and air disagreements. In the beginning I was part of these meetings. They learned how to ask clarifying questions and how to articulate a disagreement respectfully. David learned to be less critical and to take criticism from Cheryl without being devastated by it; Cheryl learned to listen more objectively to David' criticisms and to keep him up to date with what she was doing rather than avoiding him. They began to work together more collaboratively and to disagree more constructively. As a result of their hard work, they were better able to resolve important business issues.

FATHERS AND SONS

Although this book is about women working in family businesses, a brief mention of the father-son relationship will provide a sense of contrast that will highlight the uniqueness of the father-daughter relationship.

At a very young age, many boys get a strong message to "be a man." Others criticize them if they cry out of sadness or fear or call them a baby if they crawl into their mother's lap for a hug or want their father to kiss them. People think it sweet when a little girl runs to her mother in joy after a long day at school, but they think it is sissiness when a little boy does it. People often refer to a school-aged boy as "a little man."

A trend today promotes a more balanced upbringing of children, and I know parents who nurture their boys to explore and express their feelings. These families are in the minority, however, and the more traditional a family is, the less likely the family will encourage the boys to acknowledge their feelings. Learning how to be independent is important, but knowing how to trust and depend on others is equally important for healthy adult development. An overemphasis on self-reliance can make it impossible for boys to satisfy their need to be nurtured or to recognize their feelings. Little boys brought up as little men don't understand why it is inappropriate to need a hug or ask for help or be frightened, but they understand that others expect the absence of these needs. They learn early to identify with the prescribed role for men and bond with their fathers within this context.

Every father was once a son struggling to establish his masculinity. To be a man is to be independent and able to influence others, so many conflicts between fathers and sons arise, unsurprisingly, around issues of power and control. The need to be in charge can make communication and trust between fathers and sons difficult. A conversation can generate competition; a suggestion can feel like a personal attack; a criticism can lead to verbal combat.

When fathers and sons also work together, the tension between them is often exaggerated. The father who founded the business wants it to continue and wants no one to undermine his hard-won achievements. He wants others to acknowledge his expertise and put it to good use. The son who is to succeed his father also has a strong need to have his contributions acknowledged; he wants to be respected for himself, not just as "Junior" to the old man's "Senior."

Such competitive striving between fathers and sons who work together can make good succession planning very difficult. The father may assume his son will take over for him some day but also resist any discussion of a succession plan. He simply can't face his own mortality and the eventual loss of his position. Unfortunately for father and son and the business, the lack of good succession planning may prevent the son from succeeding, in part because he will be ill-prepared when he finally takes charge.[3]

Fathers and sons know each other in ways that only men can appreciate, and this familiarity also breeds a special kinship. Men know how men think and how they are supposed to act. They understand that manhood may include painful obligations and emotional isolation, but few talk about or question it. As a result, many fathers and sons commit themselves to an unspoken agreement that, as men, they can be together but not acknowledge their closeness.

FATHERS AND DAUGHTERS

What is it about the father-daughter relationship that makes it unique and so different from the father-son relationship? Daughters are as unfamiliar to fathers as sons are familiar. Daughters are mysterious, unpredictable. Fathers perceive them as living in the domain of emotions and feelings, yet the very qualities that distinguish femininity from masculinity—attentiveness, sensitivity, comfort in relationships, cooperation—often bring fathers and daughters together.

Most fathers spend more time in activities with their sons, but many report feeling more comfortable and less competitive with their daughters. My husband, the father of three daughters, understands this feeling of comfort. Raised with an older sister, a mother who stayed at home, a father who was quiet and emotionally distant, and two elderly, childless aunts who doted on him, he grew up in a world of women. For him, having only daughters recreated his early history of being the only and adored man in the household. With daughters he could teach, encourage, and rejoice in their successes without having to confront the various ambivalent feelings that plague the father-son relationship. He did not have to experience the mixture of admiration, competitiveness, and envy fathers feel with their sons' achievements. He did not have to be reminded, through a son's accomplishments, of the opportunities he missed, the mistakes he made, the failures he created.

If men have been socialized to compete with other men, women have been socialized to accept authority from men, especially from their father, the head of the household. Excess obedience can be dangerous, but comfort with authority has many advantages, particularly for an adult daughter working with her father in the family business. An excellent working relationship can develop when the daughter is willing to listen and learn from her father rather than compete with him, when she respects his concern about losing control of the business, and when she is willing to wait her turn to run the business rather than grab for it prematurely.

Competitiveness between fathers and sons often results in their establishing separate domains within a family business, while daughters more often enjoy working alongside their father and seem to have less need than sons to force their father out of the business. In fact, many a daughter wants her father around in some capacity long after he has stepped down, not because she feels inadequate to run the business but simply because she enjoys having him around.

The Dark Side of the Father-Daughter Relationship

The father-daughter relationship is far from problem-free. Where a father may cherish closeness with his infant daughter and relish flirtations from her when she is young, he rarely feels comfortable around her when she reaches adolescence. When daughters enter preadolescence, fathers tend to move away, both physically and emotionally. They give their daughters fewer hugs and kisses, they spend less time with them, and they avoid situations requiring relationship talk.

It is not unusual for a woman to tell me that she and her dad were close—and then they weren't. She can't explain exactly how or when it happened, and she worries that she must have done something that drove him away. She had—she'd grown into a woman's body—and her father no longer knew how to relate to her. Take a minute to think about whether this was true with you and your father.

When fathers distance themselves from their daughters, they make it difficult to know one another well. To know someone well you have to imagine how they feel, check with them, and listen to what they say, and then do it all over—again and again. Inexperienced in the art of relationships and uncomfortable with their daughters' budding womanhood, many fathers avoid their adolescent daughters and rely on their wives to manage the relationship. When a father does spend time with his adolescent daughter, both often feel awkward. To ease the discomfort, he may shift into task-oriented or problem-solving dialogue; this makes both of them more comfortable, but it doesn't afford the opportunity for relationship building. The following dialogue exemplifies the difficulty many fathers and adolescent daughters have communicating:

Father: How was school today?
Jackie: Angela and I planned a sleepover for Friday, and it's
　　　　gonna be cool—pizza and....
Father: That's fine, Jackie, but how's school? How is math
　　　　going?
Jackie: Fine, I guess.
Father: Do you need any help with it?
Jackie: Yeah, I guess so.
Father: Okay. Let's sit down and go over some problems.

The father and daughter join around the task of math, but when their task is completed, so is their conversation. He picks up his paper, and Jackie goes into the kitchen to tell her mom about the sleepover.

Dethroning King Dad

Idealizing a father is appropriate when a daughter is five years old; it is crippling when she is thirty-five. During infancy, a daughter requires absolute protection from her parents, but as a young adolescent, she needs the freedom to taste frustration, to feel the excitement of independent accomplishment, and to experience sorrow. During this time, a father can prepare his daughter, and himself, for the day when he won't be her hero and cannot make all her dreams come true. She must learn how to do this for herself.

From a tempered version of unqualified love, a young girl must take her father off the hero's pedestal and begin the psychological journey that ends, if successful, with her growing up emotionally as well as physically. Through this process she will experience failure as well as success, sorrow as well as joy; she will feel alone at times and feel afraid, and she will learn to depend on herself. As she matures she no longer will need her father to be an idealized hero but a man she appreciates and loves. A daughter's overthrowing of her father as protector and knower of all truths is a normal part of adolescent development and paves the way to adulthood, but how this transition occurs is important and has serious consequences for the daughter. This is how Helen, a fifty-two-year-old businesswoman, described to me the traumatic moment her adored father fell from grace:

Dad and Mom came home early from a party to find me and two of my male friends visiting in the living room. My dad had a strict rule that no friends (especially boys) were allowed in the house when they were gone. After the boys left, my father flew into a rage, precipitated in part by that fact that he had been drinking. His anger got out of control, and he was about to slap me when my mother screamed at him to stop. I was shocked that my father could be so out of control—or that my mother would talk to him like that. I remember feeling relieved, but also frightened and betrayed by my dad. Somehow Dad looked smaller to me as he turned and walked slowly into their bedroom. I could never look up to him in the same way after that night. Even today I get sad when I think about it.

Helen had not spent a lot of time with her father when she was growing up. She had not watched her father make mistakes, feel embarrassed, ask for help, or apologize. She had not cried and giggled and argued and shared quiet moments with him. Helen had not really known her father, and in that one abrupt and frightening moment her idealized image of him shattered forever—and she had nothing to replace it with. The unexpected and threatening incident revealed his flaws and left her feeling frightened, angry, and betrayed.

Another woman, Katrina, told me a very different story of how her father gently but persistently forced her to let go of her idealization and see him as real:

As I went from childhood to preadolescence, my father helped me solve problems, but he refused to be my problem-solver. One time I asked him how to handle the hateful remarks of another student at school, and he told me he wasn't sure because he didn't like the way he handled his anger or hurt feelings. He suggested that I call my favorite aunt and ask her what she did when someone hurt her feelings. He also suggested that I ask my older brother and my best friend the same question. Dad's refusal to solve my problem and his gentle coaxing helped me find my own solution, and it turned a very painful situation into a learning experience. Without my being aware of it, I learned several things: first, my father would not always have the answers; second, people other than my father could be counted on for help and advice; and third, I should listen to the ideas and suggestions of others, but I should decide the best solution for me. I still adore my father, but I know he's not perfect, thank God.

Katrina's father knew the importance of helping her to see him in a realistic way, and he approached it with compassion and gentleness. He did not force his human frailty on her but showed it to her over time in a way that she could gradually integrate. His success was evidenced in her appreciation.

The Doting Dad and the Dependent Daughter

Most fathers love their daughters and would do almost anything for them. One gift some fathers fail to give their daughters, however, is the gift of self-reliance. These doting fathers are kind, generous, and charming, but despite their good qualities, they are also overprotective and possessive. They cannot bear to lose the adoration that their little girl bestows on them, and to satisfy their needs they encourage their daughters to remain dependent well beyond what is appropriate. This dependency cripples the daughters emotionally and interferes with their learning how to take risks and develop the independence they need to grow up. The daughters pick up the message that they are only acceptable if they are their father's "little girl," and they dutifully continue to act the role of a sweet, young innocent to preserve the relationship.

Behind the close bond of the doting father and adoring daughter lies an unspoken and powerful psychological contract: he will shelter her from the bad outside world, and she will always need him. When a father and daughter bond in this way, they create a cycle that is difficult for either to break. She is overindulged and protected, but her father's love flows generously only as long as she fulfills her part of the bargain: she cannot grow up. She learns early to hide any part of her personality that does not match the contract, and over time she forgets the price she is paying for her father's love. She doesn't strive for independence because she fears it will diminish his love. She ages chronologically, but psychologically she remains buried in her childhood.

This contract between a doting father and his adult daughter not only cripples her but also prevents them from sharing a deeply personal and mature relationship with each other. The unspoken contract that began as a misguided attempt by an insecure father and his frightened daughter to avoid the pains of psychological growth eventually thwarts the possibility for either of them to grow. The daughter remains a helpless princess, and the father remains trapped behind the armor of the well-guarded, invincible white knight.

From Little Girl to Executive: Karen's Story

"Let's face it," lamented Karen, a thirty-five-year-old married woman who was nominally in charge of marketing in the consumer products division of her father's billion-dollar conglomerate. "I'm daddy's little girl, and in his eyes, I always will be." Oddly, her words had both an edge of frustration and a hint of satisfaction in them. The latter seemed odd since Karen was frustrated and thinking of leaving the company because of the lack of respect that her father, the president of the company, showed her at work.

The family had hired me as its business consultant, and Karen made it clear in our first meeting that she wanted to discuss only her working relationship with her father. "He's the president, and I'm one of his direct reports," she said. "He obviously doesn't respect my work, so it's probably time for me to move on. Let's not waste company time and money discussing family stuff that isn't going to change and doesn't pertain to business."

I assured Karen I had no interest in discussing irrelevant issues, but I also knew from working with other families that the "stuff" between family members most certainly was relevant to their roles and relationships at work. I knew I would be most useful to her if I had as much background information as possible about her family, particularly about her relationship with her father, the man behind the presidency. I reminded Karen that, though she might try, she couldn't leave her family outside the office door. Avoiding the fact that her boss was her father wasn't going to change the reality. She reluctantly agreed.

Karen could not change what she did not understand, and to change her working relationship with her father, she needed to better understand him and the complexity of their personal relationship. The same is true for all of us. The first step was for Karen to answer a series of questions, the kind anyone who wants to grow personally and change an important relationship must answer. In doing so, Karen highlighted the nature of the relationship with her father. I also asked her to give me an example of the problem she experienced with him at work.

"Last month," Karen began, "I presented an innovative and financially conservative marketing plan to Dad. He rejected it out of hand. He barely glanced at it before saying, 'Kitty, you have big ideas, but they're too expensive. Besides, there's no reason for you to waste time on this. I want you to use our outside agency for this work. In fact, I'll call and tell them what we want and what our budget is. By the way, will you and Phil be coming over for dinner on Sunday?'" Understandably, Karen felt discounted and frustrated after such conversations.

Owning the Problem

I asked Karen how she responded when her father discounted her marketing plan and shifted the discussion to dinner on Sunday.

"What could I do?" she said. "I wasn't going to throw a tantrum or cry. I couldn't force him to look at a proposal he wasn't interested in and I won't use my relationship with him to get special favors. What could I do? Nothing."

In fact, Karen had done something by going along with her father. When he referred to her as Kitty, her childhood nickname, she said nothing. When he discounted her proposal without reading it, she didn't ask for more consideration. When he shifted the conversation to dinner with her and her husband, she joined in with questions about what she could bring, arrival time, and the like. In doing what she considered nothing, Karen actually colluded with her father to keep things the same between them. The relationship was stuck, and nothing was going to change unless someone did something different.

Karen did not enjoy her father's discounting her or treating her like a child rather than a competent employee. It upset and angered her, and she felt ashamed that she allowed it. She didn't want to remain daddy's little girl, but neither did she know how to change their relationship. She feared that doing something different might hurt her father or drive him away.

Many daughters like Karen sacrifice their maturity and silence their voice to preserve the relationship with their father — or their boyfriend or husband. This sacrifice is tragic and doesn't help the relationship. In fact, it insures that the relationship will remain unsatisfying and overly dependent. Blaming her father and continuing in the role of the little girl were Karen's contributions to the problem.

First, however, she had to own her part in the problem.

Karen didn't want to leave the company if she didn't have to. "I know I'm good at what I do, and even if Dad doesn't treat me as an adult, I know he loves me." With a smile, she added, "I just have to figure out how to change him!" Again I heard the slight giggle and the hint of flirtation.

"Karen," I began, "you can't change your father. You can only change yourself, and I'm not sure you're ready to change." My comment angered her. "Why should I change?" she exploded. "I haven't done anything wrong!"

Karen's defensiveness was to be expected. It is normal to want things to change without having to do anything different. Unfortunately, it is normal and it doesn't work. For things to change, the person wanting the change has to do things differently. When people complain about a relationship — with a parent, a spouse, a child — they usually know exactly what the other person needs to change, but they rarely understand what they need to change in themselves. Karen couldn't change her father or the way he treated her, but she could change herself and the way she interacted with him.

The Consultant's Voice

I appreciated Karen's dilemma and understood that she felt helpless to change her father's behavior. I could identify with her feelings of not wanting to hurt someone she cared about and not wanting him angry at her. I could sympathize with her situation, but the reality was that the problem was hers — it was not her father's, the board of directors', or the other employees', many of whom that agreed she had an impossible situation.

The problem was hers, and only she could change it. The mutually dependent relationship she and her father had developed was holding her captive. It was easy to blame him because he was the parent and responsible for the way the relationship formed, but Karen was an adult now, and she was responsible for the way she conducted her relationships. Karen was paying a huge emotional price in resentment, diminished self-esteem, and low self-confidence to preserve the status quo. As we all know, however, change always involves some risk, and only Karen could decide what risk she could afford.

One way to assess your readiness for change in the relationship with your father or another important person is by imagining ten years into the future, and your father is deceased. I asked Karen questions similar to the ones that you will find later in this chapter in "Your Relationship with Your Father" and "Assessing Your Readiness for Change." Her answers highlighted her wish to have a different, more mature relationship with her father. The process of answering the questions also helped Karen realize that if she did nothing to change the relationship, the relationship would never change. It's like the Chinese proverb, "If you continue in the same direction, you will end up where you are going." For the first time in her life, Karen realized that she was responsible for the way she behaved with her father. And, for the very first time, she felt some control over the relationship.

The Present Lives in the Past

We often find answers in the past to problems we struggle with in the present. Karen had to decide what kind of a relationship she wanted with her father, and she feared that she would lose him if she tried to grow up in the relationship. It was time to ask more questions, and I expected that I would find clues in the past to the mystery of Karen's fears.

Karen's parents divorced when she was twelve. Her mother soon remarried and moved away. Karen stayed with her father and visited her mother once a month. Karen remembered her father being so devastated by the divorce that he couldn't work for two months. Her grandfather and uncle kept the business alive during that time, and she "kept Dad alive." It was summertime, and they went everywhere together—swimming, movies, walks. "We even went on a cruise together," she recalled. They were very close, and Karen's father often said how much he appreciated her companionship. "I have no idea what I'll do when you go off to college," he once told her. So Karen didn't, opting instead to attend the local college. She eventually married, but since her father never remarried, Karen, her husband, and her father often did things together.

At the time of the divorce, Karen had felt abandoned by both of her parents. Her mother remarried and moved away, and her father was too depressed to care for her well. Karen solved the problem by becoming her father's companion. Her plan worked to the extent that her father became less depressed and she had his company, but over the years the solution outlived its usefulness. Karen needed to grow up, and her father needed to establish a different life for himself. As long as she continued to take care of him by letting him take care of her, neither of them could move forward. Their past had become their present.

The First Step

I suggested to Karen that while it might be possible for her to develop a different relationship with her father, doing so depended on three things. First, she had to redefine the problem as hers, not her father's; second, she had to decide whether to change, regardless of whether or not her father changed; and third, she had to be committed to the change.

Karen had to learn to step outside her emotional experience and to observe herself as objectively as possible. She had to learn to watch herself as if she were watching a play from the audience. She had to listen to the rhythm of the dialogue, study the pace of the scene, and monitor the intensity between the actors. She had to abstain from the temptation to change her father or his role in the drama.

When Karen stopped focusing on her father's behavior and became a keen observer of her own behavior, she recognized the passive, frightened, and dependent role she played around him. She also saw, to her surprise, the caretaking role she still played with him. Her father had survived a personal crisis, was a well-respected small business owner, had friends, and received social invitations regularly, yet she constantly worried about his being lonely and planned his social calendar so he wouldn't spend a weekend alone. Karen soon began to notice the inordinate amount of time she spent watching, interpreting, and reacting to her father's moods. She realized that she still was trying to keep her father happy so he wouldn't leave her. She realized that, in order to grow up, she would have to take responsibility for her own happiness and life choices and give the same respect to her father. The more she directed her efforts to keep him happy and available for her, the less confident she was in her ability to make herself happy and the less opportunity her father had to get on with his life.

The Second Step

When Karen was ready, she wrote a note to her father in which she said that she'd been thinking of the painful time they shared when she was young, and she thanked him for loving her. She ended by saying that she wanted to talk with him about that experience. Karen's note was a huge step toward change. The next week, Karen sat down with her father and brought the subject up directly, saying, "Dad, I was so frightened when you and Mom divorced." It was the first time either of them had used the word divorce in almost twenty-five years.

Karen's father was quite uncomfortable when she first began talking about the divorce and her fear of his abandonment. She was breaking a twenty-five-year-old contract between them to avoid these topics. She needed considerable courage to pursue the conversation when her father gave superficial responses such as, "I can barely remember yesterday, how can I be expected to remember twenty-five years ago?" When he did this, she laughed and said she hoped his amnesia included the time she decorated her bedroom walls with red fingernail polish. When he looked distressed, she respectfully backed away from the topic with responses such as, "Dad, I know how much you love me, and I appreciate how difficult this is for you to talk about." Karen's combination of humor and respect, as well as her sense of timing, kept the conversation going for many months.

Karen found that by asking her father questions rather than assuming she knew the answers, and by seeking information rather than blaming anyone, she gained a different perspective on the past. She learned, for example, that her father had blamed himself for the divorce and for robbing Karen of a normal childhood. A child of divorce himself, he had vowed never to do the same to his child, and he had failed to keep his vow. He feared that Karen would blame him for the divorce and reject him, just as he had his father. He had taken time off from work after the divorce because of his guilt. For the first time, Karen saw the past through the eyes of an adult rather than those of a frightened child. The difference was amazing.

Karen and her father continued to talk about things they had never discussed. He admitted being depressed after the divorce and realized that Karen's companionship had helped him through it. He was surprised, however, that she had worried about him being too depressed to take care of her. He also had not known how frightened she was. Slowly, and with greater and greater openness, Karen and her father stopped overprotecting each other and came to appreciate the other's strength and courage. Karen knew that her father didn't have the patent on truth any more than she did and that his version of their past was as emotionally skewed as hers, but now she had a different and broader perspective that allowed her to see her father differently. She no longer felt compelled to keep his social calendar or to invite him over every Sunday. He no longer felt guilty about accepting invitations from friends. Their time together was more relaxed and more genuine.

Over several months, I saw a change in Karen's behavior and attitude at work. She was less passive and had more energy, and her mood was lighter. She went about her business and enjoyed work in a way I had not seen before. She demanded more of her subordinates and spoke out more with her peers — and her father. On one occasion, Karen confronted her father after he called her Kitty and spoke down to her in a meeting. She said she didn't appreciate it: "I don't expect you to always agree with me but I do expect you to be respectful."

To his credit, Karen's father apologized and said she was right to correct him. "Just don't forget you're still Kitty to me — after work hours." With a smile he added, "Enough of the unimportant stuff. I need to know if you and Phil want to come over for dinner on Sunday. I'm cooking." They both laughed and enjoyed a hug before returning to work.

From the Past to the Present

Today, six years later, Karen is in line to succeed her father. Recently she confessed, "Dad and I still protect each other more than we should, and sometimes I miss the days of feeling like it was Dad and me against the world. But I like the changes I've made. I'm less afraid to stand up for myself, and I have a closer relationship with my husband. Also, I like the thought of one day being referred to as 'Ms. President.'"

What Karen did was courageous, and her father's courage to change helped her succeed. Her story is really the story of two people who trusted themselves and each other enough to do what it took to change their relationship. Her father could have hindered Karen's attempts, and we'll look at examples of obstructions in later sections. As it was, her determination was matched by her father's, he had her best interests at heart, and both of them shared responsibility for changing.

YOUR FATHER-DAUGHTER RELATIONSHIP

If you expect to work well with your father, you must understand your relationship with him and assess whether the relationship "fit" is a good one for the family business. If it is not, but you have a strong motivation to work in the business, you need to determine what needs to change to make a better fit. You need to understand what you contribute to the relationship difficulties. You need to understand your father's history and how it affected who he became and his treatment toward you. Ultimately, you must be the judge of how much change you are willing to make and what emotional price you can afford to pay for the relationship changing.

Answer the sets of questions titled "Your Relationship with Your Father" and "Assessing Your Readiness for Change" on the following pages. The first set of questions will help you assess your current relationship with your father and how well you know him as a person rather than simply as a father. Answering the questions will help you understand more fully such issues as whether your current relationship will bar you from the family business, limit your role, or aid your career. This information will provide a better idea of what needs to change in the relationship and what you need to do differently.

Your Relationship with Your Father

1. Describe your father and your relationship with him.
2. What do you most enjoy about your relationship with your father?
3. What do you find most frustrating about the relationship?
4. What would you most like to be different about your relationship with your father?
5. What would your father have to change for it to be different? What would you have to change?
6. Who has to change first? Why?
7. What stories have you heard about your father's childhood? How do they influence the way you think about your father? Have you talked with him about his childhood?
8. Do you know what it's been like for your father to be a parent? How did his childhood influence his parenting?
9. Do your siblings have a different relationship than you with your father? What makes for the differences?
10. If you work with your father, do you have the kind of working relationship you want with him? If not, what prevents it?
11. What changes would your father need to make to improve your working relationship with him? What changes would you need to make?

Your responses to the second set of questions will assess your readiness to make changes in the relationship with your father and what stands in the way of change. Take your time

Assessing Your Readiness for Change

Before answering these questions, project yourself forward to a time after your father has passed away. Your responses will indicate your readiness to change the relationship with your father.

1. What did you not say to your father while he was alive that needed to he said? What prevented you from saying it? If you had the opportunity to say it now, would you? Why or why not?

2. What did you need to know about your father that you now can never know? What did you need him to know about you? What prevented you from telling him?

3. What do you wish you had done differently before he died? What stopped you? If he were alive today, would you behave differently in your relationship with him? Why or why not? What would be the risk in changing? The potential gain? Would your changing be dependent on his changing? Why or why not?

Review your answers. If you had a second chance and you would not say or do things differently with him or if you feel you could not change the relationship unless he changed, then you probably are not ready to forge a different relationship. The timing and circumstances are not right. On the other hand, if your responses reflect a commitment to change the relationship, even if your father does not, then it is time, and you are ready.

with these most important questions. Afterward, talk with your dad and other family members about your answers. Your mother and siblings, for example, may have different thoughts about the relationship and about who is responsible for what problem in it. Listen carefully to what they say, and try to refrain from dismissing their remarks if you disagree with them. A relationship is always complicated, and oftentimes those outside of it can be more objective than those in it.

THE GOOD FATHER

Good fathering, like good mothering, is difficult. It takes time, hard work, a willingness to acknowledge mistakes, lots of practice, and, as we learned from Karen and her father, a willingness to make the changes needed to improve the relationship. The good father holds a steady course while his daughter struggles to grow up. He tries to stay calm when she is unreasonable, provide structure when she is unable, and support her when she lacks confidence. He enforces limits when she tries to grow up too quickly and forces independence when she wants to stay a child. In effect, he gives her what she needs instead of everything she wants.

As his daughter reaches adolescence, the good father continues to provide structure but allows space for her to experiment with life on her own. He relaxes his control somewhat. This stage of parenting can be especially challenging for the entrepreneur father. As a business owner, he is accustomed to being in control, but if he attempts to control his adolescent daughter in a similar way, he most surely will meet resentment if not outright rebellion.

A father always has mixed feelings as he watches his

daughter grow up. As she matures, the good father tolerates the sadness he feels about losing his little girl and replaces it with pride in her ever-expanding maturity. In the face of her growing need for independence, he parents from a greater distance. This affectionate distance is reassuring to his daughter. It gives her permission to move outside the safety of her father's world and into the world of other male relationships.

As much as many fathers want to believe that daughters need their mothers more than their fathers, it simply isn't true. Daughters need their mothers *and* their fathers. With her father, a daughter rehearses her womanhood in relation to men. In a world that is still male-dominated, her father must reinforce the message that she can be feminine *and* independent, attractive *and* smart, capable of intimacy *and* independence. The good father knows he has succeeded when his daughter grows into a confident young woman who knows what she wants and how to get it — perhaps even without the help of a man!

Assessing your Father

Was your father perfect? Of course not. Has he made mistakes? Absolutely. Has he disappointed you? I would assume so. I am sure you don't want your father to expect perfection from you, so it is only reasonable that you allow him to be "good enough" but not perfect. If you insist that he be the knight in shining armor or you harshly criticize his every mistake, you allow no room to have an authentic and close relationship with him. Think instead of a relationship where each of you can express your feelings respectfully, even when you disagree, and where you can question each other's decisions, make mistakes, and learn from them. Just because your relationship with your father has not been perfect — or if it has been frustrating or if he is difficult to talk to — don't assume that you can't forge a different relationship with him that will enable the two of you to have a good enough working relationship.

THE GOOD ENOUGH FATHER: RUTH'S STORY

Successful businesswomen often cite a positive relationship with their father as a significant reason why they are able to assert their female identity with confidence and without shame in the work environment. The special bond between a daughter and her father is often the reason a daughter seeks to work in the family business. Such was the case with Ruth, who at thirty-three committed herself to a career in the $82 million cosmetics company her father, Larry, founded in the Midwest. The oldest of three children, she grew up "knowing my dad loved me — and that he loved the business."

Feeling welcomed, but not pressured, to join the business, Ruth worked at another company: "I wanted my apprenticeship to be somewhere I wouldn't be watched and judged because of my name." After three years of training and experience, she felt ready to work with her father. And he readily allowed her in.

Larry knew that Ruth's success in the family business depended on her competence. The managers would be skeptical of the owner's kid, and she would have to prove herself. He put her in a position with no title and rotated her through the departments. Ruth relished the opportunity to learn about the business. She asked questions, got involved, and motivated others with her enthusiasm. She developed a mentorship relationship with one of the vice presidents. Over time she established her competence, and employees respected her for her contributions, not her name.

Ruth is now in line to succeed her father. "My father loved me enough to give me a chance, he respected me enough to let me achieve, and he provided the space for both," she said. She appreciates their special relationship and respects it. "I have the ear of the president, but I don't abuse it. I make suggestions, but I know the president makes the final decision. Here, I'm not a daughter trying to sweet-talk her dad. I'm a senior vice president, and he's my boss. But it's nice going to work knowing the respects my work — and he loves me!"

Larry possesses the courage, spirit, self-confidence, and ambition that describe most entrepreneurs. He also was willing to be involved emotionally, a necessity to father a daughter well. This combination of strengths is impressive; as a result of his determination, he created a special relationship with his daughter and a successor for his business. Larry is part of a unique group of hard-working men who make tremendous sacrifices to attain their business dream, and they earn every ounce of success they achieve. He also is part of a smaller group of entrepreneurs who are able to balance their need for achievement with their need for meaningful relationships. The very characteristics that contribute to successful entrepreneurship often limit a man's capacity to do both.

A daughter's relationship with her father is critical to her development, but it is only part of a much larger context. Girls do not emerge as women who are ready to lead the family business simply because they enjoyed a good enough relationship with their father. They also had a relationship with their mother. Some of them had siblings, grandparents, and significant others who influenced their development. Education, environment, intelligence, and even luck played into who they became. There is no way to know all the variables that account for the individual "me" in each of us. However, the more we know about what makes us tick, the better we will understand how certain women develop into leaders.

CHAPTER THREE

Daughters and Their Mothers

On one thing professionals and mothers agree: mothers can't win.
—Margaret Drubble

On a quiet, leisurely evening stroll through the streets of Santa Fe, Barbara, a trusted older friend who is a family business owner and the mother of a daughter my age, struck up a conversation with me about mothers and daughters.

"Your daughter will be able to go places that were off limits to you, that I never even dreamed of as possibilities," Barbara said. "You must be excited for her."

"Yes," I said, "I'm excited for her, and a bit envious; I also worry about her."

So began a three-hour conversation about the hopes, dreams, and worries that she and I felt for our daughters. We discussed our concerns for all the daughters of today's business owners who will have to make their way in a world that offers them profound opportunity, but that also presents them with uncharted challenges and responsibility. The longer we talked, the more we realized that despite our generational difference, our feelings were quite similar.

Writing as both a daughter and a mother, I know this

chapter is necessarily more personal, less technical, and farther-reaching than others in this book. It is more about who we are as women — mothers and daughters — and less about our roles as employees in family businesses. These pages, which began as a conversation with Barbara, are intended to provoke thoughts about your relationship with your mother and, perhaps, with your daughter. This chapter explores how women develop character and self-esteem and the role that history plays in determining the way you think about your relationship with your mother, your father, other women, and the family business.

WORLDS APART

Gloria, a woman in her mid-forties and head of personnel in her family's hardware business, vividly recalls the moment — during a dinner conversation when she was twelve years old — when she realized what it meant to be a woman in her family. That realization shaped the tumultuous adolescent relationship she later had with her mother.

An argument began that evening when Gloria's father blamed women for the "mess" in Washington. "We never should have given them the vote," he teased. "All they've done is mess things up."

"Yeah," chimed in Gloria's older brother, "they're too dumb to vote." The "boys" laughed, Gloria's mother smiled, and Gloria got angry.

"How can you talk like this when you have two daughters and a wife!" Gloria protested. The more she argued, however, the more they teased her. Finally, defeated and furious, she stomped to her room.

A few minutes later, Gloria's mother came into her room

and sat down to work things out. "When are you going to learn that the more you argue with your dad, the more you egg him on?" she said. "You have to learn to take a joke. Dad was only kidding."

Even then, Gloria knew that attitude wouldn't settle anything, and she turned on her mother: "Well, it wasn't funny, and I don't think he was kidding. Neither do you."

"If you'd keep quiet, he'd stop," Gloria's mother continued. "He's doing it to get your goat. You're as stubborn as your father, and one of these days it'll be the death of you." Gloria's mother sighed, gave her a kiss, and walked out of the room.

"Instantly my anger shifted from my father to my mother, and the mantra began," Gloria told me. "Over and over again I angrily whispered the words, 'I hate you! I hate you! I hate you!' under my breath. Oddly, they were directed toward my mother, when it was my father I had argued with. I was furious. I felt betrayed. I was also scared, for in that moment I think I sensed what I didn't yet know. My mother was telling me to join her in a pact of powerlessness that would rob me of my strength but would guarantee my acceptance in the world where men held power and women held onto the men with power."

The fury Gloria felt toward her mother that day was misdirected, but it also was a courageous attempt to fight for her own voice and for the strength that would shape her life. She sensed that if she silenced her voice she would be trapped, like her mother, in a world of passivity. Instead of rejecting the misguided truths of her mother's and grandmother's generations, however, Gloria rejected her mother; in doing so, she robbed herself of the relationship that she, like all young women, needed with her mother.

Gloria's mother was not trying to rob Gloria of her strength and power; she was trying to give her good advice about how to get along in a man's world. But she and Gloria were from different generations, and neither could identify with the other's world. Gloria's mother had no idea that Gloria's stubbornness reflected her attempt to break down gender barriers and expand the men's club to include women or that Gloria had needed her support in the fight.

Gloria did not understand that, in her mother's world, people did not expect women to *be* someone, but to *be for* someone. Gloria's mother, for example, had responsibility for the children, the household, and her aged mother. She balanced the household budget from a small desk in the family kitchen, where she kept an eye on dinner while she worked the numbers. She made her daughter's clothes, ironed her husband's handkerchiefs and underwear, and hung the sheets outdoors to give them a fresh-air smell. In short, the world valued women by the amount of service they provided others.

Gloria got mixed messages from her mother: she told her to stand up to her brothers when they bullied her but to be silent when her father teased her about dumb women; she encouraged Gloria to compete academically but not to brag about her grades. Gloria's mother wanted her daughter to speak up for herself and compete with the boys, but she also wanted her daughter to fit in to a man's world.

MOTHERS AND DAUGHTERS

Every daughter has her own unique relationship with her mother, but most can remember a time when ambivalence and confusion burdened that relationship. I recall when I loved my mother but I didn't like her. I wanted to be close to her but I pushed her away; I needed to talk with her, but I refused to speak; I begged for her opinions and then criticized her for them. Nothing made me happier than pleasing my mother, but rarely would I please her. Our relationship was complicated and intense, and sometimes feelings of competitiveness, envy, and dependency overpowered it.

Few daughters really get to know their mother as another woman. Even as adults, some women long for a closeness they never had with their mother, while others spend a lifetime trying to be free of her. Many daughters find it extremely difficult to become a different woman than their mother while also remaining close to her. Gloria misunderstood her mother's intentions because she didn't appreciate the differences between her mother's world and her own. Gloria saw her mother as a powerful woman who controlled both the household and the children and who supported her every opportunity. She needed her support but felt betrayed by the most powerful woman she knew. You may share similar experiences from your childhood.

Your relationship with your mother shaped your development of self-esteem, self-confidence, and integrity. You first learned from your mother how to be a woman, perhaps a wife or a mother yourself, how to understand the differences between women and men, and what those differences meant in the context of your family, the outside world, and the family business.

The last chapter explored the man behind your father as part of your search to find the right fit for you in the family business. Let's now explore further the woman behind your mother. By reviewing her past and your past with her, you will be better able to decide your future.

Mother-Blaming

It's a strange contradiction that society considers and treats women as inferior in many ways but expects them to be perfect when it comes to motherhood. They personify unconditional love and are counted on to forgive all mistakes, accept all responsibility for their children's happiness and success, and never to criticize. The perfection expected from today's mothers also includes the capacity to compete on an equal footing with men in the workplace while carrying most of the domestic and child-care responsibilities at home.

Perfection is impossible, but when mothers fail to meet the unrealistic standards set for them, people often consider them failures and cast them in the role of a bad mother. Bad mothers are imperfect mothers. As long as the world expects mothers to be totally responsible for the physical and emotional well-being of their children, they can be blamed for anything negative that occurs in their children's lives. They can be blamed for being too intrusive or too remote, too controlling or too permissive, too engulfing or too rejecting, too suspicious or too trusting. I have worked with hundreds of mothers over the past thirty-five years, and a few of whom had some of these qualities, but certainly they have not been the norm. Most mothers I have met do a good job nurturing and encouraging independence in their children. They may err on the side of being too remote, controlling, or permissive at times, but they do a good enough job.

The concept that the only good mother is a perfect mother pervades Anglo-American culture. As such, many girls grow up feeling betrayed by their flawed mother; later, as mothers themselves, they feel like failures for not being perfect. Longstanding ideas such as these are solidly imbedded in our culture, insidiously passed down from one generation to the next. And they are very difficult to change.

Women's Development
To understand the contradictions that contribute to making

the mother-daughter relationship complicated, let's look more closely at distinguishing features of women's development, how they affect your relationship with your mother and your father, and how they may influence your role in the family business.

From an early age, girls are able to articulate their feelings and those around them with remarkable accuracy.[1] Girls usually have close relationships with each of their parents and significant involvement with their friends. In play, girls find relationships more important than rules: they spend more time insuring that everyone's needs are met than in setting rules. These characteristics that most distinguish female development can serve you well in the family business. The ability to articulate well difficult issues, both emotional and intellectual, while respecting the needs of everyone involved, is a valuable personal and business asset.

As girls reach adolescence, unfortunately, they begin to devalue their intuitiveness, they minimize their perceptiveness about people and relationships, and they speak up less and without the confidence they had as children. Many girls downplay their intelligence and turn into what appear to be boy-crazy adolescents. This transformation happens at a frightening speed and becomes solidly embedded during adolescence. Why does this happen?

By adolescence girls realize that their intuitiveness and ability to understand what goes on between people can be a liability; their words can create discomfort or conflict and may even destroy a relationship. They also have figured out that, in general, males still hold more power and get more respect than females. Less so than their mothers before them, but more so than is in their best interest, girls temper their assets to fit in and to avoid disapproval, particularly from men. Under the best of circumstances, adolescence is a difficult transition. Hormones are raging, and so are emotions. But when girls devalue their strongest character traits, they worsen the transition.

Okay, enough theory. Let's now look at what this has to do with you and your family's business.

Consequences for You in the Family Business

Let's look more closely at what women's development has to do with your working in the family's business. To be most successful, you will have to bring all of yourself to the table. Let me provide an example. Intuition is a highly desirable ability to synthesize both obvious and subtle information. Stock brokers operate as much on intuition as on numbers. When people label this skill "women's intuition," however, its worth significantly drops. To succeed, you must appreciate your intuitiveness as a desirable talent rather than as a whimsical knack because only then will you trust your (well-informed) hunches and allow them to help you make better business decisions.

You need a strong, confident voice in clarifying your career objectives to those in charge. Perception often trumps reality in evaluating leadership capabilities, and you cannot afford to sound confused when you speak with your father about your ambitions or when you worry that he would rather see you providing him grandchildren than financial statements. You need to assert your interest in furthering the family business legacy to obtain the same grooming process that men in the business, perhaps your brothers, enjoy from the start of their career.

You have to demonstrate the wisdom of collaboration and participation over hierarchical control at work. Nurturing the talents of others, listening, and including others in decision-making easily translates into teamwork, and teamwork is a definite asset for the business.

From Adolescence to Adulthood: Helen's Story

Like the entrepreneurial man so completely self-reliant that his is unable to depend on anyone else, you too run the risk of turning your strengths into crippling liabilities. Helen did this very thing, and it cost her a career. At thirty-one years old, she had a promising career in her family's infant-safety products company, but she seemed intent on destroying that career with her self-effacing behavior. Joanne, Helen's friend and business associate, described the situation to me this way: "Helen is sharp with numbers, she knows the business, and she has a sixth sense about what's going to sell. She's at least as capable as Gene, her uncle; and he's good. That's how she got to be the youngest person on the management team. But she's changed since joining the team. She goes along with whatever Gene says, even when she disagrees with him and has a strong case to back up her position. I've talked to her about this, but she says she doesn't want to embarrass her uncle or act like she's competing with him. Her intention may be good, but it's backfiring. Gene doesn't want a yes man to help run the company; he wants Helen's intuition, creativity, and brain power. He isn't getting any of them. In fact, he's beginning to question his decision to make her a manager."

Helen understood the business and was good at numbers, but her intuition and sensitivity gave her the edge over other capable managers and made her valuable to the company. Her intuition helped her respond competitively to the market, and her perceptiveness about people helped her get the most out of those who reported to her. Unfortunately, those same assets became Helen's liabilities once she became part of the management team. Perhaps she lacked the confidence to trust her intuition in the presence of other talented managers, or maybe she worried that her uncle would be angry if she disagreed with him or others would be angry if she outshined them. Perhaps she was just trying to get along with everyone or felt guilty about having the highly visible management position that her mother never had.

Joanne thought all of these things contributed to Helen's self-effacing and self-defeating behavior, but I'll never know for sure: Helen canceled our appointment two days before we were to meet. I later learned that she left the company after her uncle asked her to step down from her management position. I can only assume that at some critical point, Helen stopped trusting the very strengths that had advanced her career. In her effort to accommodate her uncle and avoid conflict, however, Helen instead disappointed him, betrayed herself, and lost the opportunity to contribute her extensive knowledge and talent to the family business.

A PERSONAL STORY

Every woman I know has had the experience of denying what she knew intuitively and ignoring what she accurately perceived in order to be liked, or to avoid the potential loss of an important relationship, or to stave off criticism. I recall a particularly painful incident from my own adolescence that exemplifies this behavior. It began benignly enough but ended in a harsh lesson about the emotional price women pay in self-esteem when they abandon their authenticity.

I was elated when the quarterback of the football team, who recently had broken up with his girlfriend, asked me to the winter prom. Doug was a senior, while I was only a junior, and he was the most popular of any of the boys who had asked me out. I felt privileged. We spent a lot of time together in the weeks before the dance. Then, a few days before the prom, he stopped calling, and I no longer saw him in the school halls. I suspected that he had gotten back together with his girlfriend, but I really didn't want to talk with him about it. I hoped that if we didn't talk he wouldn't break our date.

The day of the prom came, and I hadn't heard from Doug. I got ready for our date anyway, hoping that he would come but fearing that I would be dressed up with nowhere to go. At the hour the dance was to begin, Doug called to say he would be a few minutes late. I was furious and hurt, but I acted upbeat to avoid the argument that would leave me without a date. He arrived without a corsage (unheard of in those days) and before my father even asked said he'd have me home early. At the dance Doug stared at his girlfriend, talked with his buddies, and ignored me.

One could say many things about this story, but forty years later I am most struck by my refusal to address what was happening. Certainly I was aware and felt the pain of it, but in my desperate attempt to preserve a relationship I hoped would make me "someone" by association with a "somebody," I not only kept quiet but I also tolerated disrespect and insult. I blamed the rejection on my unattractiveness, my personality, my weight. I blamed Doug's girlfriend. I blamed everything and everyone but Doug. For all my self-defeating behavior, I got a miserable evening, a battered self-esteem, and a festering dose of anger. The only good that came from the experience is that years later it allowed me direct insight into the problems that women create for themselves, Helen and myself included, when they abdicate their self-worth to accommodate others.

Your Difficult Discussions

Try the following exercise to get a glimpse of what you may be thinking, assuming, and feeling when you have a difficult discussion with your boss or relative who works in the family business—and how you actually respond. I borrowed this model from renowned organizational consultant Chris Argyris, a professor at the Harvard Business School.[2]

Divide a piece of paper into two columns. Label the left column "What I thought, felt, and assumed." Label the right column "What I said." Then think of a difficult discussion you have had with your boss or relative in the family business and fill in the columns. Once you have completed this exercise, review it for the following tendencies:

- How you avoid feeling incompetent
- How you avoid embarrassing issues
- How you react when feeling threatened
- How you limit your learning more about the subject being discussed
- How you protect yourself and/or the other person from self-understanding

Challenging Yesterday's Rules: Anita's Story

Young women today are challenging the long tradition of female devaluation, and they are also working to stay connected to their mothers. It is not easy or without conflict, however, particularly if your life includes aspects of your mother's unfulfilled aspirations. You may feel guilty about having more opportunities than your mother and, as a result, find yourself unable to enjoy what you have worked hard for and deserve. Perhaps you deny your ambitions through self-defeating attempts to ward off the envy and regrets you worry your mother will feel as a result of your success. On the other hand, you may feel compelled to succeed professionally as a way to satisfy her unfulfilled dreams or to provide her vicarious enjoyment. Even when you know your mother is content with the choices she made and the lifestyle she enjoys, you still may feel struggle with having gone beyond her. You may misinterpret your desire for achievement as selfishness, when actually it is a normal striving for self-fulfillment.

Anita, a thirty-seven-year-old woman and the director of public relations for her family's doll-making business, made this mistake. It almost cost her a gratifying career in the family business and, equally important, a genuine relationship with her mother. Aware of her mother's limited presence in the business, Anita felt guilty about her highly regarded and visible position. She understood that things were different for her than when her grandfather founded the business and refused to let her mother work in it, but she still found it difficult to embrace the privileges and challenges she had that were denied her mother.

When Anita's maternal grandfather died, his business went to his only son-in-law, Anita's father, Herman. Since the small doll-making business had not seen a profit for a number of years, Herman wanted to sell it. Anita's mother, Mae, convinced him to hold on and to try turning it around.

The first few years were tough. Herman worked long hours, and Mae often worked alongside him. She kept the books and cleaned the tools because the business couldn't afford to hire all the employees needed. When Mae wasn't actively participating in the business, she helped in other ways. She supported her husband when he was discouraged, she agreed to drain their personal bank account, mortgage the house, and borrow on their insurance. Mae was responsible for the care of their young children and ran the household. She didn't have an official position in the business, but she was very influential. The business eventually turned a profit, and over the years it became a highly profitable specialty doll manufacturing company.

Mae was courageous, she was a risk taker, and the pressure on her was intense. Anita knew the business would have been sold had Mae not convinced Herman otherwise, and the business would have failed without Mae's participation and partnership. Anita also knew that her mother had had the ability and ambition to run the company but had not had the opportunity.

A Needed Consultation

I had been the family's business consultant for two years when Anita requested an individual meeting with me to discuss some personal issues. "My mother was served injustice," Anita began. "It's because of her that our business exists today, but no one outside the family knows it. My dad's and my grandfather's pictures hang in the hallway, not my mom's. My dad gets the civic awards, not my mom. My dad gets the credit, not my mom. Don't get me wrong. Dad worked very hard and deserves credit, but so does Mom."

"Does your father appreciate what your mother has done for the business?" I inquired.

"Absolutely. That's not the issue. The issue is that Mom would have been more involved but she couldn't because of us kids and the times," Anita explained. "She insists she isn't bitter about it. 'What's happened, happened; it can't be changed, and you just move on,' is what she says. Still…"

"Still what?" I asked. By now I was beginning to wonder what was behind Anita's fierce defense of her mother.

Anita's voice was barely audible: "I don't know. I guess I feel guilty. Back then, people didn't believe in outside childcare, and

Dad thought it was Mom's place to stay home with the kids. Mom agreed. But now, only a generation later, Dad wants me to work with him, and Mom thinks it's great that women get to have babies and also work. She teases me to fight like hell to be the next company president. But somehow it doesn't feel fair. It's stupid, but I feel guilty."

Anita is not alone in her guilt. Many guilt-ridden daughters unconsciously limit their achievements out of an uncalled-for loyalty toward and protection of their mothers. As if to pay homage to the previous generation, they disallow themselves the very things their mothers could not have.

"You can't change your mother's past," I counseled. "Holding yourself back in retribution for your mother's life will do nothing for you or your mother."

"It's just not fair...," she began.

"No, it's not fair. But life isn't fair," I interrupted.

Anita's Conversation with Mae

At my urging, Anita talked with her mother about the guilt she was experiencing. Anita said she knew she had done nothing to feel guilty about, but the guilt persisted. She confessed that she rarely talked about work because she didn't want to remind her mother of what she could never do.

I had to smile when Anita told me Mae's response: "Anita, have you been chatting with our consultant?" It reflected the wit I'd come to enjoy from Mae over the previous years.

After a hearty laugh, Anita and Mae began serious conversation. Mae again told Anita she had reconciled any regrets from her past. "I didn't have your professional opportunities, and I didn't feel I had a choice about whether to stay home with my kids. That's just the way it was. But it wasn't all bad."

Mae told Anita she felt proud when she and Herman turned

the business around; she spoke of the fun she had with her children; she bragged about having the best of two worlds at a time when women were not supposed to be in business. It had never occurred to Anita that her mother had seized every opportunity available to her at the time, and that far from feeling regret or resentment, she felt proud of herself.

Mae was disturbed by Anita's guilt and insulted by her protectiveness. "Do you think me so fragile that I would be hurt by your success? Did I give you the idea that I'd be angry if you loved the business as much as I did and wanted to be part of it? Did it ever occur to you that I wanted you to be involved in the business?"

Anita was stunned. What was going on? Had her mother always felt this way and she misjudged her, or had her mother changed?

Mae continued by telling Anita what she had long held to herself. "All these years, I thought you didn't talk to me about your work because you didn't want me to know what you were doing, or you thought I'd be critical of your decisions, or something," Mae said. "Actually, I wasn't sure why you didn't talk to me, but it hurt my feelings."

Anita and Mae were crafted from the same mold. Anita didn't share her work with Mae because she didn't want to upset her, and Mae didn't share her feelings because she didn't want to upset Anita. Neither shared herself honestly out of protectiveness of the other. Beneath the protectiveness, however, lay the fear that the relationship wasn't strong enough to tolerate strong feelings, differences of opinion, perhaps even conflict.

From Pretense to Honesty

Both Anita and Mae were guilty of dishonesty under the illusion of protecting. Now that the cat was out of the bag, as Mae put it, each knew that their pretenses kept them in a polite, pretend closeness and prevented them from having an intimate and more honest relationship. Anita could no longer use the protection of her mother's feelings to justify her hesitancy in seizing opportunities. Mae could no longer use Anita's privacy as her excuse for keeping silent.

Today, nearly a decade after their initial conversation, Anita is in line to succeed her father as president of the family business, and Mae is enjoying a new relationship with her daughter. In Mae's words, "Eight years ago, I had a nice, polite daughter, who visited me regularly and cheered me up. But I didn't know her. And she didn't know me. Today, I have a kind but not always polite, sometimes stubborn, but honest daughter, who still visits me regularly. She doesn't always cheer me up, but she always gives me who she is. I have a real daughter!"

WOMEN, COMPETITION, AND ACHIEVEMENT

It is normal for you to want to be better than your mother, to succeed where she failed, to be confident where she was afraid, to speak out where she was silent. While these are normal aspirations, they are also difficult to execute.

Striving to do one's best is healthy and enhances self-esteem, but adults often scold girls and make them feel guilty about their desire to achieve. Others criticize girls as being too aggressive if they want to win, call them selfish if they act in their own best interest and bitchy if they seek out and enjoy power. You may have experienced some of these admonitions at home, in the classroom, on the playground, or in Girl Scouts.

Reality is that many women *are* competitive and enjoy achieving as much as men do. However, competition is more complicated for women, and to fully understand the issue we must examine it within the context of women's identity. Relationships form the core of women's identity. As such, women worry, more so than men, that competition will damage the relationships they value. Women do not instinctively fear or avoid success; rather, they fear and avoid rivalries that could damage their relationships. My stepdaughter, Sarah, struggled mightily with her ambivalence about competition when she was in graduate school. She called home one night to say she had been selected as a finalist for a coveted placement in her particular field of study.

I heard the worry in her voice as she gave me the good news. "I'm so anxious I can't eat or sleep," she said. "I thought I wanted this, but now I'm not sure. Three of us were selected to interview, and it's not fair to the others for me to interview if I don't really want it. Maybe I should call and cancel my interview..."

"What's going on, Sarah?" I interrupted. "You worked hard for this achievement. It's been your goal since you began school. Why are you doubting yourself now?"

"I don't know," she moaned. "It's nuts. I don't know if I'm more worried about not getting the placement, or about getting it. I want it, but Riley and Meg want it too, maybe more than I do. Somehow it doesn't seem right."

At first blush it might appear that Sarah had what some people call "female fear of success," but that wasn't it. She had enjoyed many successes over the years. Sarah wanted to win the placement, but she didn't want to compete against her friends. She hated the thought that someone had to win and someone had to lose. If she won, two of her friends would not.

Sarah faced a dilemma: she could give up opportunity she had worked hard for, or she could compete to the best of her ability, knowing that one or both of her friends might resent her if she won. Sarah was uncomfortable with her own competitiveness, and she worried that her friends would envy and resent her if she won. She was like many young women today, well-educated and ambitious and surprised by the ambivalence they feel when they compete against others. Not only does their behavior challenge the traditional feminine stereotype, it shakes the foundation of a moral ethic that stresses the importance of relationships. They feel anxious, ill-prepared, and alone in their struggle, and it makes them question their ambition.

The more honest a woman is about her ambition, the more likely she is to pursue and obtain her goals, and the less likely she is to feel envious of others. By definition, *competition* involves gaining an advantage over another person, but not for the purpose of destroying the other person. By contrast, *envy* involves spitefulness and resentment toward another person for their superiority, possessions, or success. To compete implies striving to do one's best, but to envy implies wishing to destroy that which is best in another.

A woman who denies her ambition is likely to resent and envy other women for their well-earned achievements because she knows that she could have achieved but, for whatever reasons, she chose not to. On the other hand, a woman who is honest about her competitiveness will fight for a position, or authority, or possessions, but she is unlikely to resent what others have achieved because she also is striving to achieve. More likely, she will respect others' achievements, learn from them, and she will celebrate their successes. I wanted this for Sarah.

I encouraged Sarah to talk to her friends about her dilemma. To pretend that a competition among them didn't exist or that she wasn't worried about it would only make things worse. Besides, I suspected that her friends were suffering some of the same ambivalence and worry. Talking would give voice to their discomfort and also diminish their collective fear that envy might overpower them and destroy their friendships. I also encouraged Sarah to inform the other students that she'd been called for an interview. To remain quiet about her accomplishment would be deceit in the form of omission. When the others learned her secret, they could rightfully feel lied to, and Sarah would feel guilty about her misdeed.

The next time I heard from Sarah her humor had returned. "I decided that as long as I wasn't sleeping, I might as well use the time to sort things out," she quipped. Indeed she had. Over the course of several days, she had spoken with each of the other candidates, offered her congratulations, and shared with them her wish that all of them could win the placement. She joked with them about her "secret plot" to destroy their chances of being selected and shared her pride about being a finalist. "I found out that all of us felt the same way. We all want to win but wish that the other two didn't have to lose," Sarah said. "But we agreed we have to try our hardest to win or we'll feel crummy about ourselves and resent the one who gets it."

Competition can occur within the context of cooperation, but it takes work. Just ask Sarah.

Women who feel good about themselves also will occasionally feel envious; it's human nature. But they can use the experience of an uncomfortable emotion as an opportunity to reassess their goals and priorities, rather than as a weapon to avenge the object of their envy. You can, for example, ask yourself what you most envy about another person and why. The answers will help you create an action plan to develop in yourself that which you envy and determine what you will and will not sacrifice to attain the goal.

Taking Mother To Work: Candyce's Story

The relationship you had with your mother when you were young was powerful, and it played a decisive role in your attitude toward other women and your relationships with them today. Whether you grew up with a strong, confident mother who encouraged your self-confidence or one who expected perfection and constantly criticized you, that relationship shaped, in part, the rapport you share with other women. If your mother had a positive and strong self-esteem, she trusted other women and turned toward them for support, you probably learned to trust and to expect trust from other women. In contrast, if your mother mistrusted other women, viewed them as rivals, and failed to establish close friendships, you probably internalized a self-image as being untrustworthy and grew to expect criticism from other women. Paula, the director of information services for a family-owned restaurant chain and a woman in her early forties, came to see me because of a problem with one of her direct reports.

"Candyce is a good contributor and one of my best technicians. I have no problem with her performance. It's her attitude I'm having trouble with," Paula told me. She explained that when she gave Candyce advice or offered her suggestions, Candyce took it as criticism and reacted defensively.

"Candyce has the potential, and I'm trying to help advance her career; but unless she can learn to see the value of and accept constructive criticism, all the skill in the world isn't going to get her promoted. Quite frankly, I'm beginning to wonder if it's worth my effort to help her develop. God knows I have other things to do if she's not interested."

I had known Paula professionally for nine years and trusted that her efforts were genuine, so I suggested that Candyce and

I meet alone to discuss the problem. Since Paula was frustrated by Candyce's attitude but wanted her to succeed, she willingly arranged the meeting.

It didn't take much urging from me for Candyce to describe Paula. "She hovers over me like a hawk, really. She stops by my office several times a week to check up on me and always finds a 'better' way for me to do things."

"Can you give me an example?" I asked.

"No problem. I have hundreds of them. Last week, Paula told me I needed to have more face-to-face time with the CEO and suggested that I provide him with regular updates on the program we're developing for the marketing department. Jeez! If I had that kind of time on my hands, I wouldn't be coming to the office on the weekends. It's like she lives to control me."

"Perhaps she does," I said, "and perhaps not. Are there any other interpretations that you could make about Paula's behavior? I mean, she may live to control you, but it seems a rather odd goal." Actually, Candyce's example of Paula's hovering behavior had sounded to me like offering helpful suggestions.

Candyce saw the problem as Paula's overbearing and critical character. In fact, Paula reminded Candyce of her last boss, a woman whom she felt pretended to support her but who failed to recommend her for promotion three different times. Try as she might, Candyce couldn't think of anything other than Paula's need to "smother and control" to explain the problem between them.

The fact that Candyce was fighting a battle with a second "smothering" boss, and that she was defensive, alerted me to the possibility that she was dealing with Paula as if she were someone else, most likely a family member, rather than as the boss and fellow employee she was. I asked Candyce a number of questions to help us both understand whether her relationship problem at work reflected one that existed at home. Candyce told me that Paula did, indeed, remind her of someone from her past—her mother—whom she had experienced as intrusive, controlling, and overly protective. As we talked more, Candyce realized that Paula had not always seemed intrusive and overprotective. In fact, it had only been within the past six months that their relationship had become problematic.

"Mom and I had a rough time when I was a teenager," Candyce said. "My older brother died in a car accident when he was sixteen, and Mom never recovered from it. She became obsessed with me dying and couldn't let me out of her sight. She sometimes showed up at school just to make sure I was there. When I turned fourteen and wanted to drive, she fell to pieces. I went to college as far away as possible. Even then she sometimes showed up at my apartment unannounced. I understood that Mom had been traumatized, but still, I had to grow up. Kids need their mom to protect them, but mine hovered."

As soon as the words were out of her mouth, Candyce made the connection; with that awareness came a new and broader understanding of the problem. Paula had not chosen the role, but she had become Candyce's stand-in mother in an unresolved drama. Paula did not intend to check up on Candyce or hover over her; unlike Candyce's mother, Paula was trying to encourage her professional growth. Because of the powerful experience Candyce had with her mother, however, she heard her mother's words in Paula's voice and felt her mother's control in Paula's suggestions.

An unexpected death such as that of Candyce's brother tends to exert an enduring influence on the lives of family members. Candyce's mother feared suddenly losing another child, and her hovering was a way to reassure herself that her daughter was okay. Because she poorly understood the emotional meaning of her mother's behavior and because her reactions to it were so intense and durable, Candyce had transferred the discomfort to her boss, Paula. The understanding Candyce obtained during our discussions enabled her to accept Paula's efforts for what they were, instead of mindlessly repeating her adolescent reaction to her mother's behavior.

The first step toward changing a relationship is understanding your contribution to the problems. The next step is changing your part of the problems. This is not easy, and it takes work. In Candyce's case, her work was far from over once she recognized her role. She had to work at not putting her mother's mask on

Assessing Whose Problem It Is

1. What is most problematic about the person with whom you are having difficulty?

2. Does this person remind you of anyone in your family (past or present) with whom you have had difficulty? Is the person's style, mannerisms, or way of speaking similar to that of the family member? Are the person's life circumstances similar?

3. Do you react to this person in ways that are similar to how you react to someone in your family? What is it that triggers these reactions?

4. What feelings does this person stir in you? Hurt? Anger? A feeling of being criticized? What is it about the person that most upsets you? Why? What other person or situation does this remind you of?

5. Was there ever a time when you didn't feel as negative about this person as you do now? How was then different from now?

Paula's face. Some days she did better than others. But Paula could see that Candyce was trying to relate to her differently and that Candyce was trying to take her suggestions as helpful rather than hovering. Together they slowly formed a different and more positive relationship.

It is not always possible to change a problematic relationship without help. If this section has teased out a problematic relationship for you, and you have tried to change your part of the problem and still feel frustrated, don't throw your hands up in defeat. Seek the advice of a professional whose expertise is working with difficult family relationships.

Oh No! I Sound Like My Mother!

Women often utter these words to admonish themselves for something they've said or done. When a mother scolds her own children, she often thinks to herself, "Oh, no, I sounded just like mother." She confesses to a friend, "You should have heard me lecturing my husband. I sounded as bad as mom." She laments, "I can't believe I said that. I'm turning into my mother!"

Congratulate yourself for wanting to avoid your mother's mistakes and for desiring to express your own personality. These are important steps toward autonomy that are difficult to accomplish. Some daughters, however, fear being like their mother in any respect. When they observe a similarity, they experience it as an insult or a failure. They want to compare with their mother only for contrasts, not for the likeness. Take a minute to reflect whether this speaks to the way you compare yourself to your mother.

To be sure, some mothers are emotionally toxic to their children, but they are the exception. And yet, daughters often describe their mothers in extreme terms that make them sound like a saint or a monster, a heavyweight or a deadweight, a hero or a traitor. Reality is that most mothers fall somewhere in the middle, not at the extreme ends. Here again we see one of the consequences that comes from expecting perfect mothering.

Join the majority of daughters if, at some point in your life, you have been guilty of describing your mother in extremes. Most daughters want to have a close relationship with their mother, but they are conditioned to expect perfection from her, and, when she disappoints, to reject her because of her imperfections. Contrast this with your relationship with your father. You may remember a time when your father disappointed you by not making it to your soccer game or school play or Halloween party because he couldn't get away from work. You may also remember your mother instructing you to forgive him because he was working, to understand that he *wanted* to be there but couldn't, or she made some other comment that implied you were not to be upset with his imperfect behavior.

If, like Candyce, you are experiencing an especially difficult relationship with another person, or if a particular personality type annoys you to distraction, it may have to do with a past, emotionally significant, and unresolved relationship. Answering the set of questions titled "Assessing Whose Problem It Is" may shed new light on an old problem.

THE BAD MOTHER

Bad mothers do exist.

I am not referring to the less-than-perfect mother or the inadequate mother who understands her shortcomings but loves her children and provides what she can for them. I am referring to mothers who are incapable of loving their daughters, those who cannot or will not provide the nurturing their children need, those who are emotionally or physically cruel to their children.

If you were fortunate enough to have a loving mother, imperfect as she was, this section may make you uncomfortable. But if you had a bad mother, you will understand exactly what I am talking about, and you may feel understood for the first time in your life. Yours was the mother who was heartlessly rejecting, or abusive, or relentlessly critical. She may have deserted you.

If you had such a mother you may feel justified in hating her. It is understandable if you are terrified of being like her in any way. You may have to stay away from her to protect your own physical or emotional safety. Unfortunately, distance is rarely enough to silence the cruel voice of mother in your head. Her words still wound, the scars still burn, and the question still looms large: was I unlovable?

Often, daughters of bad mothers know intellectually that they were lovable, that it was their mother who suffered the problem, but emotionally they still feel unsure. In a culture where the possibility of bad mothering is taboo, daughters often question their memory, blame themselves, and deny their childhood experience. To genuinely believe that you were lovable and it was your mother who was at fault, you must first accept the possibility that bad mothers exist. You must find the strength to examine your mother's past, explore the family she grew up in, and understand the relationships she had with her extended family. You must understand what she experienced as a child and the adversities she survived. You need to know the family values she grew up with and the expectations that surrounded her childhood.

Do not misunderstand the purpose of this historical exploration as a way to forge a close, meaningful relationship with your mother, for the likelihood of that is slim. You need to know this information to understand clearly how she came to be the cruel mother she was. You need the historical facts to speak the truth to you, rather than relying on your intuition.

The facts about your mother will help free you of any guilt you may feel about causing your mother's problems or deserving her abusive treatment. The facts will help silence your worry about suddenly and helplessly turning into her. Most importantly, a detailed understanding of your mother's history will shatter any leftover doubt about whether you were lovable—you were—but she, for any number of reasons, could not give the love that you needed.

EMOTIONAL PARALYSIS: JUDY'S STORY

Judy sought a consultation because she couldn't make a decision about whether to continue in her current job as an accountant in a small, family-held business or leave to it pursue a dream she had had for years of owning her own business. Indecision was not typical of Judy, who usually approached decisions in a very practical manner. But this time she was stuck and couldn't understand why.

I began by asking Judy about her current work situation. She was a non-family employee who reported directly to the grandfather-president. She enjoyed a good professional and personal relationship with him and she got along well with her peers and subordinates. She liked her work but was never going to be a shareholder and had always dreamed of one day owning her own company.

I asked Judy what she thought was paralyzing her about this

particular decision. She said that her relationship with her boss, as well as his wife and daughter, were important to her and she didn't want to lose their close friendships. She worried that her departure would be an insult to them and they would hate her for it. She also secretly feared that she didn't have what it takes to be successful on her own, although the fear went against what she knew about herself. She told me that her preoccupation with the situation was affecting her work, and for the first time she had been criticized by her boss for a less than stellar performance at a board meeting.

Judy's Past

As is often my hunch when an "emotional paralysis" takes over an otherwise decisive client, I began to ask questions about Judy's personal history. Her parents divorced when she was four, leaving Judy and her younger brother with her depressed and angry mother. Judy had enjoyed a close relationship with her father prior to the divorce and his departure devastated her. The loss felt worse three months later when her father married another woman and moved out of state.

Judy described her mother as particularly harsh and critical with her. Unlike her younger brother, she was not allowed to hold her mother's hand or give her a hug. If she did, her mother reprimanded her for "acting like a baby." When she started school, her mother forced her to wear clothes that set her apart from the other kids. It wasn't because of a lack of money, and her brother was always dressed well. Judy couldn't invite friends to the house because her mother said they wouldn't want to come. When her mother's friends complimented her politeness, her mother told them not to be fooled. When Judy won a writing award in high school her mother accused her of having someone else write the essay.

In her mother's eyes, Judy was a failure who could do nothing right. In spite of this, Judy did well in school and won a full scholarship to college. She remembers the day she received her acceptance letter as the most wonderful day of her life: "It meant I would finally be free of my mother."

Judy hated her mother but also longed for her acceptance, something she knew she could never achieve. For years she wondered what was wrong with her that her mother didn't love her, but over time and with the help of good friends, she realized that the problem was her mother's, not hers. Still, she sometimes fantasized about a loving reconciliation.

Two years before I saw Judy, her mother died. Judy had been torn about whether to visit her mother in the hospital, but at her brother's urging she did. The visit was awkward and neither had much to say to the other. As Judy was leaving the room her mother said, "I love you." In shock, Judy turned around. "You love me? Is that what you said?" Her mother quickly retorted, "Your brother told me I had to say it."

There is no doubt that Judy had a cruel mother. Our culture mythologizes mothers as perfectly loving, and it ignores the existence of cruel mothers, which traps unloved daughters such as Judy in a nightmare of self-blame and self-doubt. Judy worked for a family that loved and respected her. She had good, kind friends. But it was not enough to silence her mother's voice. She feared that if she left her job she would lose the only family she ever had and she would fail in her effort to create her own business. Through tears she asked, "What if I find out I'm as stupid my mother thought?"

It is common to revisit old insecurities when making a change in our lives. The uncertainty of Judy's future made her feel insecure, and she lost confidence in herself, again listening to her mother tell her she was worthless. For Judy to silence her mother's voice she needed to understand how her mother came to be cruel. She needed to know she wasn't to blame for her mother's cruelty. She needed to put to rest the question of whether she was lovable. For abused daughters, and Judy was no exception, the thought of looking into their bad mother's background is terrifying. Judy feared her effort might reveal that there was nothing in her mother's past to explain the cruelty, leaving her to believe the worst: indeed she was an unlovable child.

Bad mothers were often the daughters of bad mothers, or bad fathers, or both. Our culture preaches that good mothering is instinctual and surfaces automatically when a woman births a child when, in fact, mothering is learned, and some women are never provided with the right instructions.

Mother's Past

Judy remembered her maternal grandmother's house as a safe haven, a place she could go when her mother was especially mean. Her grandmother was a master quilter who spent most of each day absorbed in her work. Judy remembered times when her grandmother looked up and seemed surprised to see her; to Judy the silence felt like love. Judy's grandfather had died when she was very young, so to her the house seemed to belong only to her and her grandmother.

Judy began to investigate her mother's past by talking to her aunt about it. She was shocked by her aunt's description of her grandmother as a narcissistic, self-centered woman who was so absorbed in herself and her work that she rarely noticed the needs of her daughters or the verbal abuse they endured from their alcoholic father. Growing up, Judy had been told that her grandfather died when a drunk driver hit him, but her aunt corrected the story. He *was* the drunk driver and he ran his car into a tree.

Over many months and much discussion, Judy came to understand her mother more fully. Her mother's anger toward her was real, and she meant her criticisms to hurt. Her mother had been hurt as a child and she wanted to hurt in return. Judy became the object of her mother's fury toward a father who abused her and a mother who refused to notice and protect her.

The information Judy learned about her mother did not make her forgive or forget, but it did help her understand that her mother was cruel because she did not know how to love, and not because Judy was an unlovable child. As Judy said, "My

Understanding Your Mother

You can begin the process of becoming free of your mother, distinguishing yourself from her, or simply getting to know her better as a person by asking yourself some questions that will help broaden your picture of her and force you to see her as a person with a history, a family, and unique life experiences.

1. What kind of relationship did your mother have with each of her parents? How do you know?
2. Were there particularly difficult times during your mother's childhood? Adolescence? How did she cope with them?
3. What was your mother's relationship with her siblings?
4. Who was your mother closest to during childhood? Adolescence? How did those relationships help her? Hurt her?
5. What were the greatest adversities your mother faced growing up? How did she cope with them?
6. How do you think your mother's history may have influenced her parenting?

mother's past does not justify what she did to me, but it does help explain it."

Breaking Away

Judy still sometimes fights the voice of her abusive mother, but she has moved on. She was able to leave her job without having to underperform and disappoint her boss. When she spoke with him about starting her own business, he expressed regret about losing her but understood her rationale and offered his support. He had experienced the satisfaction of owning a business and wanted the same for her. "You are like a daughter to me," he told her, "and I want the very best of life for you."

Whether you share an especially close relationship with your mother or one that is completely cut off, that relationship greatly shapes the way you think about yourself and your interactions with others. Candyce and Judy brought their mother to work with them, and you will also. Understanding your mother's history and the dynamics of your relationship with her will help you differentiate that most personal relationship from your work relationships and respond to each accordingly.

THE GOOD MOTHER

We've looked at the unrealistic expectations of motherhood and we've shined a light on bad mothers, but we have not set the standard for good mothering. What distinguishes good mothering? Who is a good mother? How do women know if their mothering is adequate? These and other questions haunt most women when they become mothers. In reality, motherhood is a relationship and a role; it is neither an idealized nor vilified persona, nor is it a career. There is no one right way to mother, just as there is no right way to be married, have a friend, work, or love. How a woman parents depends on her personality, her family history, her values, and her expectations for herself.

Margaret Ann, an energetic, fifty-one-year-old business owner from Chicago whom I met on an airplane, told me a story that started me thinking about well-mothered daughters and their reasonably good mothers. Here is her story, in her own words:

When I was about twenty-eight years old I decided I wanted to work in the family business. I had enjoyed five years at another company, but I was drawn to the idea of working with and learning from my dad, a man I loved and respected and who also was respected by his business contemporaries.

I first approached my mother with the idea because I thought she'd be most against it. She had worked in the business when I was young and had hated it. Dad and she argued about how to do things, and it nearly destroyed their marriage. As soon as they could afford it, she quit. I worried that she might be angry if I worked well with Dad, or feel left out if Dad and I shared something in common. So it was with trepidation that I told her of my dream. In a million years I never would have guessed her response.

"Okay," Mom said, "after dinner how about if all of us sit down and talk about how to make it happen."

"Is that all?" I said. "You're not going to try to talk me out of it? You're not going to remind me that you hated working in the business, or that it nearly destroyed your marriage?"

My mother's next comment floored me. "Heavens no, I'm not going to discourage you. You and I are different, sweetie, and I think you would enjoy it. You've got the training for it, you and your dad get along well, and you don't have to go home with him after work! The important thing is for us to plan your entry in a way that is best you and for the company."

I swear, I don't know if my mother had changed, or if the woman I thought she was never existed!

Good mothering, like good fathering, is difficult. It takes involvement, hard work, practice, and a willingness to let a daughter claim her own identity. It requires the capacity to be close while encouraging independence. A daughter who has been well-mothered understands that femininity is neither passive nor inferior but that it includes sensitivity and strength, attachment and achievement. Margaret Ann was a well-mothered daughter. Even when she could not distinguish between herself and her mother, her mother could and pointed out their differences. Even when she felt guilty about her closeness with her father, her mother encouraged it. Even when she was afraid, her mother showed strength.

Good mothers are not perfect nor are they identical in personality or disposition. They make mistakes, they get angry, and at times they feel envious or jealous. Good mothers do not strive for perfection in themselves or their daughters. They know that such unrealistic and impossible expectations serve only to provide feelings of inadequacy and resentment, both in themselves and their daughter. They understand that those who feel bound by expectations of perfection sentence themselves to a lifetime of disappointment, low self-esteem, and even depression. Good mothers know that independence does not require emotional isolation and that closeness is not synonymous with dependency. Good mothers are not always confident in what they do, but they have confidence that in being themselves as fully and authentically as possible, they will mother well.

FROM MOTHER TO MOTHER:
A POSTSCRIPT FROM SANTE FE

Like every woman, I am a daughter. I also am a mother. Within the duality of these complex roles, then, I add this postscript just for mothers.

As mothers, we must realize that it is impossible to have a daughter and not confront our relationship with our own mother. I have known many women who never wanted a daughter because they feared they would have the same troubled relationship with their daughter that they had with their own mother. Others worried that they could not be as perfect as their mother. Still others worried that they would turn competitive and work against their daughter. Some never wanted a daughter because they couldn't be sure their daughter's life would be better than their own. The desire we have to raise a daughter in a different way than we were raised may have come from a troubled relationship with our own mother but also may come from a loving determination to offer our daughter opportunities we never had and help them turn their dreams into reality.

It is normal to feel great pride in our daughters' achievements. It is also normal for our daughters' achievements to stir other feelings in us. After all, our daughters' achievements will remind us of what we might have achieved but never attempted, of opportunities lost to age, or of ambition we had but couldn't express.

We must cast ourselves as "good enough but not perfect" mothers in order to give our daughters permission to be good enough but not perfect. We must let our daughters know that we sometimes have conflicting feeling about their achievements; otherwise, we will give them confusing emotional messages. They will recognize our ambivalence, which will interfere with their ability to pursue their ambitions and make it difficult for them to create a life that best suits *their* needs, not one they think we wanted but couldn't obtain.

When I look at the opportunities and challenges facing our daughters, pride, optimism, and hopefulness temper my concerns. Our daughters aren't perfect, but they are good enough. And with our good-enough mothering, they will go far.

CHAPTER FOUR

Healthy Business Families

What families have in common the world around is that they are
the place where people learn who they are and how to be that way.
—Jean Illsley Clarke

Most family-business founders dream of passing their business on to deserving heirs, but few realize this dream. Less than one third of family-owned businesses survive the first generation, and only half of those make it into the third generation. The reasons for failure are almost infinite and include the lack of capital, no plans to continue the business, inadequate management, estate tax problems, and poor product. While analyzing failure may be interesting, I want to help you understand what contributes to success. We could speculate that success rests in the genius of the founder; to some degree, that certainly may account for a business's initial success. But many bright, capable entrepreneurs have failed to lead their business successfully into a second generation or to plan even for its continuation.

The success of a family business over several generations depends on a complex combination of variables, including timing, opportunity, sound planning, market, product, hard work, and good fortune, but perhaps the most powerful variable that distinguishes a successful business from those that fail is the presence of a strong, healthy family behind the venture. It is important, then, to continue to explore the family behind the family business. This chapter details the family as a complex, interrelated unit and considers the factors necessary to create and maintain a healthy family from which to build a healthy family business. At the heart of this discussion are factors that distinguish the ability of some families to do well, to provide emotional support for and acceptance of their members, to learn from their mistakes, to grow, and to produce the next generation of healthy family members.

IN THE SHADOWS — THE FAMILY BEHIND THE BUSINESS

Every family business reflects the family behind it, and no family business can be understood without understanding its family. Standing in the shadows of the business are the traditions, rules, and beliefs that the family carries and that members pass on — sometimes intentionally, often unconsciously — from one generation to the next. Business families depend on individual members to work in harmony with one another, but when families demand compliance under all circumstances, the business will suffer from lack of the constructive debate necessary to generate new ideas and solve problems. If your family, for example, values harmony, prizes the virtues of getting along, suffers disagreements resentfully and silently, and almost never challenges the opinions of its members openly, these practices will greatly influence the culture of the business. If, on the other hand, your family values direct and open communication and views differences as a normal consequence of living together, your business will reflect these attitudes. Trust and a sense of respect for one another's opinions, even when heated, will fortify your family's business discussions.

Every family, regardless of its emotional strength and resilience, has its characteristic ways of expressing feelings, resolving differences, sharing disappointments, and celebrating successes. Some relatives yell and criticize one another, while others pride themselves on their emotional restraint. Some families communicate with precise clarity and with much openness; other families struggle to be open and honest with one another, communicate in obscure ways, avoid certain subjects, or ignore one another entirely. Some families insist that parents and children accept responsibility for their actions; other families allow members to deny responsibility or blame others for what is their responsibility. The differences are endless, and the continuum runs from the healthiest to the most troubled of families.

The information I provide here to help you assess the strengths and weaknesses of your family is based on longitudinal research studies of healthy families as well as on my clinical work with troubled families and consultation work with business families. As you read about other families, you may experience a number of reactions. You may feel proud that your family imitates a characteristic of healthy families or complimented that you and others in your family handle well the tensions that are a normal part of living and working together. At other times, you may feel defeated by the number of problems you identify in yourself and other members of your family and feel angry that you can't change your heritage or control how other family members behave.

It helps, certainly, to have come from a healthy family or to be able to emulate the happy marriage of your parents, but it is not necessary, nor does having such a background guarantee your health and happiness. Likewise, having come from a troubled family or having watched your parents live in an unhappy marriage does not necessarily commit you to a troubled life or an unhappy, failed marriage. Family history influences but does not determine the way you live your life. As adults, each of us has responsibility for our own actions, the decisions we make, and the way we conduct our relationships

As you read this chapter, you may identify problems with the communication, closeness, trust, or conflict management skills in your family. Use this discovery as a first step toward making necessary changes. Keep in mind that even the healthiest of families have vulnerabilities that result from the reality of the human condition. In fact, the ability to manage human frailty is part of being a healthy adult and a healthy family. Commit yourself to the idea that change takes time; it is often difficult and always requires individual responsibility, courage, and hope.

Healthy But Not Perfect

No family escapes the hardships and emotional vicissitudes of life, and no family, of course, possesses absolute health. Healthy does not imply no problems and no stress, and it does not demand perfection. What distinguishes a healthy family or business is its capacity to create an atmosphere of closeness and trust at the same time that it encourages the expression of individual differences. This allows the system to accommodate life's changes and continue to move forward. This may seem easy, but it takes a large dose of determination—and sometimes several generations—to accomplish.

Members of healthy business families, as in healthy families in general, can build upon their common values to support and trust one another, address problems openly, exercise leadership appropriately, and plan collaboratively for the future growth of their business. Their respect for one another enables them to listen and learn from each other, exercise individuality, and manage the inevitable discord that arises within the business. These family members are able to attach a meaning to their struggles without having to blame the world, one another, or themselves, and they can master stressful situations in ways that strengthen the family rather than tear it apart.

STRENGTHS OF A HEALTHY FAMILY: THE WOODBURYS

Much has been written about healthy, well-functioning families. Thanks to the research, we know that healthy families encompass a wide range of individual differences. We also know some critical variables in the coping strategies of healthy families accentuate their strengths and minimize their weaknesses.[1] In this chapter we examine the coping strategies of one healthy business family, the Woodburys, over several decades and through a variety of difficult situations. I first met the Woodburys at a seminar for business owners and their families at which I was part of a panel on special issues for daughters. After the panel discussion, Arthur and Ella Woodbury asked me if I would be interested in talking more with their family. They had three children, two of whom worked in the business, and they had been through many of the issues I addressed in the seminar. They suggested, good humouredly, that their family would be a good case study for me. That was over twenty years ago.

In the story that unfolds here, you will follow the Woodburys as they made mistakes, misunderstand one another, shared successes, and grew over a period of more than five decades. During my time with them, they moved through their daily lives, incorporated new members into both their family and their business, and struggled to make numerous changes. Their willingness to let me observe and work with them provided a great deal of material about the attributes of healthy families. The Woodburys are not perfect, but they have learned ways to handle stress, master change, and resolve conflict that insure the health and hardiness of both their family and their business.

The Entrepreneurial Years, 1945-1965

Arthur Woodbury opened his business in the late 1940s. During the early days of the business, Arthur and his wife, Ella, worked long hours to support their family of three children, Paul, George, and Regina, and Arthur's elderly parents. Arthur ran the business, and Ella was a key employee. The children literally grew up at the factory, where they played on the swing set and monkey bars Arthur erected in the empty lot behind it. The three children recall having had many childhood birthday parties in the "backyard," as they fondly referred to the empty lot. The Woodburys had no choice but to be at the factory for long days, but Ella made sure the children felt comfortable and included there. She encouraged them to invite their friends over to play. Over the years, their backyard became the gathering spot for neighborhood baseball games and family picnics.

Of the three children, Paul showed the most academic promise. George and Regina were good students, but neither had the enthusiasm for school that was apparent with Paul. Both Arthur and Ella began to think of Paul as the one who probably would run their business one day. When Paul was thirteen years old, Arthur thought it was time for him to begin learning the business, and he put Paul to work after school and on Saturdays. By the time Paul reached high school, the factory had become his full-time summer job. He was a responsible employee, and his father relied on him more and more. It came as a surprise, then, when Paul told his parents he wanted to go to college after high school graduation. In fact, he wanted to become a physician. Though surprised, Arthur and Ella understood their son's intellectual ability, but unfortunately, they couldn't support his ambition financially. Moreover, they needed Paul to continue working in the factory. The business had survived its start-up and was supporting the family, but the Woodburys were in no position to hire a replacement for Paul. Unlike Paul, the younger children didn't work in the factory. Ella had witnessed the price Paul paid because of his work at the factory—he wasn't able to participate in sports and had little time for friendships—and she resolved not to let the same thing happen to the younger children.

Paul had not resented working in the business; in fact, he enjoyed the work, and he accepted the favored treatment his younger siblings received. He even seemed to understand that as the oldest child, his parents had "cut their teeth" on him. He was adamant, however, that now was his turn. He wanted to continue his education.

Ella took pride in Paul's ambition and felt sure they could work out a plan that would satisfy both Paul and the needs of the business, but Arthur was not so sure. He called Paul's request a pipe dream and was surprised by how irritated he felt when either Paul or Ella wanted to discuss the issue. Finally Ella approached Arthur and insisted that they talk. She knew he had assumed Paul would carry the business into the future, and she understood his disappointment; but she also knew Paul had a right to pursue his own interests, and they had a responsibility to help him. She reminded Arthur that Paul had sacrificed a lot to help them when they most needed it. Arthur didn't like what Ella said, but he knew she was right. He understood it was time to face reality, and within a few days he changed his attitude. As a successful business owner, Arthur was a committed problem solver, and he decided to redefine the problem as a troublesome challenge that the business could overcome with the proper analysis and creative thinking.

Together Arthur, Ella, and Paul researched options, and within months they found a solution to a problem that had once looked insurmountable. Paul would attend the local junior college for two years and then transfer to the state university, two hours away in a neighboring city, for his junior and senior years. Academic scholarships were a possibility, and the Woodburys agreed to take out a loan for him. Paul agreed to continue working for his dad until he transferred to the university or until Arthur hired his replacement, which ever came first.

Strength One: A Strong Partnership

A healthy husband-and-wife partnership of the kind Arthur and Ella enjoy is a necessary first step to creating a healthy, resilient family. It provides a useful model for the children to observe and later emulate. Healthy couples share power; they maintain the right to voice opinions, make decisions, and act in their own behalf. Each partner is competent, possesses areas of expertise, and respects the expertise of the other; circumstances dictate which person exercises leadership at any given time. A wife who is knowledgeable about investments, for example, may control how the couple invests its money, and a husband with expertise in real estate might lead when the couple decides to purchase a vacation home. Healthy couples work cooperatively with each other, respect each other's competency, and encourage each other's success. There is a strong bond of affection between healthy mates, and they support each other's efforts, even if they disagree about the method.

Couples who are healthy parents play a crucial role in creating healthy families. A healthy parental team, by modeling and passing on to their children the shared leadership that characterizes their partnership, supports the children's budding autonomy. Such parents listen to the children's opinions, consider their needs, and encourage their contributions to family discussions. Children gain increasing responsibility and freedom based on their ability to manage it, rather than on their particular age. Negotiations between parents and children are common and reflect the mutual respect between the generations. Because the children have seen their parents share power and leadership, an older sibling might ask a younger sibling for emotional support, or a younger sibling might offer advice to an older sibling. The first generation of a successful family business often features a strong marital partnership like that described here. Over the years I have found that most healthy business couples thrive on a shared distribution of power. This does not mean that the partners have equal control of all aspects of the business but that they broadly share the authority.

The Woodburys provide a good example: Arthur founded and controlled Woodbury Printing, but Ella was a key employee during the early years and an influential business advisor to Arthur later on. Arthur listened to Ella and valued her advice. Ella led the family and made the final decisions about domestic matters, but Arthur offered support and provided influential advice. Their partnership allowed them to create a stable home for their children while they worked to create a stable business for the family. Arthur and Ella exhibited the qualities frequently found in healthy business couples: they trusted and respected each other, enjoyed being together, understood that mistakes happen, and supported each other's efforts.

Just as the personality of the entrepreneur becomes institutionalized into the culture of a business, so the character of the founding partnership appears in future generations of the family business. Children tend to emulate their parents. Children who grow up with parents who respect each other and share in decision-making generally grow up to be adults with similar values. Many start-up businesses that begin as a dream between spouses and that become a reality because of their teamwork succeed over generations because the children and grandchildren share the couple's original values.

The Woodburys demonstrate how healthy families face change, support one another, and grow stronger together. Woodbury Printing struggled as a start-up business, and Arthur relied heavily on his wife and son to get through the lean early years. Paul went into the business out of necessity, and it might have been the only job he ever knew if he hadn't told his parents about his wish to attend college. Truth be known, Arthur and Ella might have overlooked his individual needs if he hadn't nudged them. But Paul had inherited many of his parents' traits: he trusted them, he knew he could be open with them, and he understood that his ambition was as important as theirs. Paul's strong character and his parents' sense of fairness helped them negotiate an agreement that both supported Paul's ambition and met the needs of the business.

Strength Two: Independence and Closeness Are Encouraged

Independence, as I use it here, refers to the capacity to function on one's own. Healthy families accept and appreciate individual personalities, as well as diverse intellectual and physical abilities. Children learn early from their parents to express their thoughts and feelings and to take responsibility for their behavior; in the process of expressing themselves, they learn the ways in which they are similar to and different from one another. This learning is critical to developing independence. When families respect and encourage autonomy, as the Woodburys did during their entrepreneurial years, both parents and children can pursue individual interests without fear of ridicule, of rejection, or of becoming the family scapegoat. All parties can have their own opinions, honestly say what is on their mind, and even disagree, all without feeling inadequate or fearing punishment. In fact, only in the presence of autonomy can genuine closeness flourish. While part of human nature is to enjoy being with others in a meaningful way, we avoid closeness when we fear the loss of our individuality. To accept the potential rejections and inevitable losses that come with loving, we must have a firmly established sense of self. Only then can we afford to give ourselves emotionally to others.

Even in the healthiest of families, however, it is difficult to encourage independence while maintaining closeness. Arthur Woodbury was pained by the idea that Paul was different enough from him that he planned a career outside the family business; in response he criticized the idea of becoming a doctor as a pipe dream, implying that his son was foolish. Ella's confrontation helped Arthur reflect on his initial reaction, reassess the situation, and recognize the appropriateness of Paul's request, and Arthur changed his attitude and his behavior. Less healthy parents may have discouraged Paul from going to medical school, at the least made him feel guilty, or shamed him into staying at home and working at the factory. One indicator of emotional health lies in the capacity to make adjustments in our behavior when circumstances warrant a change.

In business families, where relatives live and work together, the regulation of independence and closeness can be challenging. I have seen many business families promote togetherness, far fewer that promote independence. At work, for example, grown children often remain under their parents' tutelage well beyond what is needed, making it very hard for the young adults to feel independent. The most successful business families I've worked with understand the importance of individuality within the context of closeness and encourage that individuality both at home and at work. These families do not coerce children to join the business, nor do they exclude the children from the family's inner circle if they work outside the business. Both at home and at work, family members exhibit honest communication, trust, and a healthy respect for differences. These same business families know that the business benefits when they openly share differing thoughts and opinions. Solving problems and making changes are far easier when family members value diversity than when everyone must follow an artificial and powerful family party line.

When I consult with a family business where members describe their problem as an unwillingness to make changes, I ask many questions about the family and its way of regulating power, control, and emotions. A business always reflects the coping strategies of the family that runs it.

If you want to learn more about how your family addresses issues of control and leadership, answer the set of questions titled, "Power, Control, and Leadership in Your Family." Your responses will provide critical information about how your significant relationships, your family, and the business share power. You will learn more about the flexibility or rigidity of thinking within your family. Ask family members to answer the questions too, and then discuss the responses. The discussion will further highlight particular issues for your family. For example, does one person attempt to control the discussion? If so, how do others respond? Are some members silent? Do certain responses get ignored? What does this tell you about the way your family shares power and control? What does it say about the respect you would receive in the business?

Power, Control, and Leadership in Your Family

1. What did your parents' marriage teach you about power and control in a relationship? Who has control and of what areas in their relationship? Was there a time when the balance of power was different? Why did it change?

2. Who else has power in your family? How do you know? How do they exercise power?

3. Who has power in the business? How do you know? How do they exercise power?

4. How does the business determine leadership? Are the rules for deciding leadership the same or different than at home? Are the leaders in the family business also the leaders at home? Why or why not?

5. How easy or difficult is it to express an opinion that is different than others in your family?

6. Is there someone whom the others always consider to be right? Does this ever change? Under what conditions?

Strength Three: The Structure to Perform Critical Tasks

While healthy business families need flexibility to balance the often-conflicting needs of work and home, they also need enough structure to perform critical tasks effectively. The Woodbury family demonstrated both of these qualities. When Paul wanted to leave the business, his parents listened and responded to his request; they also put some structure around how his departure would take place. Everyone understood that another person would have to assume Paul's responsibilities in the business before he could leave. The Woodburys' system was flexible enough to tolerate a disruptive change and structured enough to manage that change successfully.

Within healthy families and the businesses they operate, members possess a relatively clear understanding of one another's responsibilities and recognize that these may be different in work and family contexts. Arthur was the boss when he was at the factory, but he was a partner to Ella and a parent to his children when he was at home. Paul was a veteran employee at work, but he was a young adult still dependent on his parents when he was at home. Healthy business families recognize that certain roles and generational boundaries may be appropriate in the family or in the business context, but not necessarily in both. While it is appropriate for parents to keep certain personal and family information from their children who work in the business, it is not appropriate to keep business information from them. Parents should not, for example, exclude children from business meetings with the banker or the CPA if those children have management positions within the business.

The amount and kind of structure needed by a family or its business will change over time, depending on such things as the age of the children, the specific circumstances, and the capabilities of those in the system. The healthiest business families I have met have a sixth sense about how much structure they need and when to provide it. To highlight what I mean, assume that a husband and wife build a business in the basement of their home by working together every evening and over countless weekends. They create a product that sells well, the business prospers, and it moves out of the basement. The children join the business when they are old enough and hold roles consistent with their inexperience. As they gain experience and their business maturity unfolds, they no longer need as much structure, and the parents slowly step back and lessen their control. Over time, the parents turn operational control over to their children but retain majority ownership of the company. They continue to participate in business decisions in their capacity as owners and board members, but since they no longer manage the business, they no longer make operational or personnel decisions.

The parents in this example encouraged their children's development while providing the structure to help them succeed. It may seem that they did what any reasonable parents would do, but many parents struggle to accomplish these transitions. To do so is a sign of family health and hardiness.

Strength Four: Efficient Problem-Solving

Healthy families cope with problems in a relatively efficient way. They usually approach them in a direct and timely manner, deal with whatever conflicts may arise, and support a mutually satisfactory resolution. In the Woodbury family, as in other healthy business families, members respect individual needs, and differences coexist with cooperation and love. Paul's needs ran at cross purposes with the needs of the family business, but he and his parents discussed them and found a creative solution to the dilemma. Their initial disagreement did not threaten their love for each other. Throughout childhood, Paul and his siblings learned to think for themselves and to say what was on their minds. Paul wasn't rebelling against his father's control in wanting to become a doctor; he was exercising the individuality his parents encouraged him to develop. A family needs considerable courage and a healthy dose of self-confidence to tolerate conflict and resolve problems as successfully as the Woodburys did in this case.

Healthy families approach problems within the context of numerous options, and they tend to be pragmatic. They first try to solve problems in one way, but if that approach doesn't work, they back off and try another solution. They act as though the best way to resolve problems is to do what any reasonable person would do under the circumstances. Would that we always could find the means of using such a simple and useful method of problem-solving!

Assessing Your Family's Problem-Solving Skills

Before you answer these questions, project yourself back to a time when you were a child living in your parents' home.

1. How did you parents resolve their differences? What did their methods teach you?

2. Did your parents allow your opinions to be voiced? If not, how did you let them know your opinions? Was your method effective?

3. How old were you when you began to have a voice in family decisions? What did you learn from being part of the decision-making? If you were never allowed to be part, what did you learn from that?

4. How did your parents respond to your efforts to assert your opinions? Did their response change as you got older?

5. Disagreements are inevitable in relationships; how does your family manage them? Who is allowed to disagree with whom and about what? What issues cannot be discussed? How do others in the family react when two family members disagree?

6. How does the family address problems in the business? Are the rules for problem-solving the same as or different from at home?

7. What rules govern how the family makes decisions in the business? Are the rules consistent with the organizational structure and lines of authority? Why or why not?

Families usually do not think consciously about the way they solve problems — they just do what they've done before — and most likely they approach problems the way the family has done for generations. To help you think about the problem-solving strategies your family uses, answer the questions in the box titled "Assessing Your Family's Problem-Solving Skills." Your answers will help you better understand the effectiveness of your problem-solving skills and those of other family members.

The Evolving Years, 1965-1985

By the mid-1960s, the Woodbury family expanded to include in-laws and grandchildren, and two generations participated in the business. The grown children made decisions, however tentative, to work inside or outside the business, and Arthur and Ella were beginning to think of a future beyond children and Woodbury Printing. These evolving years challenged the Woodburys, as changes interrupted their history of open communication, tested their trust in one another, and caused the business to suffer due to their inability to address certain key issues until a crisis occurred. What distinguishes the Woodburys is not the difficulties they encountered or the mistakes they made, but their willingness to acknowledge their mistakes, make the necessary changes, and grow from their experiences.

Paul completed his medical residency and was practicing at a teaching hospital near the family home. During his residency he met Patricia, also a physician; they married and had two children, Paul Jr. and Elliott.

George married his high school sweetheart Ruth, and they lived about a mile from the family home. They had three children, the oldest, Hannah, and the twins, Arthur and Ella, named after their grandparents. After Paul left home, George, to everyone's surprise, eagerly filled his brother's shoes at the factory. He worked hard and eventually became the factory's general manager. George completed two years at the junior college and was taking business courses part-time at the university. Ella had been instrumental in this decision; she wanted all of her children to get an education so they would not depend on the family business for a job.

Regina was working for a company in another state. She had worked at the family factory for three years after graduating from college, but her relationship with George had been stressful. He had difficulty collaborating and tried to micromanage Regina. She, in response, avoided George as much as possible and told him little about what she was doing. This in turn only made George more controlling of her. In the end, her lack of confidence in George and in their partnership led her to seek work elsewhere. Regina visited the family on a regular basis, and when she was home she had long conversations with George and their father about the family business, her work, market strategies, and management theories. She appreciated the opportunity to catch up on what was happening in the factory, but she always left the conversations thinking that George had more responsibility than his capabilities warranted.

Ella loved her children, but she was somewhat relieved when they all were grown, and it was just she and Arthur in the house again. She had time to devote to things she had put aside for thirty years. With a master's degree in English and a teaching certificate she'd never used, Ella thought about applying for a teaching job at the junior college or perhaps at the university two hours from where they lived.

Arthur turned much of the daily operations over to George, but he was very actively involved—more so, in fact, than he thought was good for him or the business. He needed to be looking toward the next stage of his life, but George always seemed to need him at work for something. Arthur worried that his involvement reflected his inability to let go of his "baby," but he also worried about George's leadership. He regretted the way George's promotion to general manager had occurred without systematic plan; Arthur had simply thought it was time for the next generation to move up. When he was ready to implement the decision, Paul had no interest in the position, and Regina was too young to be considered. If they were to keep the business in the family, George was the only choice. Now, however, Arthur wondered if his own ambivalence about relinquishing the business had kept him from planning more thoughtfully for its continuation. Unfortunately, he didn't discuss his concern with George because he didn't have an alternative plan.

Significant family events can occur without warning. While playing golf at the local club, Arthur got word that Ella and George had been in a car accident. For the first few days after the wreck, they both were in critical condition. Paul and Regina came home, and the three of them kept a close vigil at the hospital and a watchful eye on the business.

During the long hours at the hospital, Paul found himself thinking about his father, including some regrets he felt about having left the family business. He began to discuss his thoughts with his father. He said he was grateful his parents let him pursue his dream, but he worried that he had disappointed Arthur and shattered his father's dream.

"It did," Arthur admitted. "Should I have been elated that we weren't going to work together?" He went on to say that he was proud of Paul and praised him for following his dream. "Don't ever feel guilty about what you did. It was the right thing to do. I would feel ashamed, and you would resent me, if you had sacrificed your dream to live my dream."

When it appeared certain that both Ella and George would recover, Paul went back home with more energy than he'd felt in years, and Regina stayed to help her father at the factory. Together they ran the business and nursed Ella and George back to health. Regina's boss understood her personal circumstances but eventually told her she needed to return to her job. George was not yet back at work, and it would be months before he could work full-time. Regina knew her father needed her help, and she loved being back in the family business; she also knew that Arthur wanted to ease himself out and that George eventually would return to run the company. Nevertheless, Regina was enjoying herself and wanted to stay.

Ironically, while Regina was ruminating about her career, her father's needs, and the family business, her parents were discussing some of the same issues. The accident had awakened Ella and Arthur to their own mortality, and they realized it was time to make some changes in their lives and in their business. After much discussion, Arthur called a meeting with George and Regina. He told them he had made a mistake in not formally planning his retirement and the continuation of the business, and he outlined his plan for correcting his error.

Arthur had hired a family business consultant, who advised him to create an outside board of directors to help him formulate a long-term strategy for the company and to serve as advisors through the leadership transition that would greatly determine the future of the business. He told Regina and George he was acting on the consultant's advice. He knew he should have formed a board years earlier but he had been bullheaded, as Ella sometimes reminded him, and concerned about losing control. With hindsight, he understood the value of having a board that he could rely upon to give him objective and critical advice. With the help of the consultant and advisors, he was going to formulate a continuity plan that included a formal process for evaluating and selecting the most qualified individuals for all of the key positions in the business. He assured Regina and George that he wanted them in executive roles if possible, and he hoped they would do whatever it took to prepare themselves for the senior positions. But he stressed that he intended to select the most qualified individuals, regardless of their last name.

Arthur and Ella also had decided to establish a family council that would include both owners and spouses to discuss concerns arising from their involvement in and ownership of the business. Ella worried that as the business grew and ownership transferred to a larger number of family members, some of whom would not be employees, family conflicts could jeopardize the business. She and Arthur had prided themselves on being open with each other and with their children, and Ella knew that the quality of this communication would become even more important as more family members shared management and ownership responsibility in the company. Arthur thought a council would give the family a structured setting in which to learn about the business, to discuss their concerns, and to provide a boundary between business and family.

As Arthur expected, Regina celebrated his decision and viewed it as an opportunity for her to rejoin the family business. George, on the other hand, was less than satisfied with the news. Disappointed and angry, he felt Arthur had betrayed him. He tried to convince Ella to change Arthur's mind; he accused Regina of stealing his position while he was convalescing and Arthur of lying to him. Arthur and Ella listened to George but held fast to their decisions. Arthur repeatedly reminded George that he wanted and needed him in the business, but that he also needed to ensure the successful continuation of the business. Arthur admitted that George had failed to meet his expectations and that he thought the failure was due, in part, to the absence of a leadership development and succession plan. He also explained to George that he did not owe him the presidency: "I owe you, Regina, and every other employee the opportunity to develop to their fullest capacity. Nothing more, nothing less."

Strength Five: Limitations Are Acknowledged

Members of healthy families realize that everyone's abilities have limits and that everything human is subject to error. Understanding that one person cannot do it all and needs to rely on others in many situations helps healthy business families appreciate the unique contributions others can make. They know that no employee, not even the founder, has an unchallengeable hold on knowledge. Arthur Woodbury was a shrewd and intuitive businessman but he also made some serious mistakes. His need for control kept him from seeing the importance of developing managers and the need for a formal succession process, that is, until a crisis threatened the future of the business. Fortunately, Arthur's ability to acknowledge his mistakes and move forward to correct them saved the family much grief and probably saved the family business from ruin.

In healthy business families, members may respect the owner for visionary leadership and analytic skills, but they do not revere him or her as perfect. Indeed, family businesses thrive in large measure because one generation does not have to contend with the absolute knowledge and control of the preceding generation. These families welcome and encourage new ideas from anyone, and this increases the likelihood that the business will be able to respond quickly and efficiently to the changing marketplace. The family responds to problems as business opportunities, and pragmatism, reasonableness, and resourcefulness sustain this process.

Strength Six: Feelings Are Normal

Healthy families express feelings openly, regardless of their nature or intensity, and this contributes to an attitude of openness and trust. This attitude includes a belief that even ambivalent and contradictory feelings are normal. For example, Arthur Woodbury admitted he was disappointed that Paul chose not to work in the family business, but also he was proud that Paul had pursued his own passion.

In healthy families, the family considers and respects everyone's feelings, from the youngest child to the oldest grandparent. Family discussions, even when intense, are filled with respect for one another. Children grow up learning that feelings are normal, the expression of feelings is natural, and they should respect the feelings of others. They grow up knowing that their feelings are as legitimate as their parents', which results in fewer oppositional struggles between them and their parents. Healthy families can share their feelings about loss and disappointment as readily as their feelings about success and achievement.

Members of healthy families intrinsically trust one another and their motives. Their trust allows them to view situations, however painful and uncertain, from a perspective that allows for optimism and hope. These families are not without their prejudices and defenses, but in general they have the capacity to look beyond themselves in their effort to deal with problems. George Woodbury was disappointed and angry to learn he would not automatically become his father's successor, and he accused his father of cheating him out of his entitlement. In time, however, he recognized that his accusations were unfair and that he had defined the situation based on his own needs. The changes Arthur proposed made him feel threatened and humiliated, and he worried about losing his position in the business. Arthur and Ella understood George's initial reaction. They thought it was normal under the circumstances and didn't lose respect for him. Regina sympathized with George, knowing she would have felt much the same way under similar conditions, and she trusted that her brother loved her despite his anger.

The way a family communicates feelings is crucial to the health of the family and the business it operates. To learn more about your family's communication style, answer the set of questions titled "How Your Family Communicates" and have other family members answer them also. After everyone has completed the exercise, discuss together how your communications affect family relationships and the way decisions get made, both at home and in the family business.

How Your Family Communicates

1. What rules govern communication in your family? Who communicates with whom about what? Is everyone allowed to express feelings and ideas, or only certain members? What happens if someone breaks the rules?

2. What rules govern how individuals express disagreements? Who is allowed to disagree with whom?

3. Do you discuss problems openly with one another? Do family members bring others into the disagreement?

4. Are any topics off limits? If so, how and when did they become off limits? What would happen if the family discussed them?

5. What rules govern how family members air disagreements in the business? Who is allowed to disagree with whom? Has anyone ever broken the rules? What happened?

6. How do the rules governing discussion of business disagreements affect the business?

Strength Seven: Circular Thinking

Healthy families sense that any action by one member can reverberate in reactions by other members, and thus no one person is ever to blame for a relationship problem. This perspective allows them to see differing sides of a problem and to approach emotional issues with a fair amount of objectivity.

Peter Senge, director of the Systems Thinking and Organizational Learning Program at MIT's Sloan School of Management, emphasizes the axiom that every influence is both cause and effect. For example, control on the part of one person increases defiance on the part of another, which, in turn, reinforces the initial control. The father who treats his daughter like a princess encourages her sense of entitlement and dependency, and the more dependent and entitled she behaves, the more the father treats her like a princess. As a way of absolving himself of responsibility for the problem, the father may complain to outsiders that his daughter is spoiled, but reality is that he contributes to the problem by encouraging the very behavior he criticizes. A similar feedback loop existed between George and Regina: The more insecure George felt about his competence, the more controlling he was of Regina; in response, Regina shared little with him and avoided him. The more she avoided, the more George pestered her, and the more she avoided him. And so on and so on.

In families where individuals accept responsibility for their own actions, they recognize that they can prevent or break a negative feedback loop. Arthur and Ella interrupted a negative feedback loop with George by refusing to respond to his angry accusations with defensiveness or counteraccusations. They tolerated his anger because they considered the context within which it occurred and trusted that he eventually would calm down. They didn't criticize him for being upset nor did they back down from their decision in order to appease him. Their ability to remain calm in the face of George's anger prevented a negative feedback loop from occurring.

Strength Eight: Outside Interests

Healthy families are involved with people outside their immediate family. They reach out to others, they depend on others, and they are actively involved in their community. They have friendships, hobbies, and activities outside of work. They often contribute time, resources, and money to local charities; sometimes they go so far as to establish and fund charitable foundations. Healthy business families realize that they must balance their familial togetherness with a support network that extends beyond the family.

Healthy business families effectively combine a need for profit with a concern for community, and they advance programs and policies that reflect a caring for employees. Family members serve on the boards of directors for other businesses, they are active in trade groups and associations, and they participate in legislative advocacy groups. Because the Woodburys created an outside board of directors to guide the leadership transition in their family business, family members began to feel a responsibility and connection that went beyond their immediate family.

The Mature Years, 1985-Present

A final look at the Woodburys finds a third generation joining the enterprise. The business structure and the management of family relationships reveal the influence of past family experiences. The Woodburys learned from their mistakes, and they are trying to pass on their hard-earned knowledge to the younger generation in both the business and the family.

The first task of Arthur's newly selected board of directors was to assist him in formulating a plan that would insure qualified leadership for the business, both in the immediate transition and into the future. Arthur had made some mistakes that he needed to correct. His need for control and his ambivalence about retirement had prevented him from planning well for his own succession. These mistakes put the business at risk and had created a hardship for some of the family.

It was not easy for Arthur to disappoint George or for George to hear that he would have to compete for a leadership role in the company. George knew, however, that his parents were acting in the best interest of the business, The history of openness and trust that had guided the family for generations helped George overcome his anger, and over time he settled into the restructuring process. In fact, once the humiliation was behind him, George found himself relieved that a formal mechanism was in place to select the future leaders. He felt less burdened and alone, and more supported as one of a team of managers that included his sister. Over time, George and Regina came to appreciate the different strengths each brought to the family enterprise; they supported each other's efforts, and together they helped the business grow.

Today the challenge and excitement of being the president of Woodbury Printing belongs fully to Regina, and she is handling it well. Woodbury Printing is now one of three businesses owned by Woodbury Enterprises, the holding company that the family formed, which has Arthur as chairman, two family members, and two outside directors on the board. George is in charge of operations for Woodbury Printing, and non-family members head the other two companies. George is genuinely proud of Regina's success and feels he has contributed to it. Regina values George's contributions to the business. They both feel good about their success in making both the business and their sibling relationship a strong one.

George's oldest daughter, Hannah, and his son, Arthur, who is nicknamed Hank, work in the business. Hannah uses the factory for summer employment while she works on a doctorate in sociology, but Hank plans to make Woodbury Printing his career. He apprenticed at another company for three years because the family council now requires that a family member work externally for at least two years before joining their business. He respects Regina, and she enjoys his passion for the business. Regina recruited a non-family mentor to help Hank with his management development because she learned well from her father's mistakes the importance of developing family leaders and planning early for succession.

The relationship between Hank and Regina reflects how well the older generations kept their conflicts from spilling into the younger generations. If Hank had grown up listening to his father complain about his aunt and grandparents, his choices about work most likely would have been different. Had he chosen to enter the family business, he would have carried some of his father's resentment with him, which would have tainted his relationship with Regina. Worse, he may never have entered the family business as a way of showing his loyalty to his father; he may have taken his talent to a competing company.

Similarly, had Regina still carried resentment toward George, she would have seen Hank as his father's stand-in, which would have tainted her relationship with him. She might well have viewed Hank as an adversary instead of the team player he is and thwarted his attempts to become a major player in the family business. Instead, Hank and Regina seem to feed off each other's passion for the business, and they join forces in their competitiveness to drive it forward.

Ella continues to be involved in a number of volunteer and educational activities. She teaches literacy classes and is part of a task force to study gender biases and their effects on academic performance in the middle school. In addition to being chairman of Woodbury Enterprises, Arthur sits on the board of directors for another business; he often accepts invitations to speak at family business seminars. It isn't unusual for Arthur, Regina, and George to make presentations together. They share their struggles as a way of demonstrating the importance of open communication, and they stress the usefulness of outside resources such as a board of directors, a family council, and family business consultants.

Paul's youngest son, Elliot, works in the finance department of the business, and his elder son, Paul Jr., is pursuing a medical career. Paul still practices medicine, and he heads family council meetings. His leadership emphasizes the difference between family and business and creates a much more relaxed atmosphere than Arthur, as founder of the business, or Regina, as CEO, could possibly provide. Part of the middle generation, he is a non-employed owner of the business and the generations on either side of him respect him.

The Woodburys are an example of a family that has produced individuals who are both independent and close to one another. They have experienced family tragedy and managed well the inevitable stresses that come with life. They reach out to others, and they respond positively to input from others. They have made mistakes but have struggled through them without sacrificing family unity. They respect the fact that their family is a *business* family and their business is a *family* business. The Woodburys are not perfect, but they are, unmistakably, a healthy business family.

It helps to have come from a healthy family, but that in itself does not guarantee your happiness or your ability to create a healthy family of your own. Family history influences, but does not determine, the way you live your life. After reading this chapter, you understand your unique set of strengths and weakness. Use this understanding to determine the way you make decisions, solve problems, and interact with others, including your family. Use it to decide what you need to do the same or differently from the family you grew up in to create a healthy family of your own.

PART II

THE BUSINESS OF THE FAMILY BUSINESS

CHAPTER FIVE

Leadership: Competence Matters

The person who knows "how" will always have a job. The person who knows "why" will always be his boss.

—Diane Ravitch

Twenty-four percent of family businesses are led by a female CEO or president, as of 2007. This is a welcomed contrast to the less than 5 percent only ten years earlier, in 1997![1] Men in family businesses still are the most likely to be key decision-makers, but these numbers suggest that for the first time in history daughters like you may have an equal chance to compete for leadership positions.

For this to happen, certain prejudices toward women that prevent owners from considering their daughters alongside their sons must be dispelled. Overcoming a prejudice is difficult, and doing so still will not guarantee your place or success in the family enterprise. The attitudes that prevent women from advancing may change, but if you aren't competent, you won't advance. You may have a good relationship with your parents and with other family members who work in the business. Your family may possess certain characteristics of a healthy family. You may feel passionate about your job. You may have all these advantages, and they are not enough if you do not have the competence to lead well.

This chapter explores what it takes to be a successful leader and outlines the kind of leadership every stage in a family business life cycle needs. By working through various sections of the chapter, you will determine the leadership your family's business requires and assess how well you meet those requirements. You can use this chapter as a practical guide to assess and improve your leadership skills. The exercises also will help you define your leadership style and determine how well your style fits within the family business culture.

CHARACTERISTICS OF EFFECTIVE LEADERS

Many characteristics enhance the effectiveness of any family-business leader, regardless of gender or personality. Leaders vary widely, but the best leaders possess a combination of attributes. They have a compelling vision for the future of the business along with an ability to communicate that vision to others. They have the ability to motivate others and the self-confidence to share power. Effective leaders recognize the talents of other people and provide the resources to develop those talents. They can manage complexity and have the flexibility to respond quickly to changing circumstances.

Business schools teach some, but not most, of these abilities. Rather, individuals acquire these traits along the road to becoming themselves— as individuals and leaders. Use this chapter as a guide not only to clarify the most important requirements for leadership in your family's business, but also to compare your leadership skills against those that successful business leaders generally employ. Throughout the chapter, consider your strengths as well as your weaknesses and determine what you need to do to improve your leadership capabilities.

A Compelling Vision

Many of us have ideas that would be useful in business, but few of us bring those ideas to fruition. Leaders can describe a future for a business that is both compelling and better than current conditions. Good leaders excite and engage others with their passion for the success of their enterprise. They are able to hold on to a vision through disappointments and tedium, endure exhaustion, and accept criticism. At any stage in the life of a business, a vision is no more than a pipe dream if it doesn't come to reality.

Crafting a vision is difficult for the best of leaders. A vision must be specific yet broad enough to guide the business through good times and bad, succinct but captivating enough to motivate others. A vision embodies the values and personality of its owner; it provides focus for the mission and the work of the leader. The vision is, after all, the heart and soul behind the business.

Even the most creative ideas will remain unrealized without a clear vision. Janet, the director of marketing in a family-owned clothing store, was a talented and energetic manager, but she lacked an organizing vision. A highly creative individual, she had good ideas and developed new ones as she went through each day. She was gregarious and spoke with almost every employee she passed in the plant, usually offering them at least one new idea to enhance their work efforts. Janet ranked among the best in the industry in intellectual ability, but her vision lacked the clarity and focus it needed. Her ideas were creative, but she frequently got sidetracked with projects that did not strategically benefit the company. Without a clear focus, she didn't know where she was going or how she was going to get there. Her subordinates felt frustrated and confused by what they described as her erratic direction. Sales dropped under her leadership, and the company missed its sales goals each quarter for two consecutive years. Janet was ineffective in her position, and eventually she was removed from it.

Janet blamed her failure on an increasingly competitive market and the conservative nature of the family running the business. These factors may have contributed to her difficulties, but the primary problem was her lack of a clear vision. Without a focus, she spent her efforts on too many activities that detracted from increasing sales and meeting customers' needs. By not having an organizing vision, the business lost money; Janet lost some of her confidence and, in the long run, she lost a job she enjoyed.

The capacity to create a vision may not come naturally to all leaders, but they can learn it. A vision should not be idealistic but firmly grounded in reality. It must be specific and quantifiable. Plans and initiatives should be measured against the vision, and anything

Your Leadership Vision

1. Do you want to be involved in crafting a vision for the business? Why or why not? Do you have a vision for the future of the business? Why or why not?

2. Can you describe your vision so that others can see it and support it? Do others get excited when you describe your vision to them? Why or why not?

3. Do you constructively question the way decisions are made? Do you offer constructive alternatives? How do others react to your questioning? What do their reactions say to you?

If you were not able to answer the questions in some detail, then you probably do not have a well-defined vision. If you plan to advance in the business, you need to change that. Ask those in charge of running the business to help you develop this skill. Attend a leadership seminar.

inconsistent with it must be discarded or changed. The set of questions titled "Your Leadership Vision" will help define your vision for the business (or the area you manage), your ability to communicate it, and your ability to excite others to join in your vision.

The Ability to Manage Complexity

Effective leaders can understand multiple sources of information and assess data from multiple perspectives. They have the capacity to organize a large amount of information in a logical way and to understand the relationship between the data and the circumstances of their business. Good business leaders know the industry outside the walls of their company. They understand the changing marketplace and are able to keep ahead of market trends.

How do you determine optimal workforce size, motivate and retain qualified staff, respond to customer needs and stakeholder demands, and retain a competitive edge in the marketplace all at the same time? In my experience, you need brains and experience to juggle all of this, plus flexibility and self-confidence. Women often are masters in the management of multiple and competing interests and problems. Over 70 percent of working women have children, and a growing number of two-income families depend on the wives' income for financial security.[2] Even when both spouses work full time and the wife earns more than the husband, however, the woman continues to shoulder the primary responsibility for child care and domestic chores. I could point out the obvious disadvantages of this arrangement for women, but for the purpose of this discussion, I'd rather address an advantage. The experience of juggling a full-time job, child care, daycare, domestic chores, the dog, the sick child, the sick daycare provider, and so forth teaches most women how to handle numerous complex tasks simultaneously—and calmly. Women often tell me that they find a direct correlation between the situations they face at home and at work. As one woman put it, "If you can figure out whether the four-year-old or the six-year-old gets the last piece of candy and make both of them think they won, you can negotiate any contract in the world."

As leaders, most women easily manage conflicting details about multiple problems, including the interrelationships between people and their tasks and the impact of one upon the other. Sally Helgesen has noted that motherhood demands many of the same skills as executive leadership, including "organization, pacing, the balancing of conflicting claims, teaching, guiding, leading, monitoring, handling disturbances, and imparting information."[3] Women who generally view their work as only one aspect of their identity—not the totality of who they are—can view themselves as mother and manager, savvy dealmaker and leader, empathic friend and strict boss. They easily fit into and feel comfortable in many different roles, and they use this ability to their advantage in various situations and environments.

A Willingness to Involve Others

According to Max DuPree, former CEO of Herman Miller and author of the book, *Leadership Is an Art*, the most effective contemporary management process is participative management. "It begins with a belief in the potential of people. Participative management without a belief in that potential and without convictions about the gifts people bring to organizations is a contradiction in terms."[4]

Women, in general, express themselves in a way that invites others to participate. In a work environment, open dialogue encourages information sharing and teamwork, commitment to one another's success, and an ease between employees. "Women ... are likely to succeed," says Janet Harris-Lange, president of the National Association of Business Owners, "because they admit they need help and surround themselves with good people."[5] Dogmatic leaders are rarely as successful as a collaborative leader. Women often lead from the center: that is, they encourage alternative perspectives and respect the power of consensus. They refuse to favor one person continually over others, seeking out opinions not just from the most senior managers but from lower managers as well. Leading from the center fosters a sense of commitment to the mission and camaraderie which are necessary for group success.

In family-owned businesses, emotions and competition can run high. A good leader has to manage the complex relationships among family members who work together and also keep them working well together. Competition can be motivating, but if allowed too much rein, it can destroy teamwork. The most effective family business leaders understand the delicate balance between competition and teamwork. They make all employees, family members as well as non-family, senior as well as junior managers, feel their ideas are needed to produce the best outcome for the business, and this in turn encourages greater cooperation and team effort.

It takes courage to involve others genuinely and allow them to influence you, your ideas, and your decisions. This approach has risks. Subordinates may feel free to openly criticize and challenge your leadership or to express frustration when you listen to but ultimately reject their ideas. Strong leaders understand these risks but believe that the positive results of involvement far outweigh the negatives.

Participative management encourages the involvement of everyone, but it is not democratic. After ending discussions and hearing opinions, leaders are still responsible for the final decision. You can share and delegate leadership, but you should never, ever give it away.

Some women confuse cooperation with accommodation, so let us be clear about the difference. *Cooperation* is activity shared for a mutual benefit. *Accommodation*, on the other hand, is conformity and agreement for the purpose of harmony. Helen, the self-effacing woman you met in chapter three, exemplifies the distinction between accommodation and cooperation. She lost her management position because she was so overly accommodating that her contribution and usefulness to the family business became minimal.

While women tend to give attention to maintaining relationships and can be cooperative to a fault, many men find it difficult, even impossible, to work collaboratively with others. These men view others as rivals, and they tend to form relationships for the purpose of gaining additional power and information, rather than for the sake of collaboration and shared success. William Hewlett and David Packard, two notable exceptions to these generalizations about men, are superb examples of strong male leaders who exhibited a participative leadership style. Growing their business from a garage workshop to a multibillion-dollar enterprise, they kept competitive and ahead of market trends in part because they valued open communication, group participation, and knew how to invite and use the knowledge of others. In the days when authoritarian leadership was the only game in town, they used what they referred to as "management by walking around." They walked the shop floor and talked to their employees. They asked for and received suggestions and criticisms from their factory workers, who were ultimately responsible for carrying out management decisions. Workers were eager to offer ways to do their jobs better, and the business thrived within the cooperative atmosphere.

Hewlett and Packard also held off-site meetings with their senior managers to exchange views, foster creativity, and encourage group participation and cooperation. In David Packard's words, "We thought that if we could get everybody to agree on what our objectives were and to understand what we were trying to do, then we could turn them loose and they would move in a common direction."[6] Packard and Hewlett felt strongly that if written objectives were to guide their managers and supervisors, they should have a part in developing them. Today, this idea of communicating and involving others is a basic tenet of a participative leadership style; in 1957, Packard and Hewlett called it "management by walking around."

Not everyone is well suited for a leadership style that encourages participation and teamwork. Answer the set of questions titled "Motivating Others" to learn more about your interest in working with others and your ability to motivate them.

Motivating Others

1. Do you prefer to work alone or with others?
2. Do you solicit ideas from others, or do you prefer to figure things out on your own?
3. Are you comfortable asking for help from others? How well do you accept criticism from others?
4. Is your working relationship with subordinates a one-way or a two-way street?
5. Do you expect new ideas and suggestions from your subordinates? Your peers? Why or why not?

If most of your answers reflected a preference to involve others and work as a team, congratulations. You probably encourage collaboration and motivate others by involving them in the mission. If, on the other hand, your responses reflected a preference for working alone and making decisions alone, you may want to reconsider your management style and/or consider modifying it. You may want to question your suitability and interest in a management position. If you want to learn more about leadership, I recommend you begin by reading some of the books from the Suggested Reading list at the back of this book.

The Insight to Use the Talents of Others

Good leadership requires an ability to use the individual talents within the business. For this to happen, leaders must first recognize that others have something to offer and then encourage the development of their talents. Family business leaders who do this well have an indisputable competitive advantage in the marketplace. In fact, businesses that fail in this regard usually fail. The dying business is easily recognized: it has a low — or no — expectation for growth in either its products or its people. It is a business whose highest priority is to avoid risk.

In his book, Max DuPree underscores the essentials of effective leadership: coaching, guiding, serving, nurturing, and caring sincerely about others. Good leaders model the importance of learning and upgrading talents and skills by keeping themselves and their subordinates abreast of market trends, new research, technical advances, and other changes. Good leaders know that the successful future of the family business depends on the contributions of others. Female executives often bring these particular qualities to their work. Raised to cooperate with and support others, they seek out and utilize talent throughout the organization; they quickly assess what motivates employees and use the knowledge to excite and empower them to perform at their full potential. Supporting employees to their full potential guarantees that the business gets the best use of its human resources, which increases the potential for business success, generation after generation.

The Self-Confidence to Share Power

As a business grows, its problems grow more complicated. No one, not even the founder of a business, can manage everything and be an expert about all things. The best leaders understand this. They know that their success comes from knowing how to diagnose a problem and then providing support to those with the most skill to get the job done well. They also know that doing this well entails distributing leadership power among a variety of people.

Sharing leadership takes a hefty dose of self-confidence as well as confidence in others. For leaders who need all the power, who insist on making all of the decisions, a shift to including others will be especially difficult, perhaps even impossible. Entrepreneurs often suffer this problem as their business grows and requires the inclusion of others to survive.

The best leaders have confidence in their strengths and know their limitations, and they respect the talent that others bring to the table. They know that with the help of others, they can solve most problems. Collaborative leaders create loyalty by signaling that they need and respect the ideas of others.

The art of sharing leadership can be difficult for many novice managers to learn. They have not yet developed the self-confidence to know that delegating tasks will not diminish their power, and they do not yet trust that others will complete the task as well as they would. If you are a new manager, you know your performance is being scrutinized closely and you want to insure that everything is done perfectly. You want to be noticed for your successes, not your mistakes. Hopefully, you have hired competent subordinates, but if not, you must first correct that mistake. Hiring less-than-stellar employees as a way to insure your importance will eventually backfire and make you look incompetent. If you have hired well and want to keep your staff, you need to start delegating some responsibility to them. Start small and give a lot of guidance before you delegate work. This will not only help the employee but also protect you. Before delegating, ask yourself if you are going to be upset if the employee comes up with an idea or finds a solution that is different from what you would have wanted. If the answer is yes, then you need to provide guidance early on so that both of you will feel good about the outcome.

The Flexibility to Respond to Changing Circumstances

Family-business leaders must be exceedingly knowledgeable about their business. They also must be able to adapt quickly to changing conditions, shifting customer needs, market trends. In other words, they must be flexible. Good leaders are never so rigid that they can't change their mind. And change it again.

William Hewlett and David Packard again offer examples of flexible leadership. From the startup of their business, these giants in the field of electronics and computers determined they would operate the company on a pay-as-you-go basis, financing growth primarily with earnings rather than borrowed money.

In the early 1960s, it became apparent that computers were to play a major role in the field of technology. Initiated by employees in the computer division, HP designed what would have been the world's first thirty-two-bit computer. The project was exciting but it required expertise and capabilities that HP didn't have at the time. Further, it was expensive, and the company would have had to incur debt to fund it. Hewlett and Packard decided to follow their pay-as-you-go founding principle, and they canceled the project. Their decision was based on caution and founding principles. What happened next, however, is a clear example of the flexibility in their leadership.

The cancellation of the computer project greatly disappointed those who had initiated it—they were so disappointed, in fact, that some of them kept working on it in secret. When Hewlett and Packard learned of their efforts, the founders took another look at the project and concluded it had more promise than they had accorded to it. They scaled back the size of the project and gambled on moving it ahead. The result is one of the computer industry's most enduring success stories. The story would not have had the same successful ending if Hewlett and Packard had not had the flexibility to change their minds.

Leadership Needs At
Different Stages of the Business

Businesses, like individuals and families, move through somewhat predictable cycles, and, as in families, businesses need different types of leadership at different stages of the business life cycle.
A startup business needs a leader who is totally committed, enjoys
having complete control, and is willing to risk what it takes to give
birth to the enterprise. Entrepreneurs have these characteristics;
they literally breathe life into their businesses. Not all good entrepreneurs, however, are good at leading a company once they establish
it. They are a special breed of leader and, as such, many of them are
better suited to starting a business than to running an existing one.

A growing business needs a leader who can share decision-
making power with others and who is willing to explore new opportunities in the interest of expanding the business. This attribute is especially important in a family-owned business, where
the founder must motivate the second generation to share in a
vision to continue the family business. During the growing stage
of a business, opportunities seem endless; nothing appears beyond
the realm of possibility. This is an exciting time in the business life
cycle, but the excitement must be tempered with calm, deliberate,
and thoughtful planning. Effective leaders at this stage wisely in-
tuit that too much control stifles creativity, and too much flexibility creates chaos. Success requires a little of both but not too much
of either. Entrepreneurs will fail to transition the business from a
startup to a mature business if they are unable to share leadership.
Some, as Edgar Schein points out, "create (often unconsciously)
a variety of organizational processes that prevent the growth of
the next generation of leadership."[7] Founders may recognize, in
theory, the need for a different type of leadership as their business
grows in size and complexity, but they may be unable to provide

that leadership. The entrepreneur may recognize the need for a chief operating officer but not give the person, once hired, the support needed to be effective. A family business owner may name a successor but not allow the smooth transition of power, thus creating an attitude that pits *us* (founder and his or her supporters) against *them* (newly named successor and supporters). Even after the older generation passes the business to the younger generation, it often continues to exercise considerable influence over the younger generation running the business. How this influence is exercised can make the difference between a successful transition and one that fails.

The transition from one generation to another is always difficult and is fraught with some tension. The best family business leader understands this situation is an expected part of the succession process and addresses concerns directly, often with the help of an outside consultant.

A family business in transition demands a leader who can manage conflict among family members who love and rival one another with equal intensity. Conflicts will occur between the older and younger generations over who is in charge, as well as within the younger generation over who has the most power. When a younger brother is promoted over his older brother, for example, it may awaken their unresolved sibling rivalry, which then spills into their work relationship.

Effective leaders at any stage in the business life cycle must possess sound judgment about the people they empower with decision-making authority. Nowhere is this more important than in family-owned businesses, where key players share a personal history. Knowing when and how much responsibility to delegate is always difficult, but when the employee is also a relative, the leader must have a special intuitive skill. The best leaders at this stage of the business cycle have it.

Years ago I had the pleasure of working with a company president who was famous in the family for refusing to assert his authority when arguments occurred among his senior staff, most of whom were members of his family. Instead, he expected them to develop a solution and report back to him when they had it. He knew intuitively that if he stepped in and settled their disputes, he would become the disciplinarian and they would take on the role of children, rather than the president and senior executives they were.

A successful transition will find the business in a calmer stage of the life cycle because it has weathered the transition, and reestablished a clear direction. Those in charge are respected for their leadership . The mature business generates new ideas and new products, performs predictably, and expands at a controlled pace. Leaders at this stage depend increasingly on the knowledge of others, and they are committed to leadership development and succession planning throughout the organization. They select managers based on competence, not on family membership, and they enforce formal policies for advancing in the company, regardless of family relation. They know that neither they nor the business can afford to rest on past accomplishments.

Assessing Family-Business Leadership

In the boxes that follow, I have outlined the family business life cycle and the leadership needed to move from one stage to another. Using these guides, determine which stages your family's business has mastered, what stage it is in now, the type of leadership it currently employs, and the challenges it currently faces. Next, decide whether the current leadership is consistent with what the business needs at the current stage. If it is not, what needs to change? As someone committed to your family's business legacy, it is your responsibility to address your concerns with those in charge of the business.

As a final part of this exercise, I suggest you list the leadership attributes you possess. Under each, give an example that illustrates how you demonstrate that particular attribute. This outline will provide a starting place from which to judge not only your leadership potential but also the appropriateness of your leadership skills in the current business climate. You can repeat this exercise yearly as a way to grade your progress as you move through the business cycle.

The Family Business Life Cycle

The Entrepreneurial Business

- The founder conceives a dream.
- Survival and maintaining necessary financing are central.
- Business owner makes all decisions.

The Growing Business

- Business has survived start-up.
- Business explores new ideas and opportunities; business expands.
- Second generation of family is moving into business.

The Transitional Business

- Company is too large and/or complex for the entrepreneur to run alone.
- Conflict develops between older and younger generations over who is in charge.
- Direction of company is in question; vision may be temporarily lost.
- Organizational structure is in flux.

The Mature Business

- Company reestablishes clear direction after transitional period.
- Expansion of business occurs in organized, controlled way.
- Business performs predictably.
- Company reestablishes organizational structure.

Leadership Needed at Each Stage
of the Family Business Life Cycle

The entrepreneurial business needs a leader:

- Who enjoys complete ownership and control.
- Who is comfortable making all decisions regarding the company.
- Who has tremendous energy and passion about the business.
- Who is totally committed to the business dream.
- Who is willing to risk what it takes to birth the dream.

The growing business needs a leader:

- Who is willing to bring new members of the family into the business.
- Who encourages new ideas.
- Who is able to excite others to join in the business goals.
- Who can manage in a way that allows the business to grow while staying focused on the guiding mission.

The transitional business needs a leader:

- Who can delegate authority and share leadership with a number of individuals.
- Who can manage conflict, especially between older and younger generations, both of who are now in the business.

The mature business needs a leader:

- Who refuses to rest on laurels.
- Who understands the importance of balancing creativity with structure.
- Who is committed to leadership development.
- Who is committed to succession planning.
- Who selects managers based on ability, not family membership.

CHAPTER SIX

Leadership: Style Matters

This is a time in history when women's voices must be heard or forever be silenced. It's not because we think better than men, but we think differently. It's not women against men, but women and men. It's not that the world would have been better if women had run it, but that the world will be better when we as women, who bring our own perspective, share in running it.

— *Betty Bumpers*

Style matters in business as well as in fashion.

I am not talking about whether to wear a skirt or pants to the office. I am talking about leadership style, and leadership style matters a great deal.

Today's work environment demands a leadership style that includes, among other qualities, an ability to manage complex webs of connections and relationships that aren't suited to traditional leadership styles. Contemporary leaders have less autonomy and control, and they have to rely more on the knowledge of others—often part-time and contract employees—to manage the volume of communication that such networks create. The autocratic management model to which most of yesterday's business leaders subscribed simply doesn't work well in most business environments today. As Edward Schein says, tomorrow's leaders "will not assume that leadership means hierarchy and control of others, and they will not assume that accountability must always be individual. Rather, the leader of the future will both... lead and follow, be central and marginal, be hierarchically above and below, be individualistic and a team player, and, above all, be a perpetual learner."[1] This also holds true for leaders of family-owned businesses.

Well ahead of her time, Nancy Badore, former executive director of the Ford Motor Company's Executive Development Center (EDC), was practicing the type of leadership needed in today's business environment. Badore has been credited with enabling Ford to emerge from its near-collapse in the 1980s by developing a training model for executive development that forged alliances between upper management and plant workers, encouraged teamwork, and produced a corporate culture based on quality and customer service. Here is how she did it.

Badore joined Ford when the company was facing declining sales, discontented workers, dissatisfied customers, and inferior products. The company desperately needed change, but the executive force didn't know what to do or how to do it. Badore led a new program designed to get union stewards and plant managers talking to one another. In those days, the company administered each stage of auto making as a separate area of specialization, and rigid boundaries separated each department. Badore's task was to break down the turf issues that prevailed throughout the company. According to Badore, "there was little literature on organizational change of this scale, so ... the plants became laboratories in which we tried different techniques to break down boundaries, get people contributing—to see what motivated them to work with zest and spirit. I was on the team that went from plant to plant, and I became fascinated with what we were learning; pretty soon I became sort of a Dear Abby on practical things about implementing culture change."[2]

After watching and learning from those who actually did the work in the plants, Badore decided she needed to bring division heads and plant managers together so the executives could learn directly from those in the plant. Her idea met with a great deal of initial resistance — division heads weren't used to learning from managers — but it was a reasonable idea, and the company desperately needed change. So the training began. The program turned out to be extremely successful and eventually defined the direction of change for the multibillion-dollar company. The program developed into the EDC, which today trains the highest-level executives. Back then no one would have guessed that talking — that is, sharing information across divisions and up and down the hierarchal ladder — would have so profound an impact on the success of a business. Today, thanks to creative and courageous leaders like Nancy Badore, who refused to be trapped by the traditional definitions and boundaries of leadership, companies appreciate the value of breaking down hierarchical boundaries, leading from the center rather than the top, and being a team player.

While Badore represents just one example of top-quality corporate leadership, her behavior is instructive for family businesses. Today's business environment is more demanding than even a few years ago: the global financial crisis and subsequent economic downturn has put additional pressure on executives already struggling with an increasingly complex world. Leadership in family businesses must flow to those who can best inspire others, who can see reasonable risks as opportunities, and who can share the accountability of complex tasks. Today's family business leaders need relationship skills as never before. Rosabeth Kanter goes so far as to say, "Whatever the duration and objectives of business alliances ... a well-developed ability to create and sustain fruitful collaborations gives companies a significant competitive leg up."[3]

The leaders of tomorrow that Edward Schein referred to are some of today's best leaders. Anne Mulcahy is one example. When she became Xerox's CEO in 2000, the company's stock was down, it was in the midst of a Securities and Exchange Commission investigation, and advisors were urging her to declare bankruptcy to clear the company of its $18 billion debt. She concluded that using bankruptcy to escape debt was a short term and overly simplified solution to a long term and much more complicated problem. Instead, Mulcahy went on a listening tour, seeking insights from employees, customers, and industry experts on where Xerox had erred and what needed to change to get the company back on track. She told employees that they wouldn't be penalized for speaking up and told their bosses to take their suggestions seriously. She believed that executives had to create a workplace where workers felt secure in giving constructive feedback because "you can never depend on filtering information up through the company. You have to talk to frontline employees."[4] To gain the support she would need from Xerox's leadership team, Mulcahy met personally with the top one hundred executives. She let them know how dire the situation was and asked them if they were prepared to commit. To demonstrate her commitment and get their buy-in, she announced that she would "fly anywhere to save any customer for Xerox." A full ninety-eight of the one hundred executives decided to stay, and the bulk of them are still with the company today. For Mulcahy, success was about getting her people aligned around a common set of objectives.

Mulcahy did much more than put Xerox back on track. By the time she stepped down as CEO in 2009, she had transformed the company: she had paid off the company's entire debt, rebuilt its product line and technology base, and, perhaps most important, rebuilt Xerox's credibility in the marketplace. Not surprising, in 2008 *U.S. News and World Report* selected her as one of America's best leaders, and the same year *Chief Executive* magazine named her CEO of the Year.

The leadership styles exercised by Badore and Mulcahy and others you will meet in this chapter are swiftly becoming the rule rather than the exception. It is imperative, then, that we examine the characteristics that represent a more participative style, for it is the leadership face of today *and* tomorrow.

LEADERSHIP STYLES

Judith Rosener, a faculty member of the University of California at Irvine, studied more than three hundred women and men who held senior positions in major U.S. blue chip businesses.[5] She found that women often based their business relationships on trust, empathy, and engagement, while men more often based their business relationships on hierarchical positioning within the organization. She described the leadership style most often found in the businesswomen as "interactive." They encouraged participation, shared information, and got others excited about their work by involving them in the process. The female executives tended to pride themselves on being able to motivate subordinates by getting them to transform their self-interests into the goals of the organization. Their power resulted from personal characteristics, such as interpersonal skills, hard work, and personal contacts, rather than from organizational status. The women interviewed strongly believed in allowing employees to contribute and to create win-win situations.

The men in Rosener's survey were more likely than the women to use a military-type leadership style based on hierarchy, formal lines of authority, and decision-making that comes from the top. They judged work performance on individual rather than group contribution, gave rewards for superior individual contribution, and admonished inadequate individual performance. I must add that the military-type leadership style the men used is also the management style that has enjoyed decades of success within corporate America.

For our discussion, I will use the terms "interactive" and "collaborative" interchangeably, and "autocratic" and "military-style" interchangeably. Autocratic leadership has worked successfully in the past, so one could argue that all young women and men who aspire to management positions should adopt that model. In fact, throughout the '80s consultants advised women in management to imitate the leadership style of their male counterparts to fit in. The problem is that a management model based on rigid authority does not fit all leaders, nor will it fit most of today's companies.

Team Approach Leadership

Far more frequently than in the past I find that family businesses, especially second and third generation businesses, are installing a leadership team rather than a single, successor. To some extent this reflects the larger world of business thinking in which the team approach is not only the norm but also a requirement.

Kraft's CEO, Irene Rosenfeld, understands the importance of teamwork and reaching out to others for new ideas. Hired in 2006, with profits falling and the company stock flat for years, her charge was to reinvigorate the food giant to its former stature. Even with a research and development staff of two thousand employees, the company hadn't introduced a new product for a decade. Her response to the stagnation was to broaden the idea pool; she introduced an online "Innovate with Kraft" program whereby ordinary people could submit innovations and partner with Kraft to launch new products, processes, or packages. One of Kraft's most recent new products, the Bagel-fuls came as an unsolicited idea from a third generation bagel maker in a niche market. The idea turned out to be a win-win for both companies: Kraft got a new product, and the bagel maker expanded his niche business.

I recently came across a story that provides another example of teamwork at its absolute best. Indra Nooyi was one of two finalists for the position of CEO of Pepsico when the company chose her in 2006. What was the first thing she did after getting the news? She flew to visit the other contender. "Tell me whatever I need to do to keep you," she implored. They had worked together for years, and Nooyi was persuasive, offering to boost her competitor's compensation to nearly match her own. He agreed to serve as her right-hand man, creating her version of a team of rivals.[6]

Gender-Blind Leadership

Before going further in our discussion of leadership style, let's clarify a potential misunderstanding. Businesswomen leaders *tend* to use a collaborative style, but categorically linking this style to merely being a woman is a mistake. Not all successful businesswomen use an interactive leadership style, nor do all businessmen use an autocratic one. No one leadership style guarantees success; your best style is one that plays to your strengths and your personality while meeting the needs of the business. The company will judge your leadership style on its usefulness and the success it produces for the company, not on its theoretical criteria.

The notion that all women—or all men—can or should have a single leadership style is as naive as to ignore the rich variations among individuals. One common mistake young, aspiring leaders make is to obsess over other people's ideas of what a leader should be and to imitate someone else's leadership style. Don't make this mistake. Read about leadership and learn from leaders you respect—don't simply imitate someone else's image of leadership. Your best leadership style will be one you develop over time, and one that allows you to have integrity of style and consistency of character.

Gender-Labeled Leadership

The fact that more women than men lead with an interactive style raises the risk that companies—especially family businesses that often are run by tradition, family rules, and past example—will define participative leadership as being for women only. We have to be very careful not to restrict women to a "feminine" and men to a "masculine" leadership model, thereby creating yet another gender-based dichotomy that limits both women and men from utilizing their best individual strengths.

While writing *The Daughter Also Rises*, I participated in the unfortunate consequences of gender-labeling leadership style. In its first edition, I used the word "feminine" to refer to a participative leadership style, thinking it would simplify and strengthen the discussion about women and leadership. I asked Gary, the CEO of a multibillion-dollar family-owned and operated company, to read a draft of this chapter because he is a genius in his field, and his leadership style is as participative as I've ever witnessed.

After reading the chapter he phoned me. "It is sexist of me to say," he said, "but I was upset to see my leadership style described as 'feminine.' My style is interactive and inclusive, and

I'm proud that it's different from my uncle's controlling style, but feminine? What man wants to be called feminine?"

I assured Gary that his masculinity was not in question and reminded him that Jack Welch's leadership style would also be considered feminine. We laughed and moved on to another subject. However, I learned a very important lesson from Gary. Constructing leadership as feminine or masculine can, and indeed did in this case, create misleading impressions and reproduce gender-role stereotypes.

Warren Bennis, author of *On Becoming a Leader*, offers the observation that "at bottom, becoming a leader is synonymous with becoming yourself. It's precisely that simple and it's also that difficult."[7] To be an effective leader, you must listen to and trust yourself. You must lead with your own strengths, your own personality, and your own life experiences. Collaborative leadership is neither the only nor the best way to lead, but since it is a way that many successful women manage, perhaps it is your style. It certainly meets and exceeds the requirements for effective leadership in the family business.

Unfortunately, an effective leadership style coupled with the necessary knowledge and experience still may not be enough to assure your advancement in the family business. You still may have to dispel certain myths about women and leadership before the family can appreciate your value to the business.

Myths About Women and Leadership

It may seem obvious to you and to the family that runs the business you work in that neither gender nor leadership style alone makes a leader, that businesses should respect women and men equally for their competence and consider them equally for leadership positions. If this describes your situation, you have my congratulations. You have a fortunate advantage over the majority of women who still must fight the prejudices that exclude or limit their advancement in a family business.

For daughters and sons to enjoy similar opportunities in a family business, age-old myths that suggest women are ill-suited for top management must be supplanted by a recognition that competence, rather than gender, is the most important variable. These myths will work to keep you in the lower ranks of the business and will deprive the business of the expertise you can bring to it. They also are extremely difficult to change because they usually exist outside of personal awareness and they are unresponsive to new information or concrete evidence to the contrary. However, by recognizing myths that work against both you and the business, your family can take steps to deliberately shatter them.

Myth One: Women Make Weak Leaders

As you may remember from Chapter One, family businesses historically have not seen daughters as viable resources. Families rarely considered daughters as potential successors unless a crisis forced them into leadership. Unfortunately, this situation still holds true in many business families, due in part to stereotypes that prevent families from seeing daughters as capable contributors and potential leaders of the business. When an emergency prompts a daughter's succession, she has a good chance of being ill-prepared for the position, which reinforces the myth that women make poor leaders. Equally destructive, the scenario increases the likelihood that the business will falter under the daughter's leadership and that she will come away with a skewed and inaccurate sense of her leadership potential. Only when families retire the myth that women make weak leaders will daughters get the development they need to become good leaders, and only then will the business benefit from the resource they represent.

Some leaders see collaboration and teamwork as evidence of weakness, an inability to exert necessary authority. Certainly, an interactive leadership style differs from the more familiar autocratic style, but it is not weak. In a family business, where positive working relationships between family members are crucial and interruptions of those bonds can create problems for the business, the ability to work collaboratively can be an especially strong asset. The best, most creative leaders exchange and advance ideas with others *and* they think independently about the tasks at hand. Collaboration is not weak and it's not about endless meetings or group conference calls. As long as the family sees it as exclusively feminine, however, its male leaders will tend to shy away from participative leadership, and the family will judge its daughters as incapable of leading the business. Perception often trumps reality in evaluating women's leadership capabilities. Ample evidence exists that managers link management ability with being male and masculine, and they have doubts about women's leadership ability. As a result, women are generally held to a higher standard of competence than men are.[8]

Logic would suggest that if women are perceived as weaker leaders but they consistently demonstrate their leadership abilities they would overcome the gender barrier. Unfortunately, it isn't that simple. When business women act in ways that are consistent with gender stereotypes, they are perceived as less competent leaders, *and* when they act in ways that are inconsistent with stereotypes they are perceived as unfeminine.[9] Thus, competent, assertive woman leaders often receive lower evaluations and are less liked by senior executives than are their male counterparts. Men currently hold most positions of power and authority and they, in particular, evaluate competent, assertive women less favorably than equally competent male peers.[10]

What are you to do with this seemingly impossible dilemma? The answer is simpler than you may think. Strut your competence *and* your femininity. By combining the two strengths you will mitigate the doubt men hold about women leaders.[11] There is another, extremely important reason to let others see both your competence and your femininity. Once women reach the highest level positions, men often perceive them more favorably than their male counterparts, thinking that women who survive discrimination must be exceptionally competent![12]

There is another problem that many daughters—and you may be one of them—face in multigenerational family businesses: sons expect the family to hand them leadership roles, and they may be reluctant to share that power with their sisters. I recently worked with a third generation manufacturing business that had a sister and her two brothers vying to replace their father as its leader. Each sibling was well educated and had the requisite training and experience to become the company's president. The problem was that each of the brothers lacked an essential requirement of business leadership—the ability to support the work performed by others. In fact, they were willing to sabotage their sister's efforts in order to aggrandize their own stature in the business.

Ann, who had an MBA, spent five years developing a new product for the company. Working with a limited budget, she designed, tested, and then built a functioning prototype. Her father encouraged her to introduce the product in selected test markets, but he underfunded the marketing of the product. As a result, the product was only marginally successful. Ann was discouraged, but she appealed for more funding to retest it in another market. Her father supported the idea initially—he personally liked the product—but her brothers argued that the company shouldn't commit any additional capital to the new product. Instead, they argued that its patent be sold to help fund the acquisition of another business, which would provide one of them an opportunity to run his own business. The argument persuaded Ann's father, who had inherited his presidential mantle from his father, and he sided with his sons.

The struggle was contentious. The lines were drawn with Dad backing his sons, arguing that the decision was one his own father would have supported. Ann was shocked. Only after her father's comment did she realize that good old-fashioned prejudice, mixed with a bit of superstition, had blocked her. The primary assumption that influenced Ann's father to back his sons' proposal was that leadership belonged to men, as it had since the business began. The business had enjoyed success for sixty years, and he did not want to challenge the status quo. Deep down he felt he owed it to his sons to pass the baton to one of them, and having two businesses solved the problem of his having to choose between his sons. It never occurred to him that he was leaving Ann out of all consideration. As a result, he made a poor business decision that reinforced the male prerogative—and motivated Ann to seek employment opportunities outside of the family business.

Our culture teaches women to be cooperative and to be comfortable asking for and taking advice, and this can make it easier for daughters than for sons to work with their fathers. On the other hand, fathers who have created a viable business, at least in part because of their tenacious independence, may find it difficult to value a more interdependent leadership style. Your father, for example, may misinterpret advice-seeking as dependence, collaboration as tentativeness, and process-oriented decision-making as a lack of confidence. He may try to toughen you up in ways that undermine and weaken some of your leadership strengths. Don't let this happen. It's important that you network with other managers who support your style; read trade books and the most recent literature on collaborative leadership; attend seminars on the topic; and talk with your father about what you are doing and trying to accomplish.

Let's look at another way gender bias affects business decisions. Jim was a research scientist employed in the chemistry department at the local university when he began his business twenty-five years ago. He conducted soil tests for local cooperatives from a lab in the basement of the family's ranch house. As the demand for his work grew, his business required a full-time commitment. He resigned his teaching position, acquired a building, built a lab, and hired assistants from a pool of graduate students. As his business grew, he expanded the scope of services he provided and over time he developed a reputation as the best in his field. However, although Jim was a first-class scientist, Jim was a lousy leader.

Jim's eldest daughter, Sally, had begun college as a journalism major but became increasingly interested in the business while she worked summers in her father's lab. Before beginning her senior year, her father asked her to consider switching majors to business in order to help him run the expanding lab business. She agreed, and after she graduated she began an MBA program while working in the lab as de facto office manager. Within five years of earning her MBA, Sally had marketing, finance, and administration reporting directly to her, and Jim oversaw the technical side of the business.

When Sally joined the business, her father told her that the company had a hard time retaining employees because "smart people leave to work for themselves." When she was on the job, she realized it was Jim's leadership style that was driving competent employees away. He insisted on exercising control over all of the functional areas of the lab; he delegated very little authority and showed scant respect for the nonscientific contributions of others. Frustrated and demeaned, several competent managers had left under his leadership.

Sally had her work cut out for her. Her first corrective action was to meet with employees and explain her role, her management style, and her dependence of them for success. She delegated more responsibility to her managers and gave them more decision-making authority. She encouraged information sharing across units. She had an open door policy and invited employees to share their ideas and constructive criticism. With increased responsibility, greater participation, and genuine respect came newfound excitement and commitment among the employees.

Initially, Jim criticized Sally's ways as being too time-consuming and worried that she was going to lose control of her people. Sally knew that her repeated explanations for doing things the way she did fell on deaf ears and that Jim's thinking amounted to "the proof is in the pudding" argument. It wasn't long, however, before Jim was convinced that Sally's employee-focused style resulted in lower turnover rates and higher employee satisfaction. He didn't understand how her methods worked, but he appreciated that they did, and he realized that he was a better scientist than businessman.

Myth Two: Women Can't Compete

This myth is born of the traditional definition of femininity: the giving of self to others, most particularly men and children. The definition requires that women satisfy the needs of others, always, before their own. Hardly the stuff competitiveness is made of!

And yet, women are competitive. If they were not, they

would have given up their fight for equality within management ranks years ago; instead, they persist in fighting for something they value. The fact that the number of women corporate officers and top earners has stagnated in recent years instead of increasing gives proof that the struggle against formidable obstacles continues. In 2008, women held 15.7 percent of executive officer position in Fortune 500 companies and 6.2 percent of executive officer top earner positions in the U.S. largest companies. In 2011, the numbers were 14.1 percent and 7.5 respectfully.[13] The number of companies having one, two, or three women directors increased slightly, but the increase was offset by the slight increase in companies with zero women directors.

By any comparison — title, function, age — women are outnumbered in the management suite, and they continue to earn less than their male counterparts. Ilene Lang, president and chief executive officer of Catalyst, sees it this way: "No change in a year of change is unacceptable... now more than ever, as companies examine how best to weather an economy in crisis, we need talented business leaders, and many of these leaders, yet untapped, are women."[14]

Women have greater access to more careers than in any other time in history. And yet, they continually come up against the reality that to be seen as feminine, they must subordinate their needs for recognition and position to those of men. This reality can produce a particularly difficult situation for daughters in family businesses: they want their father, peers, and employees to see them as feminine, but they also want those individuals to see them as competent businesswomen.

Women and men develop and shape their identities differently but one way is not better than the other. It means, however, that men and women often craft management styles that look very different. Let's look at two examples to illuminate my

point. First, women are stronger than men at relationship building, and often this skill becomes part of their management style.
In a family business, where business and family needs at times
are at odds, this skill would prove an invaluable asset to your
leadership style. Second, women often find it easy to share credit
for accomplishments. Again, this skill would be an advantage to
you in the family business, where competition among siblings
can be intense and teamwork among family members is vital.

I met Eleanor, a dynamic woman working fiercely to overcome the odds, while providing teamwork sessions for the buy-
ers in the women's department of a retail shoe business. She
was very competitive, and she worked quite differently than her
male colleagues. She thought her particular work style gave her a
competitive advantage over the men in her department: "It's my
secret weapon. When the guys are glued to their computers and
phones, devising their strategies for next season, I'm out talking to people and soliciting their ideas. Only after I've gotten as
many suggestions as possible do I get on the computer to analyze
my numbers and choose my options. The guys tease me about
not having the guts to trust myself, but I don't get the least bit
defensive. I don't need to. My numbers have been better than
theirs for six consecutive seasons!"

Myth Three: Women Are Indecisive

This myth grew from women's willingness to involve others in decision-making—that is, to encourage consensus-build-
ing—and in their flexibility with respect to roles. Rather than
recognizing these traits as strengths of a good leader, some people
think they are a sign of indecisiveness. Take a minute and think
about whether this myth applies in your family.

In a study of leadership style and its contribution to business success, Ritch Sorenson found that a participative leadership

style, one similar to that described in the research as interactive, enabled family businesses to address the needs of both business and family.[15] Participative leadership significantly contributed to the financial success of small family businesses, and it was associated with employee satisfaction and commitment. I hardly think traits that produce these kinds of successes are weaknesses.

Generally speaking, managers utilizing an interactive leadership style not only allow others to contribute but they also actively seek out different perspectives, knowing it will increase the likelihood that everyone will be committed to the final decision. It is not indecision but a very deliberate action on the part of the leader.

Sally Helgesen was one of the first to study female leadership style by following the work patterns of successful women executives. She found that, for all of them, the sharing of information and the active participation of others were deliberate and essential parts of their management style. Far from reflecting indecisiveness or a naiveté about power, their use of information and involvement functioned to empower and motivate their employees and to keep their own workload from overwhelming them.[16]

One frequent outcome of an autocratic leadership style is a decrease in organizational creativity and vitality. Here is a brief example from a corporation we all know well, General Electric. According to a biography of Jack Welch, when he became CEO in 1981, "the company was choking on its nit-picking system of formal reviews and approvals, which delayed decisions, thwarted common sense, and often made GE a laggard at bringing new products to market."[17] Jack Welch changed that. His salient management ideas emphasized opportunism, testing ideas through constructive conflict, treating all associates as equals, encouraging enthusiasm and flexibility, and replacing hierarchical organization with teams. Welch combined a competitive drive for success with flexibility, an adherence to collaboration, and openness to new ideas. By 1998, his efforts had resulted in the creation of the first American corporation with a market capitalization of $300 billion. While not many family businesses can expect to see increased productivity on the scale GE achieved under his leadership, the employee-focused style Welch utilized has many direct applications to family enterprises.

Some mislabel flexibility as being wishy-washy. The wishy-washy label, cited as one reason women supposedly can't make tough decisions, justifies keeping women out of higher level positions. Yet flexibility, along with a willingness to embrace new ideas, enables a leader to explore alternatives and promote change. Women understand this and it serves them well in business. They are able to move easily from one task to another without becoming frustrated; they feel comfortable in different roles; they view interruptions and schedule changes as a normal part of the day's flow. The women in Helgesen's study viewed themselves as playing many—and sometimes competing—roles. They moved between their various professional and personal roles fluidly; they called home and talked to children, housekeepers, and caretakers, and they occasionally noted family matters on their office calendars. The need to integrate roles and responsibilities made their lives more complicated but also enriched their lives and made them more effective leaders.

Myth Four: Women Can't Be Good Mothers *and* Good Executives

This myth suggests women can't fulfill their child-rearing responsibilities and also be competent executives. It is firmly grounded in the notion that child-rearing is a woman's primary work and they must manage any other work as an additional and secondary responsibility. As long as company executives believe that women are the sole custodian of children, women will not compete equally with men for top positions. This is particularly true in small family businesses, where family beliefs permeate company culture. If this view is widely held by those running your family's business, the family will not consider you a potential leader or even a candidate for a management position; it will view you at best as a temporary employee—until you marry and have children. Your father, for example, is not going to put the time, energy, and money into developing your leadership skills if he doesn't believe you're committed long term to the business.

Perhaps you think, "Not a problem. I don't intend to have children." Sorry, but it's not quite that simple. If your father isn't convinced you won't have children (and remember, he may want grandchildren) and he believes you can't be a good mother and an executive, he won't take the risk on you. He will overlook you for development opportunities. When you finally reach an age that convinces Dad you are not having children, it will be too late for you to get the experience that you needed to get years earlier. You will have lost the career you aspired to—and the business will have lost a valuable resource.

The myth that a woman can't be a good mother and have a career not only keeps daughters from the top positions in the family business, but it also keeps sons from being more involved in their family life. For example, if your family tradition dictates that women alone are responsible for their children, then your brother, who works in the business, probably will not take time off after the birth of his child for fear of damaging his image as a responsible, hard-working husband. In fact, the idea of taking time off probably will never even cross his mind.

Reality is that for most women, work is not a luxury but a necessity, and women are far more likely than men to be the sole supporter of their family at one time or another. Nonetheless, people often encourage them to compromise their career ambitions and choose the "mommy track." To accept that train ride, however, women must accept less pay, forego career growth opportunities, and, paradoxically, jeopardize their ability to provide for themselves and their family.

Gender biases that keep sons in the business and daughters at home also compromise the business. In a 2004 Catalyst report, corporations with the highest representation of women on their top management teams experienced better financial performance than companies with the lowest women's representation.[18]

Most executive men are married and have children, and their wives don't work outside of the home. By contrast, about half of executive women are single or have husbands who also work and do not have any children. The numbers reflect the stereotype of the ideal corporate executive. He — and we must admit it's a he — is a married family man who can devote himself primarily to the company while his wife manages the home and children. But when we change the gender of the executive, the stereotype changes as well. The ideal executive now is a single woman with no children. The stereotype relies on the belief that only a single woman can devote herself to work. In a family business, it can be even tougher for a daughter to break out of the stereotype.

OK, now for some positive news: If some of these myths live within the fabric of your family, it may be easier for you to modify them than for a woman working in a non-family business because you are dealing with trusted family members with whom you've had a long history. Unlike in a public company, where it is difficult to know where certain attitudes originate, you know or can learn where the biases began and with whom you need to talk to begin making changes. As difficult as your family may feel to you on some days, being able to sit down in a relaxed setting and discuss your concerns is one advantage of being part of a business family.

The Bank of Montreal

From a purely business standpoint, it is unwise for a family business to hold onto beliefs that deny it the best and brightest family members, regardless of gender. The Bank of Montreal figured this out well ahead of its competitors and can teach all family businesses an important lesson. Back in the 1990s, Anthony Comper, then president and COO, commissioned a task force to identify the obstacles to female advancement and to break them down. He understood that to compete on a global stage the company had to extend its talent pool beyond white men. At the time women made up 75 percent of the bank's employee population — but only 9 percent of its executive ranks!

The task force results were staggering with regard to gender-biased beliefs. In a survey of 15,000 employees, the assumptions about women's failure to advance included:

- Women are either too young or too old to compete with men.
- Women are less committed to their careers because of their child-rearing responsibilities.
- Women haven't been in the pipeline long enough to advance to senior levels. Time will take care of the problem.
- Women don't have the right stuff to compete for senior jobs.

Facts gleaned from the human resources files proved that all of the assumptions were patently false. Astounded by the results, the task force issued a myths-and-reality report that included the following factual information:

- On average, women and men employees were the same age.

- Although women had babies and more childrearing responsibility, they had longer service records at the bank, except at senior levels.
- The percentage of women in senior positions had grown so slowly—1 percent a year—that waiting for time to take care of the problem was not practical.

An aggressive initiative to advance women began. Within six years their representation in executive ranks increased from 9 percent to 24 percent; among senior vice presidents from 3 percent to 27 percent; and among senior management it had increased from 13 percent to 26 percent.[19] Impressive indeed.

A Prescription for Change

To change the myths that keep many daughters out of the family business, perhaps you included, business families must first recognize them. This is a staggering challenge because gender-based inequities are inconspicuously but almost intractably bred into the culture of your family's business.

Prejudices are durable primarily for two reasons. First, it is very difficult to change that which we do not want to believe exists. Thus, even with the strides of the last fifty years, active discrimination against women is still prevalent. We prefer to assume that the inequities that exist result from the inferiority of people's abilities or attitude. This assumption belies the reality that women fight valiantly to be seen as equal; the view that women work twice as hard for half the pay grew from reality. Second, even when society acknowledges inequities, a need exists to perpetuate the conditions that created the problem. In short, we depend upon women to subjugate their needs and ambitions in order to preserve the status quo.

Considering that leaders greatly influence the regard of future candidates for leadership positions within the company, it seems logical that leaders will beget similar leaders—a vicious cycle weighted against women. This is even more likely to happen in family businesses, which historically the men in the family have run.

Competence Over Gender: Allison's Story

Allison, the vice president of plant operations in her family's toy manufacturing business, came to see me at the recommendation of a friend and businesswoman with whom I had worked the previous year. Allison had joined the family business at the invitation of the president, her Uncle Gary, after having worked at another company. She spent the first three years on the floor learning each manufacturing job in every department and three more as a plant director before being appointed to her current position. She loved her work, but when I met her, she was discouraged and thinking of leaving the company.

Allison was well qualified for her position, but some managers did not welcome her as the only female executive. They knew her work history, career accomplishments, and business experience, but they couldn't escape the feeling that a woman, particularly the boss's niece, should not be meddling in men's work. Women, they thought, had no place in a factory, and her advancement threatened the potential advancement of other—male—managers. They viewed leadership as the domain of one gender. Allison was up against a strong bias.

Many of the technically skilled staff in Allison's department were men who had reported directly to Gary for years. They didn't want to report to someone else, particularly a woman who was the boss's niece. They went around Allison in subtle ways and continued to act as if they still reported to Gary. They informed her of decisions they had OK'd with Gary, or they "ran some thing by her" instead of first getting her approval. Gary unintentionally sanctioned the behavior by not stopping it.

Allison mistakenly thought the problem was her — perhaps an inability to clarify expectations — or an incompetence she was unaware of, or a lack of certain experience, since she seemed unable to transfer the respect and authority she had earned outside to her work inside the family business. She didn't recognize the prejudice and couldn't see that Gary and others were undermining her position. Everyone — including her Uncle Gary — was colluding to maintain the status quo.

The reason Allison couldn't take control of the situation had nothing to do with a lack of knowledge or experience. It was because she had not understood and correctly defined the problem. The problem had to do with who she was — a woman working in a heretofore men's business. With the prejudice identified, she devised a plan to address it. First, she discussed with her Uncle Gary how his behavior was undermining her authority and contributing to the problem. To his credit, Gary listened, apologized, and agreed to support a change.

With Gary's support firmly behind her, Allison initiated the second part of her change strategy. When she scheduled meetings, she began to include employees who ranked above and below the managers who undermined her authority so that everyone at every level knew exactly what she expected. In this way, managers couldn't misinterpret her directions or "forget" to pass something along to staff. She also instituted new policies and practices for the managers, with serious consequences if they didn't follow the practices. It didn't take long for everyone to get the message. Gary stood by Allison and refused to participate in any surprise end runs; over time, their combined efforts forced employees to change certain behaviors or leave the company. The actions Allison took, and which Gary supported, introduced a new company expectation: employees would respect and follow the direction of their superior without regard to gender or they lose their jobs. This expectation created a culture that based leadership on competence rather than gender; the commitment was to a strong work group, rather than to a familiar—in this case male—work group.

For years, the prevailing belief was that if attitudes changed, behaviors would necessarily follow. But we had the causative process reversed. Behavior change creates attitudinal change. Ask Allison and Gary.

You As Change Agent

Change never happens overnight, but change does happen, and it is happening in more and more family businesses across the continent. Assume that you are (and you may be) the only woman at the decision-making level in your family's business. There are no women on the board of directors. You are concerned about the situation and want the company to hire and advance more women. But how do you convince an all-male group that hiring more women is in the company's best interest?

There is no guarantee that you or anyone else will change people determined not to change, but you will increase your chances greatly if you arm yourself with facts. Do your homework. Prepare yourself with research and information. Read some of the books and articles mentioned at the back of this book.

Sound business reasons argue for introducing more women into the system. More women in management positions will lead to better chances that women will advance in the business. Your desire to be in the company of more women is *not* a good reason to change the status quo. The future of the business depends on hiring and keeping the most talented employees, male and female, which *is* a very good reason to change the status quo.

With your research complete, you are ready to develop an action plan that fits your particular business situation. You might outline the company's policies on recruiting, hiring, promoting, training and development and family leave, and compare these policies to those of successful, more progressive companies. With sound business reasons backing you, you can argue for having policies and benefits in place to attract more women. You can suggest ways to give women line experience, where they would be responsible for profit. You might suggest cross-training to enhance women's promotability across the board. You can present guidelines for promotions into management positions. By approaching the problem in an objective way, you emphasize the business issue and minimize the discrimination issue, thereby decreasing the potential for defensiveness within the group. If your presentation achieves immediate change within the business, that's great. More likely, however, you will need to repeat the process several times. Don't get discouraged. As Allison learned, change is difficult, but it is possible, very possible indeed.

CHAPTER SEVEN

Mission Possible: Balancing Family and the Family Business

The simple idea that everyone needs a reasonable amount of challenging work in his or her life, and also a personal life, complete with non-competitive leisure, has never really taken hold.

—*Judith Martin*

Jolene loved her husband of fifteen years, her two children, and her position as vice president in the planning division of her family's financial service business. She didn't want to give up any of them. But Jolene felt hassled and tired all the time. Her eight-year-old son often was angry at her because she didn't have time to volunteer in his classroom, pick him up from school, or be home when he arrived. Her eleven-year-old daughter couldn't understand why mom rarely made it to her soccer games. Jolene's unmarried sister, Arlene, with whom she worked, felt resentful whenever Jolene arranged her work schedule around one of the children's doctor appointments or school conferences. Jolene's husband wondered why she was too tired for conversation after the kids were in bed. Her friends wondered how she did it all, but they also felt irritated when she canceled a scheduled dinner with them. Jolene knew she was trying to juggle too many things, but she didn't have time to stop and figure out how to do things differently. She felt guilty about disappointing the people she loved and angry at them for asking so much from her.

The problems Jolene faced are not unique to women working in family businesses, of course. Whenever women attempt to have both a career and a family they are likely to encounter similar situations. Intelligent, rational women know that no one can do it all and that they should not have to be superwomen to have what most men have always had—a career and a family. Fatherhood has always been one of the many roles that men play, and it should not be different when it comes to women and motherhood. Despite this, it usually is more difficult for women to combine a marriage, career, and raising children than it is for men.

While this chapter is intended for women trying to combine motherhood and work in a family business, it also applies to an increasing number of fathers who are working and trying to be involved parents. The number of families who have shared their personal struggles with me makes it possible to look firsthand at the Superwoman complex and examine why it still persists today. We will look at the attitudes that create roadblocks for working mothers, and I will offer practical strategies for striking a balance between work and family life.

How Superwoman Was Born

The 1963 publication of Betty Friedan's book, *The Feminine Mystique*, which advocated women's rights and equal career opportunities, came at a perfect time for a generation of women armed with education and post-industrial prosperity. Her book legitimized women's frustrations and gave voice to their need for personal achievement, intellectual challenge, and a life outside the home.

Between 1950 and 1985, the number of women working increased by 178 percent, while the number of male workers grew by only 47 percent. By 1995 the percent of all mothers with children who worked had exceeded 65 percent.[1] By 2010, the participation rate of all mothers with children under the age of 18 was 71 percent.[2] But let's not get ahead of ourselves.

The first generation of women who achieved equal access to employment celebrated their victory—and never could have predicted the complications their victory would create. Their entrance into the workforce not only changed the shape of the economy but also the very structure of the family. The working father and the stay-at-home mother no longer described the typical family. Wives were at the office, not at home car-pooling the children, fixing the meals, doing the grocery shopping, caring for sick children, and entertaining company. No longer able to single-handedly manage the household and raise the children but unable to afford domestic help, working wives began demanding more from their husbands. Unfortunately, most husbands were not inclined to take on more of the domestic responsibility. Their wives weren't earning enough to relieve them of the financial responsibility for the family so many husbands didn't feel the need to relieve their wives of their domestic responsibilities. The wives felt so fortunate to have been allowed into the work force that they didn't protest.

Raised in what we *still* consider the traditional family, with gender roles as yet unchallenged, men as well as women continued to act on the unspoken rule that home and children were a woman's responsibility. Men and women viewed paid work outside the home as a privilege for women, not a right, and if women wanted to change the rule, they would have to carry the burden of the change. And carry it they did. During the day, women worked in factories, offices, and the family grocery store. At night they fixed dinner, picked up the house, and did the family's laundry. Working mothers still helped the children with homework, gave them their baths, and put them to bed. After the children were asleep, they prepared school lunches and put something in the Crockpot for the next day's dinner. Then they went through their briefcase and prepared for the next day's work. Superwoman was born. She was living, breathing evidence that women could have it all—by doing it all.

WHY SUPEWOMAN BECAME A HERO

In the name of equality, women embraced the image of Superwoman. At the office they dressed, talked, and felt like equals to men; but at night, they were in charge of the dirty diapers and dishes. The Herculean efforts of these superwomen proved their strength and tenacity, but it also left them exhausted. And when some of them collapsed under the weight of the responsibilities, they felt they had failed. At the time no one realized that Superwoman actually perpetuated traditional gender stereotypes and postponed much-needed changes.

WHEN SUPERWOMAN WENT UNDERGROUND

By the mid-1980s, women recognized it was impossible to have it all by doing it all, and Superwoman was slowly retired, her persona ridiculed as too perfectly perfect. Many women, myself included, applauded the retirement. The problem was that combining work and children continued to be more difficult for women than for men. It didn't seem to make sense. What we didn't understand was that Superwoman retired but gender-role expectations were still working full time—just in a different package. Pop psychology replaced Superwoman with men from Mars and women from Venus. The theory posited that men and women were categorically distinct; they couldn't be expected to understand one another or to perform well in one another's "natural" area of expertise. Women always would be the better nurturers; men the better warriors. Popular folklore turned men into emotional and domestic incompetents. Office jokes ridiculed husbands as lacking the gene for noticing dirty laundry, for saying "I'm sorry," for knowing when the children needed a bath. No matter how the expectations were packaged, women were still responsible for child care and household management as well as their work, while men were responsible only for work.

It is hard for today's women to admit they think of children as fundamentally their responsibility and work as an option. It's hard for men to admit that they think of their income as the real one and that they have less responsibility for raising their children, being emotionally involved in family life, or managing the household. It's not modern; it's uncool, old-fashioned. Unfortunately, new spins to old rules don't change the rules, and unless we face the reality, we can't hope to change them.

Few marriages today resemble the days of the working husband and stay-at-home wife, but neither do they resemble an equal partnership. Betty Carter, in her thought-provoking book *Love, Honor, and Negotiate*, argues that "the force of the traditional marriage has become even more powerful precisely because everyone believes traditional marriage no longer exists."[3] Today's young, educated, career-minded couples approach marriage with the idea that it will be a contract of equality. And it usually starts out that way. At no other time in a marriage is the balance of power more equal than early on, when both spouses work and they have no children. The balance of power shifts, however, when children are born, or when one partner—usually the man—begins making significantly more money than his partner, who then no longer "has" to work.

It isn't your imagination. Gender is still the best single predictor for who is spending how much time doing housework, and it's not just true in the United States, but also around the world.[4] Husbands do much less housework than their wives, and when they do it, they see it as helping out their wives rather than fulfilling their own responsibilities. In a study published in 2000, Suzanne Bianch and her colleagues found that women put in an additional five hours a week in housework once they marry, while marriage does not significantly affect the number of hours for men.[5]

Babies and Backslide

Women and men may not come from different planets, but one undeniable difference that makes combining a career and children more difficult for women is that women have babies, and men do not. When babies arrive for couples, the backslide into traditional roles becomes exaggerated. Even the most progressive couples—those who share equal responsibility for earning a living and doing the housework—regress to more traditional roles after they have a baby. The wife spends more parenting time with the baby, and she increases even more her share of the housework. During the same time period, the husband spends more time at work and less time at home with the baby or his wife, and he decreases the amount of time he spends on housework.[6] In her early study of women in family businesses, Patricia Cole found that worrying about adequate child care and balancing work with motherhood created problem after problem for women working in their family's business, much more so than for the men.[7] For example, a middle-aged man responded to the researcher's child-care question by indicating that it was something he never thought about; his wife and co-owner of the business took care of it.

You may argue my concerns are outdated but recent research results would argue against you. A study from Cambridge University suggests that support for gender equality is in fact *declining*, with growing sympathy for the old-fashioned view that a woman's place is in the home.[8] The results showed that the percentage of men *and* women arguing that family life does not suffer if a woman works plummeted from 51 percent in 1994 to 38 percent today. Husbands *and* wives expressed concerns that a mother's job comprised the welfare of children and of the family, implying that caretaking is women's work. According to Jacqueline Scott, who conducted the research, "the notion that there has been a steady increase in favor of women taking an equal role in the workplace and away from their traditional role in the home is clearly a myth."

The thought that putting women back in the home would solve the problems created by combining work and family is naive and preposterous. First, the majority of women work out of necessity, not as a choice; second, women who work to satisfy personal ambition have no intention of giving up that right. Reality is that the traditional workplace, the one made by and for men with wives at home, can't meet the needs of working *parents*—men as well as women.

SPECIAL OBSTACLES FOR WORKING MOTHERS

At one time or another, all of us confront obstacles in our work lives. We rely on our co-workers, our bosses, even the senior management to help us succeed—for ourselves and for the company. When the structures and support are not in place, the stress of it all can take the best out of us. Since married working women still do more of the housework and assume more of the child care responsibilities than do their husbands, the imbalance creates particular complications for them. Even if you are not married and/or you do not have children, do not skip this section. You may one day be married and/or have children, and most surely you will be working with other women who feel the stress of trying to "do it all."

Family Leave

Many small businesses argue that they can't afford to provide more family leave time than legally required. The fact that small businesses cannot afford to lose experienced and committed employees is precisely why they *do* need flexible leave policies and family-friendly benefits. A very conservative estimate of the cost of replacing one $8.00 per hour employee is $3,500.00. To replace a middle level employee costs approximately 150% of the annual salary. Let's do a quick calculation: Assume you have a supervisor whose annual pay is $40,000. Multiply this by 150% and the cost is $60,000 to replace that one employee. If you lose two supervisors in one year the cost has now doubled. For a small family business the expense can be staggering.[9]

When faced with the cumulative stress created by rigid company regulations and child-care responsibilities, many new mothers opt to leave their jobs, taking years of training and experience with them. However, most of these women don't stay at home but move to companies with more flexible leave policies — and those companies may be the competition!

Women are more likely to return to work after giving birth *and* stay at the job if they have greater control over their work schedules, according to a recent Baylor University study.[10] A flexible schedule allows them to meet work demands while also caring for their newborns. It just makes sense: when working moms are more in control of their work-family related stress, they are less likely to leave work out of frustration. Wives today expect more from their husbands on the home front, and more men are willing to give up an advancement or part of their pay check to be involved with their family, but many companies still are slow to create the conditions that make it possible for them to parent well. This can prove a competitive advantage for family businesses. Smaller, family-owned businesses have the latitude to provide greater flexibility for personal concerns, which is especially important for new parents. A working woman or man who is not preoccupied with family concerns makes for a more productive—and loyal—employee.

Child Care

Businesses must approach child care as a problem they share with working parents if change is ever to occur. Several years back I consulted with Kathleen, who owned and operated a house-cleaning business with her brother, Fred. The business had enjoyed success, and what once had been a small sister-and-brother shop was now a moderate-size company. Kathleen came to me to discuss what the company should do about supporting the child-care needs of its staff.

The issue was highlighted for Kathleen when an employee, Mary Beth, called early one morning and asked if she could bring her three-year-old son to work for the day. Her child-care provider was sick, and she couldn't find an alternative arrangement, but she had a training session to conduct that day and she didn't want to postpone it. Thirteen employees were scheduled to attend the session, and canceling the meeting would be expensive.

Kathleen sympathized with Mary Beth, and she was impressed with her concern for the business. She agreed to the arrangement, but later that day she realized she had unintentionally set an untenable precedent for the company. She couldn't allow the same privilege to all her employees without creating utter chaos; having several employees running after toddlers would interfere with their work and disrupt the work of others. Most of the company's employees were women, and Kathleen wanted to address their child care concerns, but she couldn't think of a reasonable solution. The company was doing well, but it certainly couldn't afford on-site day care.

The problem Kathleen faced is increasingly common today, but her response to it was remarkably modern and far-sighted. Too often, smaller companies avoid setting policies to address work and family concerns, choosing instead to let the employees figure it out. This is a mistake. Smaller businesses already have a difficult time staying afloat with their larger competitors, and family-friendly benefits can offer the competitive edge they need to retain good employees.

Kathleen was correct in deciding not to set a precedent for bringing children to work when child-care arrangements break down. Being sensitive to the needs of working parents does not mean ignoring the needs of the company. Children distract parents at work, disrupt others in the office, and interfere with productivity. Kathleen also was correct in her assessment that the business could not afford, nor did it need, on-site day care. However, that was only one of an endless number of alternatives available to the company. Some family businesses have found it worth the investment to hire a child-care provider on retainer who is available for emergency child care when employees need it. With this arrangement, both the company and the employees who expect to use the service contribute to finance the benefit.

After looking at a number of options, Kathleen put together

a task force made up of management and staff with small children and directed it to develop several proposals for consideration. The final result, which the company supported, was a company-wide emergency child care co-op. Participating parents had to sign up for days when they would be responsible for emergency child care for the other parents in the company. They could contribute their own time or pay for the services of a licensed child-care provider to do their duty. Through the co-op, parents had guaranteed child care when their arrangements broke down. Management contributed to the expense of the project and offered guidelines and flexibility for parents on duty.

Kathleen's approach to the problem was brilliant on several levels. First, by forming a task force (which included both women and men) she got employees invested in solving the problem, which would virtually guarantee their buy-in to the final decision. Second, she defined the problem as *ours*, rather than *hers*, to solve. Third, by including men in the problem-solving, the unspoken message was that men as well as women were responsible for their children. The final result was a policy that included the participation of all parents, not merely the mothers.

Paper Policies

Family-owned businesses usually operate within the culture and tradition of the founding family. There may be formal company policies, but everyone knows that the unwritten, informal policies are the ones to be respected and followed. I have heard countless stories from working women that speak to this issue. Ruth, a non-family member working in a family-owned travel agency, is one particularly poignant example. She refused to take the full eight weeks of leave allowed her after the birth of her son because no family member had taken more than two weeks off following childbirth. "I wasn't about to be stigmatized as the one who 'abused' the policy," Ruth said. "If the family doesn't believe in taking eight weeks off, then I don't believe in the leave policy."

Company policies aren't worth the paper they're written on unless its leaders strongly support them, insist that they are implemented, and categorically refuse to allow the careers of capable employees to be jeopardized because they have children. Keep in mind, however, that in many small family businesses, the senior managers are men who have non-working wives at home; this arrangement makes it especially difficult for them to appreciate the difficulties of working mothers or for them to create a company culture that is sensitive to and responds to the needs of working parents. If this situation applies in your family's business, you may want to discuss the issue with those in charge. They may not understand the role they play in a family-friendly policy being ignored, thereby increasing the likelihood of the business losing good employees who otherwise would have stayed.

SUPERWOMAN DOESN'T LIVE HERE ANYMORE

For the purpose of this discussion I have made several assumptions: you are a working woman who understands that unrealistic cultural expectations, family values, and company practices are not going to change tomorrow. You don't have a wife at home to take care of everything but your career, and you understand that life as superwoman will kill you; but still you want a career, a personal life, and children. What are you to do?

There is no single prescription for juggling work, family, and personal needs — and no perfect way to keep all the balls in the air all the time. What works for the woman with one young child, a live-in nanny, a husband, and two demanding but flexible careers will be different from what works for the woman with three young children, a career that includes a two-hour commute, and a husband who works nights. You must write your own prescription that addresses your particular needs, responsibilities, aspirations, and life choices. You are the best judge of what motivates you, how much challenge you need, and how much stress you can manage. You are the only one who can carve out the lifestyle you want. And you are the only one who can make it happen. With these thoughts in mind, I have a number of suggestions for you to consider.

Decide to Have Some of It All

Having it all — that is, all of it all of the time — is unrealistic and impossible to achieve. For example, no working mother can spend as much time at work as a childless employee can, and she cannot spend as much time with her children as the stay-at-home parent can. It's impossible; the available hours simply are not there.

Having some of it all, however, not only is possible, but also is what most women and men desire, probably you included. Having some of it means that you can simultaneously enjoy the satisfaction that comes from work and also the emotional rewards that personal relationships bring. Having some of it all is about having the most of what is most important to you at any given time. This necessitates prioritizing, making trade-offs, and understanding your limitations, as well as being honest and realistic about what is important to you. It is about having the conviction to follow through with what is most important to you, regardless of what others think. It is about owning your own life.

Admit that you are only human. Superwoman exists only in comic books, TV sitcoms, and romance novels. You may want to do what it realistically takes two or more people to accomplish, but you can't; it's humanly impossible. Instead, define what you can and cannot reasonably accomplish. Your success depends on a realistic rather than an idealistic plan for what is possible for you to have at any given time in your life.

Prioritize: Susan's Story

A smart executive carefully defines her priorities as well as her limits. Know the trade-offs and make conscious decisions. Don't let the trade-offs just happen. Prioritizing is not child's play. It requires that you identify, among a number of options available to you, those which are most important to you. It demands that you take responsibility for how and where you spend your most valuable, albeit inelastic, resource—time. Prioritizing does not guarantee that you will always make the perfect choice, but it does put you more in control of the decision-making process and increase the likelihood of your making the most beneficial choice among your options.

Susan represents a modern day example of how family wishes and societal expectations discourage women from defining and carrying through with their set priorities. Like many of today's professional women, she planned to have a career regardless of marriage or children. By age thirty-two, she had completed college, married, and worked for several years. Then she accepted an entry-level job in the family's mattress business. Susan didn't mind starting over because she was determined that one day she would succeed her mother as president of the company. She was prepared for the challenges work presented her. She ran machines, worked in the shipping department, in the planning department, on the floor, and in the sales office to gain the experience she needed.

After five years, she became vice president of operations. She also was pregnant with her first child.

While prepared for the challenges work presented her, Susan was not prepared for the challenges pregnancy presented. Everyone in her family had a different opinion about what Susan should do now that she was going to be a mother. Her mother, who had encouraged her education and was proud of her career, ignored the fact that Susan was going to have a baby. She was preparing for retirement, and she wanted Susan to take over the business. When Susan pressed her to talk about what it was like to work full-time and parent two children, the response was short, but telling: "Don't make a mountain out of a mole hill. I dealt with it, and so will you."

Susan's father, who had retired from the company ten years earlier, was adamant that she should give up her role in the family business "at least until the little one is in school." He regretted not having spent more time with his children, and he didn't want Susan to repeat his mistake. "Mark my words, you'll regret it," he told her.

Susan's husband was supportive of whatever she decided, but he wanted her to understand that he had no interest in being a househusband. He would do his fair share of the parenting (whatever that meant), but no more than that, and had no intention of quitting his job or moving to part-time work. It seemed everyone—except Susan—knew exactly what they wanted and what they would do to have it.

When Susan came to see me, she was too anxious to think about her own wishes and needs. The only daughter and youngest child, she had always been close to her parents, and she didn't want to displease them now. Regardless of her decision, however, one of them was likely to be disappointed. Susan trusted that her husband would be a partner in parenting, and she respected his ability to know just how involved he wanted to be in work and parenting. But she resented how men's clear-cut role in society allowed him to make such choices without apparent guilt or ambivalence. On the contrary, Susan's husband seemed proud, almost self-righteous, that he was going to be more involved with his child than his father had been with him. Susan, on the other hand, was paralyzed with ambivalence in the midst of conflicting role expectations from family and society.

If you identify with Susan's struggle, I suggest you do a couple of things. First, define *your* priorities regarding work and family. Let's assume that like Susan, your husband knows that he will continue to work full-time after the baby is born; what do *you* want to do? Your mother chose to run a business and have children and she wants you to also; but what do *you* want to do? If you are ambivalent about how to answer the questions, don't despair. It's impossible to know for sure what you want to do about a situation you have yet to experience. But ambivalence will only keep you stuck, and the need to please others will prevent you from defining that which is most important to you.

Talk to other women you know who have chosen to work and to have children, and some who have chosen to work part-time or not at all. Talking to others can provide useful information and help you clarify your thinking. Ask them how and why they made the decisions they made. Don't overlook the probability that working in your family's business provides you greater flexibility than that of other working mothers. Use this to your advantage.

Take the time to answer the set of questions titled "Your Career and Children." Contemplate your answers and the emotions they generate. This will help you clarify what *you* want and need (rather than what you think others want from you) regarding these most important and personal issues, and your answers can be used to guide further discussions with your husband, family, and those you work with.

Your Career and Children

If you want to learn more about your commitment to a career and children, answer the questions below. If you have a spouse or significant other, have that person also answer the questions. After both of you have completed the questions, compare your responses and have some discussion.

1. How important is it to you to work? To have children?
2. Do you think it is possible to combine a career with marriage and children? Why or why not?
3. Do you expect to interrupt your career while raising children?
4. Are you comfortable delegating child care to someone outside the family? Do you have the financial resources to pay for outside child care?
5. Have any women in your extended family had both a career and children? How well did it work for them?
6. Do you know women outside your family who have a career and a family? Have you talked with them about the trade-offs they have had to make? What did you learn from these conversations?

Susan's Choices

I asked Susan dozens of questions about her career, marriage, and children, to help her focus on *her* life, *her* goals, and *her* priorities. The process calmed her nervousness and helped her think about what was most important to her. Once Susan realized that she didn't want to make choices primarily to please her parents, who would love her regardless of what she decided and who would survive their disappointment, and that she didn't want to quit work simply because her husband wasn't going to and society dictated that someone should be at home full time, she was able to define her own career and personal goals. Susan had been trying so hard to be the good daughter and trying to figure out how to do everything everybody expected of her that she no longer knew what she wanted.

Soon after our initial consultation, Susan began to feel energized and in charge of her life and career again. She realized that she wanted to play a significant role in the family business, and she wanted to be an involved mother. Once she understood the importance of her own pursuits, she worried less about the wishes and expectations of others. She was ready to talk with her family.

Susan calmly told her mother how much her work in the family business meant to her. She expressed the hope that she could find satisfaction and accomplishment within it and reiterated her hope to be the president some day. When her mother said, "Good, I can retire!" Susan laughed and interrupted her. "Mom, thank you for the vote of confidence, but it's more complicated than that. I plan to work, and I also want to spend time with my child. I'm not ready to take over for you at this time. I like what I'm doing, and I want to stay in my position for two more years. In fact, I'd like us to work out a plan for me to work four days a week so I can spend the fifth day at home. I want an arrangement that will satisfy both of us. I also understand that the business is yours and you have to do what is best for the business—and for you. If we can't work something out, I'll be disappointed but I'll respect your decision."

Susan also was prepared when her father again admonished her that if she didn't stay home with her child she would regret her decision. She told him, "I think you are talking about your regrets, Dad, not mine. It makes me sad that you didn't have as much time with your kids as you wanted, and I don't want to repeat your mistake. But you and I are different, and I have to do what I think will work best for me." Susan had regained her confidence in her ability to make good decisions in her own behalf.

Today, years after we worked together, Susan remains married and has two children. She struggles somewhat with the trade-offs she had to make to achieve her priorities, but she has no regret about the decision. She is president of the family business — and she still works four days a week. Susan and her parents have a close relationship; her father worries about his grandchildren and spends a lot of time with them, but he knows that Susan is a good mother and tells her so often. Susan's mother gets exasperated by Susan's "newfangled ways of managing," but she respects the leadership Susan has brought to the company. Susan is proud of her parents for respecting her decisions — and she is proud of herself.

CHOOSE THE ONE YOU LOVE — CAREFULLY

If your life plan includes a career, a marriage, and children, my advice is this: choose your spouse as carefully as you do your career. And choose both very carefully. Keep in mind that it's much more difficult to leave a marriage then a job. After marriage is a little late to learn that you've chosen a man who intends to make all the major financial decision, or expects you to scale back or quit work once children come, or who has no intention of sharing child-rearing responsibilities!

Your answers to the previous set of questions, "Your Career and Children," clarified your intentions and expectations about combining work and children. If you have a significant other, and you have not explained yourself on these most important issues, now is the time to do so. If you think it will be easier after you are married, I can assure you that you are wrong.

Now answer the set of questions titled "Your Career and Family Life" to clarify your expectations about a marital partnership and partners combining careers and a family. If you have a significant partner, have that person answer the questions also. When you have completed the exercise, discuss your responses with each other. Your responses will highlight both the similarities and differences in your expectations about combining careers with a family. If there are considerable differences, further discussion is in order. If certain issues are too difficult to discuss, I would suggest involving a professional counselor to help with the discussions.

Choose a Business Partner — Carefully

If you are one of the growing number of women who work with their spouses, either in a business partnership or within a family business, you know that the arrangement can offer significant benefits. But it also presents special challenges. Not all couples enjoy working together nor are they all compatible business partners. Finding out these things after the business is under way will not benefit your marriage or the business.

In some important ways, a business relationship between spouses is no different from one between any two people. For it to work, you must trust and respect each other, work well together, complement each other's strengths, and above all want to be in partnership together. However, in other important ways, a business partnership with your spouse is unique from any other relationship. When you work with your husband, you also sleep with him, raise children with him, make budgets and do estate

Your Career and Family Life

1. How much time does your career require? How much travel is involved? How much evening and weekend time is required? How predictable is your work schedule?

2. How important for you is it that your partner support your career?

3. How important for to your partner is it that you support his/her career ?

4. How important is it for you to have children? How important is it for your partner?

5. If either you or your partner don't want children, how will the decision to have or not have a child be made?

6. How would the presence of a child or children affect each of your careers?

7. How would you divide child-care responsibilities?

8. How important is it to you that your spouse is a parental partner, rather than a parental helper? Partners share equally in responsibility while a helper is a subordinate without ultimate responsibility.

planning with him. As business partners, you and your husband are dependent on and responsible for each other's future. Working together can enrich your relationship as well as the respect and appreciation you feel toward each another. It can also stir competitiveness and disagreements over such issues as how you distribute compensation and who does what; it may be difficult to leave business problems or disagreements at the office; it can be especially difficult to address marital problems because the failure of their resolution can have major and destructive consequences for the business. A shared business venture with your spouse represents a special kind of commitment to and dependency on each other. Like parenthood, a shared business comes with celebration and sleepless nights, excitement and overwhelming stress, rewards and setbacks, and uncertainty.

My spouse is also my business partner, and I can't imagine a more satisfying working arrangement. But I repeat: it is not for every couple. If you and your spouse are considering a business partnership or plan to work together in the family business, I suggest you first talk with a business consultant who will help you examine the pros and cons of it for your particular relationship.

REMEMBER THAT MONEY TALKS — LOUDLY

My daughter was two years old and at home with her nanny when an article reporting the results of a survey of three thousand working women mysteriously appeared on my desk at work. It read, "The more money a woman earns, the more likely she is to share the family's financial power — and the happier the marriage."[11] I don't know who left the article, but it came at an important time. At the time I was feeling guilty and selfish about leaving my daughter in someone else's care, and the article helped me stay with a career I loved. It supported my belief that she was better off with happily married parents who had full-time careers and a nanny who loved her in their absence, than with an unhappy mother or divorced parents! I believed it then and I still believe it today.

Children learn early in their lives that until they can support themselves financially they are not free to do as they wish. As long as parents hold the purse strings, they get to set the rules and make the decisions about how and when and if money is spent. In fact, the wish for financial independence is what propels many young adults to leave home. Why, then, do so many women forget the importance of financial independence when they marry? Too many young women still dream of the day when they will enjoy the security of being taken care of by a man. These women may find protective men who want to take care of them, but the dependency will leave them unprepared to take care of themselves financially if a divorce occurs or their husband dies prematurely.

We all know the truth in the saying that money is power, yet few couples discuss the power of money in their relationship. Fewer still discuss how to balance the power when one of them (usually the woman) becomes financially dependent on the other one (usually the man) during their child-rearing years.

The powerful force of tradition continues to dictate the way relationships work. No one wants to think that she or he would dominate a marriage with money, and the phrase "my money is our money" is often the mantra of the spouse who makes the most money. Betty Carter, cofounder and director of the Family Institute of Westchester and author of several books, considers this one of the last great myths of romantic love. She asserts that the more accurate and unspoken agreement between most couples is, "I will share my money with you as long as you make me happy."[12] As clear evidence of her argument, she cites divorce proceedings where couples try to prove that what's mine was never yours and what's yours is really part mine.

Money can create a striking imbalance in a relationship. Its power can be neutralized, but only if its force is recognized. Unfortunately, this rarely occurs. One partner (usually the economically dependent woman) is aware of the resentment she feels about asking for money or waiting for her partner to approve a decision that would allow a purchase, but she is unaware that it is his power and control over the money that she resents.

Rarely does the economically independent partner (usually the man) consciously or malevolently try to control the relationship with money. More often he is surprised, hurt, and angered to learn that his wife thinks of the money as his money. He considers himself generous with their money, he gives his wife whatever she asks for, and he doesn't squander money on boy toys for himself like other men he knows. The husband does not realize that the issue is not whether he is considerate of his spouse with his money, but whether he and his spouse feel the same ownership of their money.

Let me assure you that the spouse who earns the most money rarely asks permission to spend money. It is equally rare for the financially dependent spouse not to ask permission, even when the couple insists the money is their money. The verbal agreement — my money is our money — is overridden by the nonverbal addendum, "until I (the one who makes the money) no longer want to share it with you (the financially dependent one)." He — and usually it is a he — who makes the most money, controls the largest expenditures of money. For example, it is not uncommon to hear from a husband who earns the money in the marriage that he surprised his wife with expensive jewelry or a new car. He is pleased with himself, and his wife appreciates his love and generosity. However, in over thirty years of working with couples I have yet to hear from a woman financially dependent on her husband that she surprised him with a room full of expensive furniture or a new car. She simply would not feel comfortable spending that kind of money without discussing it with her husband.

Ironically, the one exception to this rule that I have seen is when the wife has significantly more money than the husband. Many women from successful business families are wealthy in their own right from ownership in the family business, trust funds established by parents or grandparents, or investments they have made on their own. In these situations, one would expect the woman to have equal or more power in the relationship. More often what occurs is that the woman downplays

Money and Your Marriage

1. Do you usually ask your spouse for permission to go on a trip (hunting, visiting a friend, etc.), or do you inform him/ her of your intent to go and then discuss how best to do it? Now answer the question in regard to your spouse.

2. Do you usually ask your spouse before making a major purchase such as a new television, lawn equipment, washer etc., or do you inform him or her of your intent and then discuss how best to pay for it? Now answer the question in regard to your spouse.

3. Who has the final decision about whether a major purchase will be made? How do you know?

4. Do you and your spouse ever argue over money? What is the nature of the argument? How do you usually settle the argument? Does someone win and someone lose?

5. Does one of you nag the other about money? What happens as a result of the nagging?

6. Who makes the most money? Who has greater access to the financial assets?

her wealth, or the couple denies themselves opportunities her money could provide them, choosing instead to save her money and wait until he makes money for them to spend. On the surface this may seem prudent, but it occurs even when the woman has enough money for them to save and spend, and couples rarely exercise the same prudence when the man makes the money.

How you spend the household money can illuminate much about the balance of power in your marriage. Both you and your partner will need to answer the set of questions titled "Money and Your Marriage." After each of you has completed the exercise, discuss your responses. As with previous sets of questions in this chapter, a discussion about who spends the money and how they spend it may be difficult. Even so, I encourage you to do so, perhaps with the help of a counselor if needed.

Money Matters: Becky and Ted's Story

Ted and Becky, a couple I saw because their marriage was falling apart, could barely make it on their combined salaries. Ted was fresh out of law school, having gone back to school to change careers in his late thirties. He loved his work as an environmental attorney for the state, but it paid very little. He worked three evenings a week at the local Legal Aid office to earn extra money.

Becky was a writer and poet who worked out of their home, and she cared for their infant son. She had worked for a magazine for ten years prior to going out on her own. Becky also did freelance editing, but the work was sporadic. Becky's parents, with whom I had worked years earlier, referred the couple to me. Becky's mother ran an insurance business that had been in the family for three generations. Becky's older sister and younger brother worked in the business, and Becky was one of the family owners.

It seemed reasonable to me that Ted and Becky would be overwhelmed with the stress of trying to launch two new careers and adjusting to a new baby after ten years of marriage. What they complained about, however, was not having enough money to pay their bills or to hire the child care needed to give themselves more time for work. The discussion struck me as odd, since I knew from working with Becky's family that she had a sizable trust from her grandparents. Ted and Becky seemed surprised when I asked about it.

"Oh, that," Becky began. "We would never spend that. It's our security and Jordan's college fund."

"We've always contributed equally to the relationship," Ted interrupted. "No need to change that now. Besides, another five years and we won't need it anyway. I'll be making enough money to take care of things."

"You may not be together in five years if things continue as they are," I reminded them. The reality of what I said startled them. I addressed my next comment to Becky.

"If your trust represents security, why aren't you using some of it to help insure your future? Why aren't you investing money in yourselves and your relationship?" Becky's trust was large, and I knew that the annual interest from it was more than Ted's present salary. Becky could use some of the interest to hire the child care they needed and to make their lives easier, and she would not have to touch the principal of the trust. Instead, she and Ted were behaving as if the money didn't exist.

Becky and Ted had a fairly egalitarian relationship; they loved each other, supported each other's careers, and they were enjoying their infant daughter. They thought their only problem was a lack of money and the stress it created for them. In reality, there was no shortage of money. Unconsciously, however, Becky felt guilty and worried about having significantly more money than Ted, and Ted felt ashamed that he couldn't provide for his family sufficiently. They were stuck, in large part because of their unconscious, traditional beliefs about how a marriage should operate. They wanted to be equal partners but they worried that Becky's money would give her more power and make her less feminine; it would make Ted more dependent and thus less masculine. They resolved the problem, not by talking about it, but by downplaying the importance of the money. Unfortunately, their solution created other problems that almost destroyed their marriage.

Ted and Becky were fortunate. They came to counseling before it was too late, while both of them still were committed to making the changes needed to save their relationship. We talked about the unconscious expectations and family stories that each of them brought to the marriage, and the influence that gender stereotyping had over the decisions they had made about Becky's trust fund. Over time, they came to view the trust as a luxury that gave them a number of choices. They hired a part-time nanny so Becky could work uninterrupted, and Ted quit his second job to spend more time with his wife and daughter. They decided that they would take a trip by themselves once a year to renew their emotional relationship. When I last saw them, they were well on their way to being the equal and intimate partners they intended to be.

Balancing the Power of Money

Olivia Goldsmith, author of *The First Wives Club*, understood the importance of women having equal financial power in a relationship. She lost most of her cash, her Jaguar, and both of the marital homes during a bitter, six-year divorce from her husband. At one point, her $300,000 capital shrank to less than $40,000, most of which was in an IRA, and she had to borrow money from a schoolteacher friend. Given her scenario, it is hardly remarkable that the theme of financial independence ran through her advice to women.

"I think a woman getting married today has to have her own identity and her own money," Goldsmith said. "I don't mean that couples shouldn't have funds in common. But it is very, very important that you have your own investments and money that is clearly yours."[13] Goldsmith's comment is as timely and important today as it was fifteen years ago when she spoke it.

To be real partners, couples must find ways to balance the unequal power that money creates in a relationship. I'm not suggesting that partners must earn the same amount, but they must assess contributions to the relationship equally. For example, in a traditional marriage that is also a partnership, the spouse who carries responsibilities for the house and the children would be seen as contributing as much to the relationship as the one who earns the money. Each would have equal access to the money and equal decision-making power. This kind of partnership is possible to achieve in even the most traditional of relationships, but only if the couple genuinely acknowledges and reckons with the power of money.

If you want to further your understanding about the power of money in your significant relationship, answer the set of questions titled "The Power of Money in Your Relationship." For most couples, the balance and power of money changes over time and under different circumstances. It may be time to examine the balance in your relationship.

The Power of Money in Your Relationship

After both you and your spouse have answered the questions, discuss your responses with each other.

1. Do both you and your spouse work outside the home? Who earns the most money? Whose career is viewed as most important? Why?

2. Who most often leaves work early or misses work because of the children's needs? Why?

3. Do you have an unwritten contract about money in your marriage? How would it read?

4. Was there ever a time when the power of money was balanced differently than it is now? How was it different? What shifted the balance of control?

5. Is it time that you and your spouse update the unwritten contract about money in your relationship?

Feeling Selfish: Emily's Story

Feelings of guilt and selfishness are epidemic among women, regardless of education or economic status. Encouraged to be selfless in their pursuit of caring for others, generations of women have felt selfish when they considered their own needs. Thousands of women today feel selfish about having a career unless they need to help support their family, or they have no children. My work with Emily, the office manager in the family-owned floor covering business, highlights these struggles.

Emily's job demanded that she be out of town two or three nights every other week. She enjoyed her work, and the travel was not a problem for her or her husband, Pete. In fact, Pete teased Emily that her travel kept their romance alive. "Absence makes the heart grow fonder," he would say.

After they had children, however, things changed. Emily's travel became their number one problem. When I saw her, the children were ages two and five. Emily reported that they cried each time she left, didn't sleep well, and acted out more when she was gone. All of this, on top of his full-time job, made the periods of parenting alone very difficult for Pete. He yelled at the children in Emily's absence, and the children complained to her about him. Emily worried about all of them and felt guilty about being gone. When she returned from a trip, exhausted by the travel, Pete's complaints often greeted her: "The kids haven't slept for two nights, and they've been acting like animals. You don't know what it's like when you're gone. I never get a break. You act like traveling is hard, but at least when you get to the motel room at night, your time is your own. It's not fair."

At times Emily felt defensive and angry. Did Pete really think that sitting in airports, attending meetings until 11:00 P.M., and sleeping in motel rooms was a break? She resented his trying to make her feel guilty for traveling, and the more he tried to make her feel guilty, the more she resented him. When Emily's anger subsided, however, she found herself paralyzed by other feelings. She feared she was a bad mother, worried that her selfishness was damaging the children, and considered looking for less-demanding work. But she loved her job and knew she'd resent Pete more if she gave it up.

Sometimes Emily's guilt made her cancel a trip or send someone in her place, but then she worried about whether the work was getting done well. She felt guilty about delegating her responsibility, and she resented the family pressure that kept her at home. She was short-tempered with the children, and she avoided Pete to prevent an argument. At other times, Emily made sure not to mention an upcoming trip until the night before she left, hoping to avoid the children's sorrowful pleas and Pete's criticism. It didn't work, of course, and Emily began to fear there might not be a solution to reconciling the family needs with her own. At the suggestion of her father, Henry, with whom I had consulted when he was planning his retirement, she called me for a consultation.

Emily, like thousands of women who work and have children, couldn't figure out how to be responsible to her husband and children and also be responsible for herself. It seemed a no-win proposition to her. If she selfishly kept her job, she could lose her marriage and emotionally damage her children; but if she selflessly sacrificed her work to please her husband, she still could lose her marriage and damage her children because of her resentment.

Emily was confused, guilt-ridden, and angry. She no longer knew exactly what she wanted or why she wanted it. She no longer knew whether she was traveling to move toward her career goals or traveling to get away from her husband and children. She no longer knew what she wanted in her career, her marriage, or her relationship with her children.

I encouraged Emily to talk with other women in her family about how they had grappled with similar problems, and what she learned cast a different light on the problem. The women in Emily's family either worked and didn't have children, or had children and didn't work. Interestingly, marriage wasn't a part of the equation. For example, Emily learned of a great aunt who bore twins by a man she didn't marry. The man didn't provide support, and the aunt didn't work, but the extended family supported them because of the family's strong belief in mothers' being home with their children.

In another branch of Emily's family, there was an aunt who had a successful career and also was married, but she had no children. During a conversation with this aunt, Emily learned that the couple had been unable to conceive a child. "I desperately wanted children, but I suppose it was a blessing in disguise," explained the aunt. "Had I had children, I wouldn't have my career." With these family values, it's no wonder that Emily experienced ambivalence and confusion about combining a career and a family!

Following these conversations, Emily needed to talk with her father about the most influential woman in her life — her deceased mother. Emily told her father what she had learned from talking to the other women and asked him whether her mother had struggled with similar problems. Henry said that Emily's mother, Vivian, had been a gifted artist and had dreamed of teaching art and owning a gallery. "I'm part of the reason she never fulfilled her dream," Henry confessed. He had discouraged her because it would have looked like he couldn't provide for the family, and he wanted her to be home when he was there. "It was selfish of me," he told Emily.

Emily's father said more. He had been the mayor of the small town Emily grew up in, and he frequently was gone. The family lived hours from a large city; since Vivian didn't drive, she rarely visited the museums and galleries she loved. She was lonely and suffered depression for years before her death. "Your mother loved me, and I her; but it wasn't enough. She needed her work. I wish I'd known then that what was best for each of us — not just for me — would have been best for both of us."

Emily did a lot of soul searching after her conversation with her father. Unlike generations of women in her family before her, she did not want to choose between a career and a family. She wanted both, but she had no family role models to follow. The legacy of regret that her foremothers had left, however, made Emily see that she felt a passion both for her work and for her family. Perhaps it did not have to be an either/or choice. Perhaps it was possible to forge a new path in the family.

Emily decided it was time to talk with her husband. She told Pete about her family's longstanding dilemma surrounding work and family, the conversation with her father, and her mother's un-fulfilled dream. "Perhaps I feel the same passion for my work that my mother felt for her art," she explained. "If I give it up, a piece of me will die."

But Emily didn't stop with a passionate expression of her own need. She went on to say that she understood Pete's resent-ment at having full responsibility for the kids, the house, and his job when she was gone. She admitted that she treated his com-plaints as childishness because she didn't know how to address the real problem. For the first time in two years, Emily and Pete talked in earnest about their work, their children, their marriage, and their future.

It took months, and the course wasn't smooth, but Emily and Pete made changes. Emily traveled when her work demanded it, and she stopped springing her absences on the family. Before a trip, she showed the children on a map where she was going, gave them each a picture of her, and one of her T-shirts to wear to bed. She telephoned them while she was gone. These things helped her children feel less anxious about her absence, made her feel less guilty about being gone, and supported Pete in his parenting efforts. Emily actually increased the number of days she traveled, but Pete no longer resented it. He knew she loved her work, but he also knew she loved him.

Together, Emily and Pete built some alone time into Pete's schedule that gave him a needed break from child care and gave Emily time with the kids. Since she no longer needed to avoid them to avoid her guilt, she enjoyed being with them more. Emily and Pete also arranged for a babysitter to come in twice a month so they could go out. They enjoyed being together again and felt like the partners they had been in the early years of their marriage.

PART III

THE DAUGHTER
ALSO RISES

CHAPTER EIGHT

Joining the Family Business

The best career advice given to the young is "find out what you like doing best and get someone to pay you for doing it."
—*Katharine Whitehorn*

A decision to join the family business will affect your life in many ways. You should make that decision only after a great deal of personal reflection, as well as extensive discussion with people working in and outside of the business. To succeed you have to be competent in your work, committed to the business, and enjoy what you do. Even though it may seem obvious that you must make the best decision for you about joining the business, many daughters—and sons—join for reasons unrelated to their professional or personal interests: convenience, family expectations, easy money, obligation, not wanting to disappoint a parent (or other family member), and so on.

I have heard many reasons for working in the family business that have absolutely nothing to do with business needs, personal interests, or legitimate career goals. Harriet, for example, decided at the age of ten; she overheard a conversation between her parents and her older sister, Elsie, who was lobbying to work at an ice cream store for the summer instead of in the family business. Her father's angry words abruptly ended the discussion, but they left a lifetime impression on Harriet. "If you're part of this family, Elsie, you're part of the business. If you're not, you're not. You decide." In that moment, Harriet made her choice.

Linda was another woman who entered her family's business for reasons unrelated to the work. Unconscious motivations drove her decision, like those of many children of family business owners. Twenty-six years old at the time I saw her, Linda came for a consultation because she had lost interest in—perhaps even hated—her work. We talked about her work, her life, and how she decided to join the business. Her father traveled three to four days a week when she was growing up, and when he was not on the road, he was often at the office or talking about the business with Linda's mother. Linda considered the business to be a magical place where her father was happy. On those rare occasions when he took her to the office, she sat in his chair while he finished reports at the conference table. She tried to imagine being there with him every day and dreamed that one day she would work at the office too.

After Linda graduated from college, she joined the business and set out to fulfill her dream. When reality met fantasy, however, the result was less than ideal. She and her father worked in the same building, but Linda saw him no more than she had as a child; when she did see him, they met to discuss business issues. Linda felt lonely and angry and betrayed by both the business and her father. She could not understand why the business held her father's attention and why it didn't hold the same fascination for her. She didn't understand why she and her father had not become closer by working in close proximity to each other.

Unaware of the unconscious motivation that drove her to join the business, Linda could not understand the disappointment and anger she felt. She knew only that she hated her work. Without understanding why she decided to join the business, Linda would never be able to enjoy the work that she blamed two decades earlier for taking her father away from her.

Exaggerated memories, like those of Harriet and Linda, can skew your impressions of the family business and make it difficult to discover what it can offer you. Facing the reality of the family business can be difficult, even for those without distorted impressions. For some, joining the family business is as easy as expressing the interest. For most, finding success is much more demanding and may take years or involve several transitions into and out of the business. Even though you may love the product the business sells and have something of value to contribute to the enterprise, you may confront an unexpected challenge along your way to success—learning to work well with those in charge, perhaps your father, and perhaps other family members as well. You must not minimize or discount this challenge. To work together successfully, you will have to confront and reconcile past experiences and memories. You may have to forge a different, more egalitarian relationship with your father or with a sibling with whom you've had a strained relationship.

Deciding whether to enter the family business is momentous. A wrong decision can create painful consequences for you, your family, and even the business. There is no way, of course, to guarantee that you will make the right decision, and it is naive to think all feelings can be eradicated from a decision that involves family. You can, however, increase the likelihood of making a decision that is right for you and that your family can support by making sure that your reasons accentuate what is best for you and the business, rather than depending on an inflated sense of entitlement, obligation, old fantasies, or convenience.

This chapter is designed as a workbook to help you decide whether to join the family business. You will need to think about many issues, including your personal interests, career goals, knowledge of the business, and work experience. You will explore your relationships with those who run the business, your expectations about a career there, and the value you can bring to it. You will distinguish your needs from those of others in the business. Following each section, you will answer a series of questions. At times they may seem tedious, but answering them is absolutely necessary to make the best decision possible about your career. Don't rush through the task.

SHOULD YOU JOIN THE FAMILY BUSINESS?

There is no time like the present to begin assessing the options open to you. As you evaluate the costs and benefits of joining the family firm, keep in mind that most heirs have a wide range of feelings about working in their family's business. You will likely find that your own mixed feelings surface as you work through this section. Pay attention to what you feel and try to separate your feelings from your expectations.

To make a good decision about your career, you need to weigh elements such as your ambitions, personal values, life goals, and family relationships, as well as the fit between your needs and the needs of the business. For purposes of simplicity, I define a good career decision as one that balances the key factors mentioned above. It is also one that will satisfy you for a long time and one that has a low probability of causing you regret later in life.

Personal Interests, Values, and Goals

Two of the most important reasons for joining a family business are that you love the product or service the business sells and that you love the idea of working with your family. If you do not get excited by either of these ideas, you probably shouldn't sign on. You will lose interest, you probably will bring little value to the company, and you may complicate or worsen your relationships with family members. Working with family members is not child's play. Such a work environment usually exaggerates your weaknesses and takes your strengths for granted. You need patience and a capacity for forgiveness. You have to form strong, positive work relationships with certain family members, some of whom you may not like. You may have to terminate—or be terminated by—a family member.

Your decision to join the family business should be the most rational, thoughtful one you ever make, but it is very difficult to think clearly about a decision that involves family. Emotions frequently interfere with the process; at times they may override it. Some people believe there will be less pressure in the family business while others expect to have more authority there than they would in another company. Some join out of sheer entitlement and laziness. They don't think they should have to do what hundreds of thousands of other young people have to do: compose a resume, find companies with openings, compete with others for the job, suffer the humiliation of not being hired. Some children need to prove something to their dad (or their mom or Uncle Albert or whomever). And many young people join the family business because they feel that others expect them to do so.

Family expectations develop over time and for many reasons. They may evolve as a way to justify a behavior, explain a tragedy, lessen a pain, keep a secret, provide reassurance to the family. Sometimes families create them for the purposes of one generation, but the family preserves them in memories. These expectations continue to influence—or even govern—how future generations think and feel about themselves and treat one another, make life choices, and view the world beyond the family. Unless you uncover the family values and expectations that influence your behavior, the decision you make about joining the family business may not be your own, and it may not be in either your best interest or your family's.

The sets of questions in this and the following chapter function differently than those in the previous seven chapters. The earlier question sets helped you gain personal insights relative to the information presented. The exercises in the next two chapters will help you decide whether you should join the family business and what your role in the business might be. Give the questions thoughtful reflection, have conversations with other family members, and ask trusted friends and advisors outside of the business to discuss your answers with you.

Your Personal and Work Goals

1. As a child, how did you imagine yourself when you grew up (an astronaut; a famous journalist; a mother; a dancer; president)? To what extent does your current career incorporate your childhood ambitions?
2. What are the three most important things in your life? How much time do you devote to each?
3. Does your work and lifestyle permit the time you need for those things that you value most? If not, what needs to change? What might prevent you from making those changes?

Family Relationships

The next step in making a good decision about your career is to assess your family relationships honestly. If it was difficult for you to grow and flourish in your family, it most probably will be difficult for you to do so in the family business. On the other hand, if you thrived in your family and enjoy strong, positive relationships with family members, you probably will enjoy working with them. A family business tends to imitate the family behind it, and yours is probably no different. Good family relationships do not guarantee good business relationships or business success, but they do increase the likelihood that working with your family will be gratifying and that you will spend more time executing business strategies than negotiating family disputes.

You and Your Family

1. What beliefs do your family value most (for example: family problems shouldn't be discussed with outsiders; women will stab you in the back; a bad attitude will kill you; love and money don't mix; never cry in public; money makes happiness etc.)? What family experiences have influenced these values?

2. How do family beliefs influence the way you and your family think about the business?

3. What stories has your family passed down about women and work (for example: women can't manage money; mother is the bedrock of the family; women and work don't mix)? Why are these stories meaningful to you?

4. Do you like being around your family? Do you avoid certain members? Why? Do they work in the business?

5. Growing up, how often and on what types of projects did you and your siblings, or your family as a whole, collaborate (for example: having a garage sale, household chores, decorating the house for the holidays etc.)? How do you remember the experiences?

6. Do you think that working with your family would be an advantage or an obstacle for you to overcome?

Your responses to the next set of questions, "Your Family's Expectations for You," highlight the influence your parents' expectations have had on your career choices and your interest in or avoidance of the family business. Take time to contemplate your responses and what they mean in terms of decisions you have made about your life and your career. Is it time you reconsider what *you* want to be doing and what is in *your* best interest?

Your Family's Expectations For You

1. What are your parents' expectations for you now? How do you know? Are their expectations similar or different? Have you tried to live up to their expectations? Rebelled against them? Avoided them? What have been the effects of your efforts?

2. How have the above expectations influenced the work you are currently doing? What was your mother doing when she was about your age? Your aunts? Your grandmother? What influence have their lives had on your career choices?

The Power of Relationships

Family businesses often exaggerate the qualities of relationships; they can make good relationships great and poor relationships terrible. They cannot, however, magically change relationships. The members of your family are who they are, and no amount of wishing, complaining, arguing, or demanding is going to change them if they don't want to change. You must accept this reality if you expect to work successfully with them. Do not fool yourself into thinking that joining the family business will resolve a family problem; it will more likely worsen it. The best *and* worst thing about working in a family business is, in fact, working with your family.

Some families try to deny or downplay the importance of positive, strong relationships among family members who work together in the business. They emphasize the business and ignore the relationship part of their association with one another. This is a mistake, of course, because denying the importance of relationships can have devastating consequences. Years ago, I saw a classic example of this phenomenon. When Roy, the founder of a small and successful custom tile business died, he left 50 percent of the common stock in the business to each of his two sons and named them co-presidents of the business. I never would have recommended this arrangement without the consent of all involved parties. It might have worked, however, if the brothers, Roy Jr. and Elliot, had had the competence necessary to run the business, a trusting relationship, and the desire to work together. Unfortunately for everyone, they had the competence but not the relationship. The brothers had competed fiercely with each other since childhood, and now they could barely be in the same room without arguing. They worked in different areas of the business, in part to avoid having to work together, and each had tried unsuccessfully to buy the business from their father before he died.

As you may have guessed, the founder's ownership and asset distribution proved disastrous. The brothers mistrusted each other's motives and couldn't agree on anything. Each offered to buy out the other, but neither would sell. Each was afraid the other would end up with the better deal. They began taking more and more time away from work as a way to avoid each other and their inevitable arguments. The business foundered without the leadership it needed, and ten years later the brothers were forced to sell the business to an outsider at a loss. They blamed the sale on decreased customer demand and increased external competition, both of which were accurate but insufficient to explain the failure. Although competition had increased and larger companies had taken contracts away from them, the business had enjoyed a good reputation in the region, each brother was experienced in certain aspects of operation, and they employed an excellent management staff.

The business could have succeeded with the right leadership, but the contentious relationship between the brothers made the leadership structure impossible and eventually destroyed the business. The father denied the competitive relationship between his sons and may have hoped that by naming them co-presidents he would force them to be close. The brothers denied their competitiveness with each other but fiercely acted it out. No one could change what they refused to acknowledge. In the end, they lost both the business and the opportunity to have better family relationships. In this scenario, the brothers blamed each other, their father, and the business climate, but they couldn't face the relationship issue that was at the core of the business problem. Make no mistake: acknowledging family relationship problems is difficult and addressing them is more so. But if you are serious about joining the family business, you *must* understand the relationships within the family and the business.

In contrast to the family mentioned above, successful business families recognize and respect the powerful role that relationships play in the success of both their family and the business they run. They understand that when relationships are strained family communication breaks down, so they encourage open and honest exchanges between family members. While they respect the power of relationships, they also appreciate the need to separate business relationships from family relationships, and business issues from family issues, even though the two are inseparably joined. In the most successful family businesses, the company clearly defines in writing the roles and responsibilities of family members as well as non-family members, rather than relying on oral agreements made over a family meal. These businesses base performance appraisals, bonuses, and even terminations on the ability of individuals to fulfill agreed-upon responsibilities. They discuss business issues and strategies openly, and no one assumes that everyone in the family thinks alike. The firm hires and fires family members based on their ability to fulfill particular needs of the business, not to pay off a personal debt or settle a family feud.

Working With Your Family

The three question sets in this section are similar to the many difficult questions I ask daughters considering a career in the family firm. Your responses will lead to self-discovery about your family relationships that will help determine whether you want to work with your family, whether they want to work with you, whether

Disagreements and Your Family

1. Are you able to disagree openly with others in your family? Are there certain family members you cannot disagree with? Why not? Have you ever tried? What happened? Do those you cannot disagree with work in the family business?
2. What are the rules for discussing disagreements in your family? Who speaks to whom about what? What happens when someone in the family doesn't follow the rules?
3. How are decisions made in the family business? Who makes them? How do you know? What happens after a decision is made?
4. What skills do you need to acquire to improve your method of disagreeing with others in the family?

it's in your best interest to do so, and the potential consequences of your decision for you, your family, and the business.

No family or its business is without problems. If you plan to work with your family, you need to have a strategy for resolving conflict. Your answers to the set of questions titled "Disagreements and Your Family" will indicate how well you and your family solve problems and whether you need to address this issue further before joining the family firm.

Should you decide to work in the family business, at some point you probably will report to a family member. Answer the following set of questions to assess the influence your family history has had on how you respond to authority.

You and Authority

1. What did your parents do effectively in exercising their authority over you when you were growing up? What did they do unfairly?

2. How did you respond to your parents' authority (for example: ignore it, rebel against it, not question it etc.)?

3. Who has the most authority in your family? How do you know? Does this person(s) work in the family business?

4. How do you respond to the above person's authority? How effective are your responses?

5. Would working with this person(s) create difficulties for you? Why or why not?

6. What would need to change to make working together satisfying?

7. What would you need to do differently to work well with this person? Is it realistic? Why or why not?

Congratulations! You have completed a critical and very personal part of your decision-making process. You have determined your personal and work goals and considered your relationships with your family. You know who has most influenced your ideas about work and family and how their influence has affected your thoughts about working in the family business. You understand how you respond to authority as well as the influence it might have on your working relationships with family.

Some of your responses may have confirmed what you already

Your Family's Business

1. Were there any critical events that affected the family business: a financial disaster, a death, a problem with a family member? How did the family deal with the crisis? What did you learn from the way the family handled the crisis?

2. What lessons has the family passed down about the business (for example: be cautious of outsiders; hard work will carry you through; take care of the business and it will take care of you; the business is about family)?

3. What meaning did you take away from the lessons about the family business (for example: everyone deserves a second chance; money destroys a family; short men can't be trusted etc.)?

4. Has anyone in the family chosen not to enter the business? How has that decision affected his/her relationships with family? Has anyone ever been disinvited? Terminated? How has that decision affected his/her relationships with family?

knew, while others may have surprised or alarmed you. It would be a mistake to discard those that don't fit your current thinking. No amount of denial will improve your relationships with family members, and all the aptitude in the world isn't going to make up for a lack of interest in the product or service of the business. It may be difficult to acknowledge certain things about yourself or your family, but your honest appraisal now will help you make a good decision that you will be satisfied with for a long time.

CAREER APTITUDES, INTEREST, AND READINESS

It is time to consider your readiness to enter the family business. Your decision will affect you, your family, and the business. You probably don't need to be reminded that if you do not possess certain abilities and if you do not bring value to the business, your career isn't going to offer you much personal satisfaction, and it won't benefit the company either.

I suggest you be honest with yourself about whether you are prepared to enter the business. It is selfish and unfair to expect the business to take care of you because you don't want to go through the hard work of finding a job. If you have neither the necessary skills nor the motivation to acquire them, your presence will harm the business, and the entire family may pay the price for your decision. If, on the other hand, you get excited by the idea of working with your family and you feel you have something to contribute to the business, I would encourage you to pursue a career there. I cannot repeat enough that you should join because it fits your interests and aptitude, and not because it offers the easiest path for work or you owe something to the family. Find other ways to pay your debt. You and your family will be glad you did.

Misplaced Loyalty: Fran's Story

Fran, a thirty-two-year-old woman who sought my consultation because of her unhappiness in her family's business, is an example of the darker side of family loyalty and obligation. Today Fran lives with her two daughters in a small country home. Her two-acre backyard consists of waves of vegetables, patches of strawberries, and latticework screens full of snow peas. Her displays of flowers reflect her talent and good taste, as well as her competitiveness and triumph over the enemy — weather, insects, time. Fran knows what she is good at, and she pours herself into the work, determined to be the best at her craft. The success of her nursery and the enjoyment she derives from it are evidence of the good decision she made about her career.

At one time, however, Fran poured her substantial talent and winning attitude into the real estate business her family owned. She was determined to follow in the path of her older sister and brother, both of whom loved their work and were quite successful at it. Fran's attempt was earnest — but she failed miserably. She never came close to the sales of her siblings, and she felt guilty about not doing her part for the business.

By answering questions similar to those in this section, Fran uncovered the reasons behind her failure: a disinterest in the service of the business and a considerable lack of training and experience because of her disinterest. Fran's loyalty and obligation to her family, as well as her need to achieve, had blinded her to these important facts. In reality, she would never contribute substantially to the business; it would be better off without her.

The following sets of questions will help assess your readiness for joining the family firm. Pay close attention to your responses. You may need to question your motivation if, for example, you have not worked outside the family business even though those in charge of the business have determined that doing so is important.

If you cannot answer the next set of questions, "The Needs of the Business," do not skip them. Instead, talk to those who can answer the questions for you. The information you gain will be invaluable for determining whether you want to work in the business and, equally important, whether the business needs you.

THE RIGHT FIT

Working with family can be challenging and more complicated than other business arrangements, but, with the right fit, it can be more rewarding than any other arrangement. If there isn't a good match between you and the business, however, nothing is going to make it work well. Don't cheat yourself and your family like Fran did by pretending to be interested or by over inflating your value. Everyone will lose.

You have assessed your readiness to join the business and whether the fit is right between you and the family business. However, while your internal dialogue is important, it is insufficient for this most important decision. Talk with some trusted friends about what you are discovering about yourself. Friends can be an invaluable resource in any process of self-discovery and self-assessment. Talk with them *and* listen to their feedback, think more, talk more, think more, and so on. If you practice this process with friends, it will help prepare you for having meaningful conversations with your family about what it will be like to work in the family business.

Your Needs and the Family Business

1. What do you need most from your work (for example, recognition from family, challenging work, money, satisfying and stimulating work, job security, etc.)?
2. Have you communicated your career needs to those in charge of the business? What was their reaction?
3. What do you hope to achieve through your work? Have you communicated your aspirations to those in the business? Why or why not?
4. What do you want to do in the business? What strengths would you bring to the role? What would you hope to learn and accomplish in the role?
5. What are you doing to prepare yourself for the work you would most like to do in the business?
6. Have you worked outside of the family business? If yes, why did you leave? What did you enjoy about the work? What did you dislike? What are you looking for from the family business as a result of your previous work experience?

The Needs of the Business

1. What do you know about the family business?
2. What problems does the business currently face? What will it take to correct these problems?
3. Why should the family business hire you?
4. What do you offer the business that is different from what anyone else in the family has to offer?
5. How could your skills help improve the business?

You and Your Family and the Family Business

These questions assume your father started the business but insert the appropriate name if otherwise.

1. Why did you father start the business?
2. Does your father enjoy his work? How do you know? What does he most/least enjoy about his work? If other family members work in the business, do they enjoy their work? How do you know?
3. Do those operating the business envision it extending beyond their lifetime? Are you part of the future plan? Why or why not?
4. If you were not part of the family business, what would you be doing? Why?
5. Are you the first child to join the family business? The first daughter? The last of many? How does your placement in the family influence the way others already in the business will treat you?
6. If your siblings work in the business, what legacy do they leave you? How might their legacy influence how family and non-family members working in the business see you?

Beginning Conversations

If you cannot have honest dialogue about the business and your potential role in it with family members who work in the business, you are asking for trouble. I have a number of suggestions for having these important conversations. For the purpose of this discussion, I assume that your father owns and operates the family business; as a result, he has an enormous emotional and financial investment in the business. Therefore, if you are considering a career in the business, you must talk with him about what the business means to him. You would use the same approach, of course, if the leader is another family member.

These talks should take place over an extended period of time. Prepare for them carefully so that you know what information you are seeking and so that you can articulate clearly what you want to say. Ask him what the business has meant to him as well as how its meaning may have changed over time. Ask him to describe what he has most enjoyed and most disliked. Ask him what his frustrations and satisfactions have been and, perhaps most importantly, what his dreams are for the future of the business. Keep in mind that his dreams will shape the business you may devote your career to.

Your father may be a private man of few words who will not converse with you about his feelings or his work. You must understand that these affect the business even if you do not discuss them. They still reflect the motivations behind his business strategy and the way he makes decisions. They still will color your working relationship with him once you are in the business.

Perhaps you may never persuade your father to talk with you. He may, for whatever personal reasons, thwart your attempts to learn what the business has meant to him and what he thinks about the future of the business. It may be frustrating, but his refusal to talk provides you important information for making your decision about working with him.

You may want to talk to others in the family about the history of the business, what they know about your father's relationship with the business, and what they know about his hopes for the future. You may want to talk to those working in the business to learn about how your father's silence affects their working relationship with him. They may provide some insight that will help you decide how best to interpret and respond to your father's silence.

Discussing Potential Problems

Assuming that you have been able to glean a basic understanding of the business and what it means to your father, you are ready to discuss potential areas of conflict that might arise with him should you decide to become a part of it. This topic may be uncomfortable and difficult, but you should not avoid this necessary step.

It usually is easier to talk about problems when you are dating someone than when you are married to them because the outcome of any conflict is less consequential. The same is true about courting the idea of joining the family business versus being part of it. As difficult as it may be, talking with your father about potential conflicts will be easier before you are in the business than it will be after you are part of it.

The experience you have had living together will shape the scope of your discussions with your father. There is no way to avoid it. My own history underscores the point. I grew up in a large German Catholic family. An unspoken and strongly enforced rule held that my father was the absolute head of the household. His opinion was beyond question and his rule reigned. I, in turn, became a rebellious adolescent. Over the years, my father mellowed and I grew up; he became more tolerant and I less immature. We became friends, but the childhood lessons I learned about male authority never completely left me. Even as an adult it was difficult for me to say something that I knew would meet with his disapproval. He sensed this, and on occasion he would tease me as a way to help change my perspective. "If only I'd had this kind of control over you as a teenager," he would say with a smile on his face.

You should expect some discomfort when talking with your father about issues that you'd rather avoid, but don't let that stop you from initiating the discussions. Differences and disappointments are part of every healthy relationship. Within a context of respect, they can provide you and your father the opportunity to understand each other and to resolve problems that would otherwise show up later in your business relationship. Spend the considerable time needed to discuss areas of potential conflict, as well as how these might be resolved or used to advance the interest of the business.

It may not be possible for you to have these discussions with your father if he refuses to share his thoughts about himself or the business. On the other hand, perhaps you assume he will not want to talk because you never have tried to engage him. You may recall that Karen, a woman you met in chapter 1, assumed her father would never change. "Let's face it ... I'm Daddy's little girl, and in his eyes I always will be" is how she put it. To Karen's surprise, however, when she quit acting on her assumption, expressed her concerns, and, perhaps most importantly, changed her own behavior in relation to him, she discovered that her father was willing to talk and that he found the courage to change his behavior. By assuming her father would never change, Karen had rationalized her own behavior and felt justified in not challenging the status quo of their relationship.

Your father may not respond as positively as Karen's father did, but don't be too sure. Don't just assume it can't happen. Those we love can and do change — often in response to a change we make.

Your decision to join the family business demands a critical assessment, and it takes time and effort to arrive at the best choice for you, your family, and the family business. Let's review the work you have completed toward reaching your decision. You have defined your personal interests and career ambition;

you can articulate your motivations for working with your family. You have uncovered some of the history that makes up your family's story; you understand the unspoken rules that influence the way your family and the business operate. You have decided whether there is a good fit between your needs and those of the family firm. You have had extensive conversations with family members working in the business. While there is no sure method for predicting the future, the research you have completed to this point provides information—very good information—with which to make your decision.

Making a Decision

Most heirs have mixed feelings about working with their family, even when they are certain the decision is the best for them. If, after working through these exercises, your ambivalence prevails and prevents a decision, I suggest you talk to an outside consultant who is trained in this area. You owe it to yourself and your family. On the other hand, if you are convinced that being part of your family's business is a good choice for you and those working in the business agree with you, it is time to make a decision. Carpe diem!

CHAPTER NINE

Advancing in the Family Business

If you think you can, you can. And if you think you can't, you're probably right.

—Mary Kay Ash

Congratulations! You've done your homework, critically weighed the positive and negative factors of working with your family and prepared yourself as well as possible for entering the business. You've had meaningful conversations with family members working in the business and enjoy their support for joining the team. While you can't predict the future with certainty, you're confident you've made the best decision and will be satisfied with it for a long time. Your course is set, and the hard work is over. Right?

Not quite so fast. Women have made remarkable strides in the past fifty years; you can find them in all areas of higher education and in virtually every profession. As a recent hire to your family's business, you are now among an ambitious and elite group of women. Unfortunately, entering previously inaccessible places is only half the battle. Remaining inside is the other half, and it can be difficult, very difficult.

This chapter is about a set of obstacles that confront daughters who make it into the family business and want to advance to a leadership position. These obstacles are of a particular nature, they are extremely subtle, and they are powerful. Far too often they go unrecognized until it is too late to overcome them. Please read this chapter carefully and do not assume you are an exception to the problem.

THE DARKER SIDE OF AMBITION

I have a confession to make. Though I am a fierce supporter for women in the workplace, I once questioned whether women were ambitious, or at least whether they were as ambitious as men. I never stated this publicly, but privately I worried about it. Why else did I keep meeting successful businesswomen who went out of their way to disabuse me of the idea that they had earned their success through hard work and fierce determination? Repeatedly, women working in their family's businesses told me that luck got them where they were. It made no sense to me that after working hard to accomplish many things, these women shied away from the recognition they deserved.

I had met men who were humble about their achievements and men who shared credit for their successes, but never had I met a man who denied his achievement or refused recognition for it. In fact, my experience had been quite the opposite; generally, men tended to exaggerate their contributions to their successes. Strikingly different, women tended to undervalue or deny their accomplishments and to avoid any recognition for them.

Did this difference indicate ambivalence about success on the part of women? A fear of competition? Denial? As I studied this question, history gave me part of the answer. Women have fought long and hard for their successes, they have achieved the right to vote, educational opportunities, and access into any career. But as they have reached each of these milestones, a backlash of intolerance—sometimes overt, more often subtle—always underscored the dangers to women when they venture outside their expected gender role.

Sarah Palin, Christine O'Donnell, and other conservative female politicians understand and have used this backlash to promote their ambitions. Christine O'Donnell has stated that wives should "graciously submit" to their husbands—while her website touts her "commitment to the women's movement." Sarah Palin opposes abortion and comprehensive sex education while she describes herself as a feminist. These conservative, antifeminist, extremely ambitious politicians have rebranded a negative label and in doing so they have reached the top tiers of the GOP. It is impressive that these women, the faces of what is being called "new conservative feminism," are being recruited to run for office by a party that historically has kept women out of its mostly male club. Impressive, but the "new conservative feminists" also are the faces of the backlash of intolerance. The party supported only female politicians willing to subjugate women's rights, oppose abortion, and graciously submit to their husbands. In this light, the only achievement these politicians advanced for women appears to be additional support for more rigid gender stereotypes.

The Price of Ambition: Tessa's Story

Let's look at another, more personal example of the darker side of ambition. Tessa, a very successful systems analyst, had worked as a consultant for many top firms in the country. A major business magazine featured her, and she was frequently mentioned as one of the up and coming women in the business world. Tessa had what many would envy: a career that she loved, a salary that surpassed most, and a husband who had retired from public service and stayed at home with their two preteen children.

Tessa came to see me because she felt miserable. As she explained it, "I'm a failure as a wife and a mother. I'm on the road constantly. My kids complain I'm never at their school activities, and when I am home my husband, Brad, complains that I neglect him. I love my work and my clients think I'm wonderful, so it's easier to stay away from home than to be there and feel like a failure. And that makes me feel more guilty."

Tessa's father, a college professor, had reared her after her mother's death when Tessa was four years old. Tessa's mother had worked as a chemist until Tessa's birth and then quit her job to stay home. Both of her parents valued education and expected their daughter to one day go to college and have a career. Tessa never considered otherwise.

Tessa was the last of her friends to marry and have children. She had been worried that either or both of those life changes would prove too hard to manage with her demanding career, and she was wary of boyfriends. With Brad, however, it was different. He was devoted to his career as a firefighter and understood her passion for her work. Their friends described them as the perfect couple, and Tessa's father liked Brad.

They eventually wed and waited five years before having children. Tessa had worried that she couldn't balance a career and motherhood, but Brad had reassured her that he'd come from a large family, loved kids, and didn't expect her to be a stay-at-home mom.

The couple had twin boys and, as agreed, Brad carried the lion's share of the child care. Tessa managed their finances and continued working. Both of them seemed to enjoy the arrangement, but their friends found it a bit odd. One of Tessa's friends even said that she couldn't imagine not wanting to "be there for my children."

Tessa's colleagues, most of them male, also found her life choices strange. One "complimented" her for not being like other women, "who care more about being home than making a dollar." Sometimes, colleagues overtly criticized her for being too aggressive; more often the criticism was subtle. "Holy cow, Tessa, you'd think you were a man the way you acted in that meeting. Calm down." They told her that she was lucky to have a husband who could do his work and hers too. It seemed to Tessa that the amount of criticism directly correlated with her level of success. "But that makes no sense" she said, "because the work I bring in helps all of us."

Tessa said nothing in response to the criticisms because secretly she wondered what was wrong with her that she loved her career and didn't want to be home full-time. She worried that she was a "weirdo woman," as she put it, because she loved to chase new contracts, reveled in the thrill that went along with competing and winning, and took great pride in being one of the best in her field.

The problem was not that Tessa was a weirdo woman but that she was living a life different from the stereotype that defines women. She was reeling from the powerful backlash against her decision to follow her ambition as well as to marry and have children. Her ambition made her different, and that made her less feminine.

From Guilt to Understanding

As Tessa began to understand that the problem lay not inside her but within the culture, her attitude about her situation began to change. She felt less like a weirdo woman and more like the talented woman she was. She heard the criticisms of co-workers as an affront to both her ambition and her femininity, and she was offended. She began addressing the criticisms directly and, over time, they subsided. Tessa assumed some co-workers still criticized her behind her back, but she no longer cared.

Tessa's experience helps answer the question about why I kept meeting women who denied or downplayed their considerable successes. The answer was twofold: first, personal recognition flies in the face of how women have been raised and what is expected of them; second, women, understandably, do not want the assault on their femininity that recognition might bring.

Stay the Course

A poignant example of the subtle denial of one's accomplishments appears in a PBS interview with the president of Liberia, Ellen Johnson-Sirleaf. A Harvard-educated economist and former World Bank official, she won a landslide victory in late 2005 to become Africa's first woman president. An interviewer asked her if she grew up feeling that she was born to lead or had a duty to lead. Her answer: "…(I) had no idea I'd be president or (sic) certainly would not be great. In fact, I'm not great…I think the evolution of my life just led me in this direction."[1] This comment came from a woman who married and had four children right out of high school, divorced her abusive husband and lost custody of her children, was imprisoned, tortured and exiled for speaking out against an oppressive government, returned, and was elected president of Liberia!

Women who want to make a career in the family business must be prepared for the pressure they may encounter to delay or give up their ambition for the sake of a brother, a husband, children, or even a peer, most probably a man, at work. They must be willing to talk to family members about the importance of pursuing their career goals. At times they may have to remind their husband that they cannot always be the one to leave work when a child is sick; they may have to push their father to reward their work contributions with a promotion or salary raise, rather than merely a thank you. They may have to compete publicly with a coworker for advancement. In short, they must be willing to hold on to their ambition.

This is a huge challenge. But to quote President Johnson-Sirleaf once more, when asked what message she wanted to convey to young Liberians, she said: "That you can be anything you want to be, as long as you're willing to have the courage of your conviction, and to stay the course, that there will be difficulties in life, but the potential to surmount those difficulties are there. It's just left with you."

ESSENTIAL BUT INVISIBLE

Businesswomen are competent; they work hard and they are persistent. They are like men in these qualities, but these qualities are not enough for women. Regardless of the value they bring, women often do not receive appropriate recognition for their contributions.

Women, in general, are stuck in middle management, and their status there appears to have little to do with their degrees, how long they've been employed, or their persistence. Although women make up half of America's labor force, as of 2011, only twelve Fortune 500 companies have women CEOs or presidents, down from fifteen in 2010 because three women left their posts and men succeeded them. This in spite of the fact that companies with the highest representation of women on their top management teams experience better financial performance than companies with the lowest women's representation. Fortune 500 companies with the highest percentage of women officers experienced 35 percent higher return on equity and 34 percent higher return to shareholders than those with low percentages of women officers.[2]

Business leaders increasingly want hard data to support the link between gender diversity and corporate performance. These numbers give them unquestionable evidence of the link. According to Tony Comper, the chairman and CEO of the Bank of Montreal whom you met in chapter six, "the study confirms my own long-held conviction that it makes the best of business sense to have a diverse workforce."[3]

The same legacies that have made it difficult for women to reach the top of the corporate ladder also have played an important part in keeping women invisible in the family business. In a study involving women and men working together in their family business, Patricia Cole found that even when women felt supported by their father or brother or other male family member, they often felt invisible to the public and nonfamily employees.[4] Male respondents agreed that customers and suppliers ignored or undervalued the work the women did. One supportive father said that when a customer ignores his daughter, wanting to speak with him instead, he listens attentively and then tells the customer to talk to his daughter because "she's the one in charge."

Ideally, the process of making daughters visible in the family business begins at home, with parents teaching both their sons and their daughters to think of the family firm as a possible career choice. Families must include daughters as well as sons in conversations about the business, encourage them to work part-time during school holidays, and give them opportunities to train in the business. Mothers as well as fathers must pass on the values of the business. Ernesto Poza referred to this important leadership role of the mother as "senior advisor and keeper of the family values."[5]

In a study of 702 family firms, Colette Dumas found that when daughters learned the values of the business at a young age, had an initial positive experience of working in the business, had the support of their family, and received genuine opportunity, they not only actively participated in the business but often eventually assumed a leadership role in the business.[6]

You can't expect that your family and others will notice and reward your every contribution in the business, nor should they. However, you can and should expect that your hard work will get the same recognition as that of other, usually male, employees. You can and should expect to receive comparable salary to male employees. You can and should expect the same development and training opportunities as other, usually male, employees. You can and should expect to be visible, very visible, in the family business.

REVISITING PRIMOGENITURE

Now that you are in the business let's take another look at how primogeniture may block your advancement.

Primogeniture still casts a long shadow over succession decisions, and many more sons than daughters advance to leadership. Family businesses rarely consider daughters as serious candidates to succeed the founder. When the family businesses eliminate daughters from leadership positions without consideration, they not only rob daughters of well-earned advancement but also cheat the business of valuable executives.

Primogeniture can create difficulties even when the business considers daughters for leadership positions in the business. When daughters advance beyond their brothers, they challenge the norm of transferring leadership from father to son, which can upset the gender balance within the family.[7] Cynthia was just such an example. She and her older brother, Will, both worked in the family's construction business. Cynthia kept the books for the business and handled the administrative office. She loved her work and got along well with her father and the employees. It was more complicated for Will, who worked closely with his father and was his expected successor. He and his dad often disagreed, and sometimes the arguments occurred in front of employees. When the arguments were especially intense, Cynthia stepped in to mediate between them and calm the worries of the staff. Over the years the arguments intensified, and Will eventually left the business, moved out of state, and started a small business of his own.

After Will's departure, Cynthia gradually took on more responsibility and began working more closely with her father. Their skills complemented each other well. She appreciated her father's instruction and didn't need to compete with him as Will had. No longer working together, the relationship between Will and his father also improved, with both father and son sharing business information and advice with each other over phone calls.

Then tragedy struck. Dad had an aneurism and was dead before reaching the hospital. Following the funeral Will stayed for two weeks to help Cynthia and assure employees that the business would continue.

A month later, Will called Cynthia to say that he planned to sell his business and return home to run the family business. He thought she would be relieved and grateful. Instead, Cynthia was shocked and angry. She could not believe he assumed the right to take over the business after being gone from it for years. She had worked hard and well with their father and had every intention of now running the business. Will thought otherwise. He reminded her that their father always expected that he would one day run the firm.

As it turned out, succession was not a decision either Will or Cynthia could make. Their mother, Esther, had inherited most of the company stock; she and she alone was in a position to name her husband's successor. Esther came to me for a consultation because she knew she had to make a decision soon, and she knew the decision had to be in the best interest of the company. She also knew her husband's recent death and the unrealistic wish to make both children happy clouded her thinking.

I had to ask Esther only one question to clarify her thinking: "Why do you suppose your husband left you in charge of this decision should something unexpected happen to him?" Esther knew the answer and knew the decision she had to make. She named Cynthia president. Esther went a step further and asked Cynthia to consider a position for Will within the company. She reminded Cynthia that Will had considerable expertise to offer the company but also said that she would respect Cynthia's decision. After considerable thought, Cynthia offered Will a position she felt would benefit the company and be a good fit, but in making the offer she made it clear that she was in charge and he would report to her. He declined her offer.

Fortunately for all, this was not the end of this particular consultation. Almost two years after Will declined Cynthia's offer, he phoned her to discuss returning to the business. He had thought long and hard about the situation and could now accept that she was the boss. She thanked him and said she'd consider it. She then contacted me and asked if I'd work with them to find a satisfactory solution. She could see many benefits in having her brother in the business, but she didn't want to jeopardize their relationship or create a problem within the business.

During our first visit, I was impressed with the candor and maturity that each brought to the consultation. Will had long since given up his sense of entitlement and acknowledged that Cynthia had done a stellar job of running the business. Cynthia admitted that Will possessed superior knowledge and experience in certain areas and that the business would benefit from his expertise. It took several months for them to work out a solution they both felt comfortable with, but five years later they continue to work together — very well.

Women executives have to prove their competence longer and more frequently than do their male counterparts, and this also is true in most family businesses. There is more skepticism about their ability, even when they are more experienced than their male counterparts. They face higher standards and lower rewards then male leaders.[8] Their commitment is questioned and they face pressure to prove they are serious about making the business their career. In was Cynthia's good fortune that her mother owned the majority stock and that she based her decision about succession on the best interest of the company, not primogeniture. In the end her decision proved to be in the best interest of the family also.

Father-son succession still dominates in family-run businesses but father-daughter succession is often more harmonious and less competitive.[9] As a psychotherapist and business consultant, this makes sense to me. More often than not, father-son and mother-daughter relationships harbor more difficulties, especially in the area of competitiveness and conflict, than cross-gender relationships.

A necessary final step to increasing the likelihood that the business will groom you and consider you for leadership is to talk directly with those in charge of the business about your ambitions. For example, talk to your business founder-father about your career goals rather than hoping he'll figure them out. Let him know that you intend to make a career in the family business and that you are interested in leadership training and experience.

If you can advance the hiring of additional women into the business, do so, as it will increase the likelihood that the business leaders will notice your and other women's accomplishments. Over time, the more women the company employs, the more likely that some of them will advance to management positions. The more women there are in upper-level positions, the more commonplace they become, and the more natural it will be for them, and you, to advance.

Finally, and perhaps most importantly, keep talking to those in charge. Don't assume that one conversation with your father about your career is enough. It needs to occur at least yearly. And don't assume that once you've expressed your career aspirations that your father is responsible for making them happen. He isn't. Ultimately, your professional development is your responsibility. That said, let's look more closely at the formal steps you must take to develop into a leader in your family's business.

PROFESSIONAL DEVELOPMENT: A KEY TO SUCCESS

Begin by formulating an action plan that will guide your professional development. Through professional development, you can acquire the necessary skills, adopt the necessary attitudes, and maintain the required motivation to be a good leader. One day in the not too distant future, you may be an executive, and the challenges of leading your family's business will be many. Business conditions will be demanding, competition fierce, and resources limited. Change will be constant, and the amount of information you must process will be staggering.

Professional development is a crucial variable in determining your success in the family business; a passion for the business and a wish to work with family will not, by themselves, sustain your career over time. You must continually demonstrate not only the commitment but also the ability to continually develop your skills. You must convince management to support your development by offering you increasing responsibility. And you must get regular evaluations as part of your leadership development plan. To achieve all these things, you must create a professional development plan that is well formulated, well executed, and strongly supported by senior management. At times the process will be arduous, but it will provide huge payoffs in your long-term success.

It is one thing to work in the family business, but as you may have realized already, it is quite another to be a key player. Becoming a leader takes time and a concentrated focus, and it depends on many complex and interrelated variables, some of which you have little control over. Ambition, commitment, and determination are necessary, of course, but they are insufficient. To make it to the top, you also must have knowledge and experience and the skill to manage and motivate others. You must have the support of management as well as the other owners of the business. Finally, as a family member, your success will depend on your ability to manage relationships with other family members, both those working in the business and those who do not.

These factors fall into four major areas that you should include in any professional development plan:
- Motivation and commitment
- Knowledge and experience
- Support from management
- Ability to work with others

I have included sets of questions to help you assess yourself in each of these areas. After you have worked your way through them, you will be ready to begin formulating your development plan. The second section of this chapter will show you how to do it.

Motivation and Commitment

You need to reassess your motivation and commitment to your role in the business regularly, since they change over time and are influenced by how long you have worked in the business. They will wax and wane at various stages of your life. For example, you may be more committed today than you were the day you joined the business but less interested in your work than you were a year ago. At any given time, your commitment and motivation levels depend on such variables as whether you are making a real contribution to the business, whether your work continues to be meaningful, and whether you feel challenged.

Knowledge and Experience

To become an effective manager, you must work hard, know your stuff, and be motivated by your work most of the time. Many good managers regularly attend management programs offered by their trade association or a business school, study the practices of competitors, and work continually to improve their business. If you can continue to grow and help the business grow, you will earn the respect of employees who work with you. If you view a position in the family business as your birthright, you will probably spend little time developing the skills you need to be effective in your position, and you will probably never earn the respect of the other employees. You can't fake involvement, sweat, and a willingness to learn, and you can't fool employees for long. To be a key player in the company, you will need to know how the business makes money, who the major vendors are, how the business is financed, who your competitors are, why people do business with your company, what kind of talent is needed to run operations, and what technology makes the business more effective. If you aspire to a management position, you eventually will need to know more than the current management. The business has probably grown since its founding, and to continue that success, you will need to keep learning and growing.

You can't know it all, of course; you will need to hire the knowledge, expertise, and experience you do not possess. This means you

Assessing Your Motivation

1. Do you like your work most of the time? Why or why not? Do you have fun at work most of the time? Why or why not?

2. What do you enjoy about your work? What do you dislike about it? What is most difficult about it? What percentage of your time do you spend doing tasks that fall into each of these areas? What do your answers tell you about your work?

3. What needs to change to increase your motivation and commitment to your work?

4. Is there a job you would prefer to the one you currently have? What needs to happen for you to get that job? What are you doing to prepare yourself for the job you want?

will not always be as experienced as those you hire. I add this admonition because business leaders often overlook their own shortcomings, and you cannot afford to do this. An indispensable attribute of today's best family business leaders is a willingness to surround themselves with competent subordinates and provide them the necessary resources to succeed. If you cannot bear to take those steps, make changing that attitude a priority in your development plan. An excessive need to control is a leadership liability.

Support from Key Managers

Support from key managers is indispensable to your success in the family business. If you don't have it, find out why immediately. You will not succeed if key employees in the business do not

Assessing Your Knowledge

1. What were your goals and objectives when you began your career? Have they changed? How?

2. Do you have, or are you acquiring, the skills to insure that you can attain your goals?

3. With whom did you identify in the early years of you career? What are the most important things you learned from them? Do those things still apply in your work today? Explain.

4. Would you describe yourself as someone who values the knowledge and contributions of others within the business? Would others describe you this way? Explain.

5. Do you receive evaluations at regular intervals? If not, why not? You must get regular evaluations of your abilities and performance if you want to continue to advance.

accept you enthusiastically. If past events have strained relationships, or if you have a reputation that works against you, address those issues as soon as possible. To do so, you may need an outside consultant who understands both family-owned businesses and family relationships.

Ability to Work with Others

Cooperation and collaboration can motivate and empower employees and enhance the overall effectiveness of the work of a whole team. Nowhere are these traits more valuable than in the

Assessing Your Ability to Work with Others

1. Do you work for a family member? If yes, how does the family part of the relationship help or hinder the business part of the relationship?
2. What would you change about your business relationship with certain family members if you had the power to do so? What prevents this change from happening? What else?
3. What are the good and bad aspects of your relationship with your boss?
4. What are the good and bad aspects of your relationships with your subordinates?
5. What are the good and bad aspects of your relationships with your peers?
6. How do you handle problems that arise with your boss, peers, and subordinates? Is the way you handle problems the same for both family members and non-family members? If it is different, why and in what ways?

family business, where the complicated relationships among family members add a dimension to the business that its leaders must manage sensitively. You may have to supervise your older brother, whom you once looked up to as a wiser, trusted advisor, or you may have to disagree with the president, who is also your father-in-law. You might have to deliver a poor performance appraisal to your cousin or encourage your sister to allow the company to redeem her stock. How well you understand and manage your relationships with family members will be a major factor in deter-

Assessing Your Future in the Business

1. What struggles, if any, have you had with other family members who work in the family business? With family members who do not work in the business but who share an interest in it?

2. Would you describe your current role in the business as formal or informal? Explain.

3. Did the family members working in the business support your entrance into it? Do you have their support now? If not, why? You will need their support if you want to advance in the business.

4. Is there room for you to advance in the business? Have you expressed your aspirations to the principals in the business? What do their answers tell you about your future?

5. Does the business have a formal succession plan in place? Have you spoken to those in charge about the importance of succession planning? Why or why not? What do your answers tell you about your future in the company?

mining your success in the company.

You need to be as certain as possible that other family members will support, not undermine, your involvement in the business. Competitiveness, jealousy, and unresolved differences among family members have sabotaged many businesses. To be the best leader in the family business you will need excellent communication skills, a good understanding of relationships, and sensitivity to the family history that influences the business. Few managers make the effort to acquire the relationship skills they lack. Do not make this mistake. It could mean the difference between your being a mediocre manager and a great one.

DEVELOPING YOUR PLAN

If you want to be the best at something—performing on the piano, debating politics, or playing baseball—you must have the resolve to develop your skills. In *Outliers*, bestselling author Malcolm Gladwell noted that it takes 10,000 hours of practice to become proficient at a task.[10] You don't have to reach for perfection, but the same guidelines apply to your professional development. You must hire good coaches, listen to their advice, make necessary changes, and practice, practice, practice. You learn good management over time, and your success in building them depends on several things: your ability to identify both your strengths and your weaknesses, your willingness to learn new ways of thinking, and, finally, the opportunity to put these elements together through practical, on-the-job experience.

As a first step in your professional development, complete the self-assessment questionnaire that begins on the next page. Rate the degree to which you think you currently possess a particular attitude or skill and the degree to which you want or need to possess the same attitude or skill. Some of the questions may not pertain to your current role in the business, but try to answer them all. Take your time, and be honest with yourself. No one but you will see your responses.

After you have completed the questionnaire, study your answers closely to determine the areas where you need the most improvement. Look at the difference between your current skill level and the degree to which you think you need

Self-Assessment Questionnaire

Rate yourself on a scale of 1 (low) to 5 (high). Put an "x" through the number that represents your assessment of where you are now. Circle the number that represents where you think you ought to be in five years.

Management Skills

1 2 3 4 5   Understanding of the business and its mission.

1 2 3 4 5   Understanding of the current marketplace.

1 2 3 4 5   Ability to work as part of a team.

1 2 3 4 5   Ability to work alone.

1 2 3 4 5   Willingness to share power and authority with others.

1 2 3 4 5   Ability to tolerate and acknowledge errors in self.

1 2 3 4 5   Ability to tolerate and acknowledge errors in others.

1 2 3 4 5   Ability to keep going after an experience of failure.

1 2 3 4 5   Degree to which others think of you as the one to get the job done.

1 2 3 4 5   Degree to which you delegate to others.

1 2 3 4 5   Interest in management responsibility.

1 2 3 4 5   Degree of tolerance for ambiguity and uncertainty.

1 2 3 4 5   Responsibility for decision-making authority.

1 2 3 4 5   Degree to which you supervise others' activities.

1 2 3 4 5   Degree to which you help others succeed.

1 2 3 4 5   Degree to which your position is free of functional and technical concerns.

1 2 3 4 5   Degree of personal investment in developing your career.

1 2 3 4 5   Willingness to take risks even when doing so may lead to errors.

Analytical Ability and Skills

1 2 3 4 5   Ability to identify problems in complex, ambiguous situations.

1 2 3 4 5   Ability to sense quickly what information you need about a complex problem.

1 2 3 4 5   Ability to obtain needed information from others.

1 2 3 4 5   Ability to assess the validity of information gathered by others.

1 2 3 4 5   Ability to learn quickly from experience.

1 2 3 4 5   Ability to detect errors in own actions.

1 2 3 4 5   Flexibility—ability to think of and implement different solutions for different kinds of problems.

1 2 3 4 5   Creativity—the ability to be original, even fanciful, in your ideas and solutions to problems.

1 2 3 4 5   Breadth of perspective—insight into a wide variety of situations.

1 2 3 4 5   Degree of self insight—the ability to understand your own strengths and weaknesses.

Relationship Skills

1 2 3 4 5   Ability to develop open and trusting relationships with peers.

1 2 3 4 5   Ability to develop open and trusting relationships with superiors.

1 2 3 4 5   Ability to develop open and trusting relationship with subordinates.

1 2 3 4 5   Ability to listen to others in an understanding way.

1 2 3 4 5   Ability to communicate thoughts and ideas clearly and persuasively.

1 2 3 4 5   Ability to motivate people over whom you have no direct control.

1 2 3 4 5   Ability to influence superiors.

1 2 3 4 5   Ability to influence subordinates.

1 2 3 4 5   Ability to diagnose complex interpersonal and group situations.

1 2 3 4 5   Ability to develop processes that ensure high quality decision-making by others.

1 2 3 4 5   Ability to develop a climate of collaboration and teamwork.

1 2 3 4 5   Ability to design processes to facilitate intergroup and interfunctional coordination.

1 2 3 4 5   Ability to create a climate of development for subordinates.

to possess the attitude or skill. Next, rank in order the areas that need improvement. You can't concentrate on improving everything at the same time. Some areas can wait, while your immediate circumstances may demand that you improve certain areas right away.

You must decide whether and when you want to bring someone else into your development process, but keep in mind that this is a very good time to utilize the support of a mentor. Identify a person from senior management who has the experience and interest in your career to provide you some guidance. Request a meeting with that person. Let her know you want to develop your management skills and how you think she could help. Ask her to look over your self-assessment questionnaire and your list of priorities for improvement, and invite her to add others. The way we see ourselves sometimes is different from the way other people see us; your mentor most likely will provide a somewhat different, and quite valuable, perspective concerning your developmental needs.

The next step is to have your mentor complete the Skills Checklist. Have three other people who know you and your work well also fill out the questionnaire. I would suggest that they include your father (or whoever is in charge), at least one other family member who works in the business, and someone who reports to you. The completed checklists will help you and your mentor assess your organizational, intellectual, and relationship strengths and weaknesses and determine the areas of greatest developmental need.

Then, you are ready to design your Career Development Plan. You can use the one I provide at the end of this chapter or you can devise your own. The format is not important. It is important that you formulate specific, measurable goals that you can achieve in a systematic and timely fashion. You may want to outline both short-term and long-term goals. Establish monthly meetings with your mentor to review your progress. Ask to receive a variety of assignments that include learning opportunities where you will be accountable for a measurable result and have the chance to succeed or fail. You need to be challenged, but not too much too soon, and you need a mentor who appreciates that no one develops management skills overnight or in a vacuum. Ask for support in the form of regular feedback about your strengths, weaknesses, and professional progress.

Skills Checklist

Does the employee have the organizational, intellectual, and self skills necessary to be a manager in the family business? Specifically, using the three-point scale provided, rate the degree to which the candidate does the following. (N = Needs Improvement; A = Average; E = Excellent)

N A E   Think and act strategically?

N A E   Have the knowledge required to use company resources well?

N A E   Appropriately delegate responsibilities?

N A E   Have good time management skills?

N A E   Have good analytic skills?

N A E   Think creatively and flexibly?

N A E   Accept responsibility for decisions?

N A E   Have good business judgment?

N A E   Have good personal judgment?

N A E   Have integrity?

N A E   Have well-developed communication skills?

N A E   Understand the skills of employees/ colleagues?

N A E   Have the ability to include others in setting goals?

N A E   Motivate and persuade others? Show appreciation for others' work?

N A E   Understand her own motivations and behavior?

Career Development Plan			
Skills, behaviors, capabilities needing improvement	Activities, training, experience needed to make it happen	Timetable	Desired Outcome

Use Your Plan

The final and crucial step is for you to use the Career Development Plan you and your mentor worked hard to develop. Far too often I have witnessed someone take the considerable time to formulate a development plan — and then toss it in a drawer and forget about it. Don't do this. Your professional plan is not a one-time exercise but an ongoing process toward your ultimate career development. You must get regular evaluations if you want to advance in the family business. You must be continually challenged if you want to be one of its leaders.

PART IV

Q & A

CHAPTER TEN

All You Ever Wanted to Ask About Family Businesses But Were Afraid to Know

What is the answer? ... In that case, what is the question?
— *Gertrude Stein*

In a question-and-answer format, this chapter addresses situations that families who work together routinely encounter *and* customarily avoid. The questions asked here come not only from women working in the family business but also from business founders, their spouses, their male children, and family members who are owners but not operators in the business enterprise. All family members as well as non-family members working in the family business need to read this chapter. But even if your parents or other family members decline to read it, you need to know the kinds of questions they may be asking about the business and about you.

While I have probably not heard every possible problem that families working together encounter, I've heard a lot of them over the past thirty years. Family members often keep their concerns and questions to themselves, verbalizing them only within the confines of a consultant's office. They don't want to upset someone they love or create a problem for the business or family. Unfortunately, this kind of secrecy does not protect the family from its problems; it only makes it more difficult for the family to solve its problems. It's like the proverbial elephant in the living room: you can try to ignore it but you can't get around it, and it's not going away by itself. Living and working with family is not for sissies. It can be difficult for a daughter to question the wisdom of a decision made by her father, for a sibling to criticize the performance of another sibling, or for a younger sibling to be promoted over an older sibling.

You will not find easy-to-follow directions or simple solutions in this chapter. As you already know, complex business and family problems don't lend themselves well to simplicity. Keep in mind that no single solution works for everyone, and no one example will do justice to your unique circumstances. What works well in a small mom-and-pop business will most likely fail to work in a large family enterprise. In the following scenarios, I suggest solutions to a series of family business situations I have encountered. They may give you insights into solving problems you encounter in your family business.

When is the best time to bring my daughter into the business?

Sam has an ambitious daughter, Michele, who wants to join the family business. She has almost completed college and has worked four summers in the business. Sam's brother and business partner, Nick, thinks she's too young and inexperienced to join the company; Sam thinks her summer employment has sufficiently prepared her.

Michele may be bright and ambitious, but if I were in Sam's shoes, I would not invite my daughter to join the company until she works somewhere else first. At the least, let her test herself and gain valuable working experience on someone else's payroll! More seriously, by working somewhere else Michele has a better chance of being treated like a regular employee than like the owner's kid. If she works in a larger, more sophisticated company, she will have an opportunity to learn the basics of management and be evaluated regularly and fairly by people more objective than her family can be. It is difficult to get the criticism and fair evaluation one needs to learn and grow in a family business. Experience outside the family business not only will enlarge Michele's repertory of management skills, but it will also help strengthen her sense of self-esteem and business confidence.

A good rule of thumb is to have family members work elsewhere for five years before joining the family business. There's nothing magical about five years, but there needs to be enough time to gain real experience. If the time frame is too short, it's easy for the family member to coast while waiting to join the family business.

When Michele does join the family business, she will benefit from a good mentor, ideally an experienced nonfamily manager. She could be at a disadvantage without one. Nonfamily employees, particularly younger, less experienced ones, may be hesitant to criticize her, they may envy her "special" position as a family member, and they may compete with her by withholding information or good training. It is an unfortunate but all too common occurrence in a family owned business.

Michele will need a mature mentor who is secure in his or her position; who will evaluate her against high standards; and who will support her leadership development. She most likely will need more than one mentor to learn all that she will need to know to advance successfully in the business. If Michele is brought into the business and not provided the necessary and appropriate mentoring she won't reach her potential, and the business will suffer from her lack of good training.

*I enjoy my work, I'm doing a good job, and I'm well
compensated for my work. Is it important to have a title also?*

Amelia has worked in her parents' pharmaceutical research company for eight years. Her many responsibilities include overseas operations, but she has no formal job description and no title. This might never have become a problem except the company is very successful; as it expanded, it created separate divisions and needed people to run them. That was when the company hired Tom, a gifted chemist with an MBA, to run the domestic side of research and gave him the title of senior vice president.

Tom's arrival delighted Amelia. She respects his work, likes his leadership style, and works well with him. Over time, however, a strange thing has happened. Customers began treating her as if she were Tom's subordinate instead of his peer. She knew Tom was not creating the situation nor was he trying to undermine her authority, and she decided to speak with him about it.

Amelia's concern didn't surprise Tom. "I knew from my interview process that no one except your father had a title around here," he said. "That worried me, and I insisted on a title as a condition of my employment. I've worked in operations a long time and for several large companies. I know that titles matter.

"You need a job title, Amelia, and one that accurately reflects your responsibility. It embarrasses me when a customer — or worse, an employee — asks if you now work for me."

Amelia was dumbstruck by Tom's comments. She had never thought about a job title, but she now wondered if the absence of one was creating the problem. Could a title have so much power?

Job titles aren't always needed, especially in small family businesses. But in larger companies and in the marketplace, titles are like resumes — they convey credibility and open doors. In this situation, the family business has grown into a major enterprise, and Amelia needs a title to distinguish her position both within and outside the company.

Had Amelia worked for a public company, this problem would not have arisen; position descriptions and job titles are a matter of course. But like so many family businesses, this one had started small and gradually grew. No one had thought about titles. Until now.

It is time for Amelia to approach her father and address the need for titles as a byproduct of the company's growth. This issue affects Amelia and everyone else in the company. The company needs to create titles as well as job descriptions for every employee. It will take considerable time, and the business may need to enlist outside help to complete the work, but it will be worth it in the long run.

I hope to make my career in the family business. How important is it for me to have a mentor?

Rhonda has worked in the family business since she graduated from college three years ago. She likes the work, and her evaluations reflect that she's doing well. She wants to advance, but she worries that without a mentor this won't happen, and she doesn't have one. Her grandfather, the founder of the company, insists there's nothing special about having a mentor. He never had one. Truth be known, he thinks "mentor" is another word for crutch. Rhonda's uncle, a senior vice president in the business, feels just the opposite. He credits two mentoring relationship as important factors in his successful career. Rhonda isn't sure what would be best for her.

A mentoring relationship is nothing magical. I have known successful women and men who benefited from having a mentor and other successful individuals who never had one. That caveat aside, I have to side with Rhonda's uncle. My bias is that a good mentor can provide invaluable advice, support, perspective, and constructive criticism.

Female or male, it is difficult to succeed in an organization, particularly a very large one, without people who will pull for you. In a smaller organization, it is easier to achieve visibility for your work efforts. If your family owns the company, that connection may pull you along for a while, but it won't make up for the lack of a good mentor.

First, understand what a mentor is not. A good mentor is not a more experienced clone of yourself or someone who simply sings your praise to anyone who will listen. A good mentor is someone you respect but is somewhat different from you in style, experience, talent, and outlook. These differences will deepen and enrich your professional growth and leadership style.

How does Rhonda go about finding a good mentor? First, she first must identify one or two people she respects, has good communication with, and can learn from. Next, she has to secure the person's willingness to work with her. Gender is not an issue. What matters is that the person has credibility within the organization (or understands the business, if he or she works outside of the organization), respects her professional abilities, will commit to helping her succeed, and will take the time to work with her over an extended period of time.

Rhonda may have a difficult time finding a good mentor because her last name is on the company's door. That fact will intimidate all but the most accomplished and confident managers. All the better! It means that when she does find someone to provide critical advice and guidance, she can trust the person's motivation for working with her. The best mentor will have no need to compete with Rhonda and will, in fact, feel personal satisfaction from seeing her succeed.

It will be important for Rhonda to listen, ask questions, take advice, and seek constructive criticism from her mentor. He or she is there to assist her advancement. On the other hand, it is equally important for Rhonda to remember that she has no obligation to follow the advice; a mentor is not a boss. But the right mentor will provide her an invaluable opportunity that she would be foolish to miss.

My father inherited the family business from his father and he feels obligated to pass it on to my brother, even though I also work in the business and want to be considered for the CEO position when Dad retires. I accused Dad of favoritism and he didn't disagree, but he didn't put a formal succession plan in place either. Should something happen to Dad it will create a problem between my brother and me, and a problem for the business. What can I do?

First, let me make it clear that Harry has the right to do whatever he wants. He currently owns the business and he can choose whomever he wants to succeed him. However, if the company fails because of poor leadership there will be no business to pass onto the next generation, male or female. If he had a board of directors, he could consult with them about succession but, unfortunately, he does not have a functioning board.

Carol, like many women her age, is ambitious and competent and she wants to advance her career. She is correct to question Harry about where she stands as his potential successor. She worries that the business will be compromised if primogeniture is used to decide succession, and she can't compete within such an arrangement. Neither she nor her brother is ready to take over for Harry but Carol has potential and a passion for the business that her brother lacks.

Carol has an advantage over some children of business owners: Her relationship with her father allows her to talk openly with him. She needs to continue talking with him. She needs to tell him that she worries about the lack of a formal succession plan and also she understands his hesitancy to put one in place. However, the business needs it, the family that depends on the business needs it, and she needs it to plan for her future. Carol can say a number of other things to Harry. She can suggest that the best way to honor his father is to do what's best for the business; she can remind him that there is room in the business for both she and her brother; she can suggest that Harry hire a consultant to help with such an important issue.

Carol respects her father and his personal dilemma. She should end each of her discussions with him by saying that she will respect whatever decision he makes. None of this will be easy for Carol, or for Harry, but standing up for what is in the best interest of the business will increase the likelihood that Harry will make a good business decision – and that Carol will have a shot at the corner office!

How do I convince others I can be a CEO—and a mom?

Let's continue with Carol and Harry 's situation and address another common concern I hear from family business owners who also are fathers. Harry encouraged Carol's career, but when he thinks of succession, only his son comes to mind. He thinks the business is Ken's birthright; and he thinks it would be a liability for the business if Carol were CEO. Should Carol marry and have children, Harry is convinced she would leave the business and he would lose her as a potential successor.

Statistics about working mothers argue strongly against Harry's thinking but, unfortunately, statistics don't change his thinking. Prejudice makes him minimize Carol's business potential and overestimate his son's ability. It most certainly will limit Carol's advancement and could harm the business if Harry chooses a less than capable successor.

Harry based his reasoning on his experience of having a spouse at home with their children while he ran the business. It doesn't occur to him that if Carol marries it might be to a man who would assume the child-raising responsibilities, or that Carol and her spouse might each have a career and figure out child care differently than did Harry and his wife. In Harry's mind, choosing Carol to succeed him means she loses the opportunity to have a husband and children, or he loses a potential successor when she marries. Period.

Harry thinks by using primogeniture to determine succession that both his children get their birthright: Ken would get to run a business and Carol could marry and have children. We all have blind spots—and Harry is no exception.

If Carol wants a shot at the top position, she will have to talk seriously with Harry about her ambitions. She can begin by telling him that she appreciates his concern; she understands that having a career and a family is not for sissies. No woman or man can do it all. Should she choose to have both a career and a family she will have to make choices, set priorities, and accept that life requires many tradeoffs. She will need a husband who is a partner or who is willing to be a stay-at-home father, or they will have to assign much of the day-to-day childcare to someone else.

Carol should tell her Dad that she may not make the same choices about work and family that her mother made, or that he would make for her, but she needs him to respect her choices. The fact that she and her father can have such discussions together bodes well for their ability to reach a decision that is both personally satisfying and meets the needs of the business.

My manager daughter is incompetent. What do I do?

Larry is facing one of the most difficult decisions: terminating a family member who is not performing well. It can be heart wrenching to terminate a relative, but the business cannot afford to retain incompetence.

First let me say that Larry is asking the wrong question. He knows what he must do — terminate Diane's employment. The question is *how* he should do it and how he can preserve his relationship with her after the termination.

An owner, obviously, should never terminate a family member impulsively or for personal reasons. If Larry can use other options, such as reassignment or training, he should do so. But if he has already taken those measures and his only option is termination, then he must do it with the same thoughtfulness and fairness he would use with any employee. He must document his reasons well and in writing.

Hopefully, Larry has spoken with his daughter repeatedly about the problems, and she will not be completely surprised with his decision. However, we all use denial at times to avoid matters we don't want to address, so Diane still may be surprised and angered by his decision. Larry also may face criticism from other family members who think he should have overlooked Diane's incompetence because of her family membership or think he was overly critical of her or think he simply didn't want her in the business. If Larry knows his decision was the only reasonable option left to him, he will need to take the heat as best he can; it is one of the unpleasant responsibilities he took on as CEO and chose to include family in the business.

I have witnessed too many situations where the unexpected termination of a family member has led to lawsuits and family estrangement. Emotions run high, and too often the firing is done poorly and without the forethought that would be part of the termination of a nonfamily employee. Larry would be wise to consider a procedure I recommend managers follow before considering termination. It may save him, Diane, the business, and the family unnecessary grief:

- Determine if the employee's skills are inadequate or she is in the wrong job. If the latter, provide training and place her in a more suitable job.
- Document the problems. Keep detailed job performance records that reflect recommended solutions and the outcomes. If faced with legal action, it is imperative to have documentation that reflects the reasons for the termination.
- Be sure that she receives ample notice that her work is substandard. At least two written warnings should precede any termination.
- Give her time to improve—be specific about the improvements she needs to be make and set a timetable for their accomplishment. Review her performance midway through the probation period.
- Keep the issue between the two of you as long as possible. There is no need to humiliate an employee, most especially your child, in front of her peers.
- Be straightforward when you actually terminate her. Avoid referring to personal inadequacies. Focus on her failures as an employee and make clear that you based your decision on work performance and business needs. Leave the relationship out of the discussion.
- If possible, provide her a severance package and offer outplacement assistance.

As owners of a small family business, we can't afford to offer on-site daycare as a benefit for our employees, but we'd like to support our employees who are trying to balance work and family. What can we do?

Everett and Maureen should be congratulated for wanting to help their employees balance family and work responsibilities. With over 70 percent of mothers with school-age children now in the workforce and with single-parent families growing, child care is a very real issue for companies of all sizes. Companies that are insensitive to family needs will find it extremely difficult to recruit and retain good workers. But not all companies—Everett and Maureen's included—can afford the expense of on-site child care.

Everett and Maureen can do much to support their employees shy of on-site daycare. Flexible maternity leave policies, part-time work or job sharing, and elder care leave are just a few of the benefits that small, family-owned businesses can implement.

The problems associated with balancing work and family affect most Americans—male as well as female—and it takes cooperation between employers and employees to find creative solutions to the problems. Everett and Maureen should start by having brainstorming meetings with their employees. The employees know best their most pressing needs and their greatest sources of stress in trying to balance work and family.

The next step is to research what other companies are doing to address similar needs. Assign someone to visit the local bookstore or library and read about how other companies are managing work and family issues. Gather information on companies that have succeeded as well as those that have failed in their endeavors. This research will provide ideas and models for responding to particular needs as well as suggestions for avoiding mistakes.

The final step is for Everett and Maureen to discuss with their employees ways to take what they learned and tailor the ideas to fit their situation, without sacrificing the business needs. There is no substitute for employee involvement in this process. Their involvement not only will produce better solutions but also will produce greater commitment to the results. Nothing is quite as empowering for employees as knowing they have an impact and make a difference. In the end, the effort Everett and Maureen put into helping their employees balance the stress of work and family will pay off in higher productivity, increased employee loyalty, and higher morale.

As weird as it sounds, ever since I can remember I've talked to my mother through my father. He's easier to approach, and he understands me better than she does. Now I'm working in the family business and it appears I soon may be reporting to my mother. How can I learn to talk with her directly before the change at work occurs?

Nancy's father is a photographer who works out of a studio in their home. She has fond childhood memories of riding through the countryside with him to photograph windmills or barns or sunflowers along the Midwest country roads where she grew up. Even as a teenager, she found it easier to approach him with a problem than her mother, who is president of the family's home construction business.

Ironically, Nancy followed her mother's career path into the family business, where she was recently promoted to head the design department, a position that reports directly to the president. As much as Nancy loves and respects her mother, she has never talked easily with her, and she worries that their communication problems may impair their working relationship.

Nancy is wise to anticipate that she may have problems reporting to her mother, considering the two of them talk through her father. Nancy's father is the communication conduit, sending and delivering messages between Nancy and her mother. As common as this communication style is, it is also inefficient since it prevents individual family members from having direct communication with one another.

The fact that Nancy and her mother don't talk directly to one another is reason enough for them to have a conversation! How else are they going to work well together? Of course, beginning to talk with one another won't be easy or without discomfort. Initially, she and her mother probably will feel awkward and uncomfortable, and they each may find excuses to bring Nancy's father into the conversation. Practice will help her surmount these obstacles. It is clear that Nancy understands the need for the relationship to change, however, or she wouldn't have raised the question.

First, Nancy needs to define the problem as hers, which it is, and ask for her mother's help. Neither of her parents has voiced a concern about their communication pattern and they may not want to change it. The fact that Nancy's mother promoted her to a position that reports directly to her without any mention of potential problems leads me to think that Nancy is the one most uncomfortable with the arrangement.

Nancy can tell her mother that the promotion has her thinking about how they communicate through her father. She can lightheartedly say that calling Dad to resolve an issue with Mom, the President, who is in the next room, might be a bit cumbersome.

Nancy must recognize that changing the triangle will cause some discomfort for her as well as her parents. As Nancy and her mother learn better how to talk to one another, for example, her father may feel less needed by two very significant women in his life, and he may feel hurt, angry, and left out. Nancy can antici-pate this and let her father know that even though she needs a different kind of relationship with her mother, she still needs a close relationship with him.

If Nancy attempts to alter the triangle and fails, she shouldn't despair. Family communication patterns are quite resistant to change. She may need assistance from a consultant. Her parents may support this idea; but if they do not, she should seek the advice of a consultant independently of them. It will be well worth her effort.

I'm frustrated and angry at my Dad because I never got to work in the family business like my brothers did when we were teenagers and today I'm not part of the business. I told my Mom how unhappy I am about the situation but nothing changes.

This is an all-too-common situation that I encounter when working with families. I call it the blame game. In this family, Stephanie prefers to blame her father rather than understand his perspective and the problem it created. Blaming others is a hu-man fragility. It impedes understanding problems and it does not accurately depict what has happened. Understanding needs to precede trying to fix a problem. If Stephanie does not un-derstand the problem she will not be able to fix it. Attributing blame won't help.

Let's look at what each person in the family contributes to the problem and then some suggestions for resolving it. Since Stepha-nie blames Dale for her unhappiness, let's begin with him.

Dale did not understand Stephanie's resentment and was somewhat miffed by it. He never made Stephanie work in the business and thinks she should feel grateful rather than resentful about it. According to Dale, "Stephanie has nothing to complain about. She never wanted for anything. She had a couple of summer jobs during high school, but only because her friends did, and she never kept them for long because she got bored with the work. I never made her work in our business like I did her brothers. My sons complain that I was harder on them than on Stephanie—and they're right. I swear I can't win."

Here's what Dale contributed to the problem that he didn't understand: As a father, he thought it was imperative that his sons learn the value and importance of work so that one day they would have a successful career. He thought a career was optional for Stephanie, and he didn't put the same demands on her to work. When the children were young, the boys resented the arrangement and Stephanie liked it, very much. When they became adults,, however, the boys appreciated the experience they gained from working in the family business, and Stephanie resented that she didn't receive the same opportunity.

Is Dale to blame for Stephanie's anger? Absolutely not, but he did contribute to the problem. For the situation to improve, Dale needs to stop acting so defensively. He must try to understand Stephanie's current point of view, be willing to listen to what she has to say, and accept his part of the problem. He needs to acknowledge to Stephanie that he made a mistake in not giving her that same work experience he gave his sons and explain that he did not callously exclude her from the business.

Now let's look at Stephanie's contribution to the problem: she angrily blames Dale for her exclusion from the business and complains to her mom that he is to blame for her not having a career in the family business. She complains to her mom about it—but she doesn't talk with her dad about it.

Is Stephanie to blame for the problem? No, as a child she had no way to understand the future ramifications of the favoritism she received. But Stephanie is no longer a child. It is time for her to take responsibility for her career.

I'm not blaming Stephanie *or* Dale for the problem. Dale intended to take care of his daughter, but his good intention excluded her from valuable work experience. Stephanie has a right to be angry or regretful about her lack of work experience, but staying angry and blaming her father isn't going to provide her with work experience she didn't get as a teenager.

If Stephanie wants to change the situation, she first has to give up her self-righteous blaming and take responsibility for her part of the problem. She needs to decide whether she is interested in being part of the family business or whether she's simply angry at being excluded from it. If she actually wants to work in the business, the next step is to initiate a discussion with her father.

Stephanie can tell Dale she realizes that blaming him and complaining to her mom wasn't a productive solution to the problem. She can say she wants to learn more about the business in order to decide whether, and in what capacity, she might want to be involved in the family business. She can ask Dale to think about the same. These conversations will take time and thoughtful effort to reach a productive conclusion. The process of talking can also provide Stephanie and Dale the opportunity to develop a different relationship with one another.

Finally, a note about Stephanie's mother's role in creating the problem: she thought she was helping Stephanie by listening to her complaints and she thought she was protecting her husband from Stephanie's anger. In reality, she was keeping the problem unresolved. Stephanie's mom needs to get out of the middle. When either Stephanie or Dale complains to her about the other, she needs to direct them back to each other. Stephanie and Dale have to talk to one another, not to mother, to improve their communication and their relationship.

I love working with and for my family, but the business seems to consume us. It's all we ever talk about at family gatherings. How do we change this?

When you live and work together, the tendency to talk about business is normal, even expected. However, if business is the primary and predominant subject of conversation at every family gathering, this is extreme; it may be a sign of other problems, and the situation probably needs to change. Good family relations depend upon frequent and meaningful conversations among members. These conversations need to cover a variety of subjects, the business being only one of them.

Consider Lynn's family. Like most business families, her family has a difficult time not taking advantage of its time together to discuss business matters. Whether it's Christmas dinner or a casual encounter on a Sunday afternoon, work seems to consume the conversations. Lynn and her mother, father, and older sister own and operate a health food chain with stores across the state, and it necessarily takes a good deal of their time and attention.

Lynn's family is enjoying decent profits from their business, and since the individual members enjoy their various jobs, it doesn't seem that work should always dominate their conversations. I suspect that they have gotten into a communication habit that needs to be broken: they use the business as the only vehicle to interact with each other. Allowing business matters to dominate family time prevents personal conversations from occurring. This may be the unconscious intent of the family, but it works against healthy family relationships, and it increases the likelihood of emotions' exerting excess influence in business decisions. Talking can damage relationships, but not talking can be more damaging.

This family needs to draw a better boundary between its

work and its family life. One remedy other business families have used to deal with the tendency for business discussions to permeate family activities is to establish a family council. A family council is a formal meeting, generally held two to four times a year, of family members who have an ownership stake in the business. It provides an excellent vehicle through which family members can discuss a variety of issues related to their ownership of the business enterprise. It also provides an opportunity to educate non-operator owners about the business, to discuss the family values that can and should shape the business, and it is a vehicle for discussing individual family members' expectations about the business.

The membership of a family council typically changes as the owners and family move through different life phases. The initial membership usually comprises the CEO, his or her spouse, and their young adult children. In the second or third generation of ownership, the council usually includes siblings, cousins, and other relatives who own significant shares in the business. Most families choose to involve in-laws as permanent members of the family council since this can foster a spirit of openness in the family.

A family council is an excellent forum for educating family members about the rights and responsibilities that pertain to their ownership stake and their current or potential employment in the business. It can provide a structure to help families create a shared vision to guide their ownership of the business. Well-informed owners can make a positive contribution in planning for the growth of the business. They can tackle such questions as who can work in the business and what they need to do prior to employment, what the family will do if a member's performance detracts from the success of the business, and how the business will handle the termination of a family member if that step becomes necessary. Having a forum to discuss such issues can reduce misunderstanding and family friction when problems arise.

Finally, a family council fosters an awareness of family history and underscores the value of being a family member. The constructive dialogue that occurs around significant issues related to the family business helps to build trust and a sense of constructive collaboration among family members. The collaboration that develops in these meetings has the additional benefit of helping the family cope constructively with difficult business or family issues that may arise in the future.

How do I get the younger generation to take more interest in the business that will one day be theirs?

Lou and his siblings own and run a large cement business. Lou is the CEO; his brother and sister hold management positions in the business. Their children are still young adults, but Lou and his siblings hope that one day some of them will join the business. The older generation wants the younger one at least to be knowledgeable shareholders. To Lou's credit, he is trying to teach the next generation about the business through family council meetings, readings, and retreats.

The problem is that the younger generation doesn't seem willing to take the time to learn about the business and become responsible shareholders. As chairman of the family meetings, Lou sends out articles and financial reports for everyone to read prior to the meetings, but rarely do the children read them. As a result, he has to go over the material during the meetings. He invites them to co-chair meetings with him but they decline; he suggests they work in the business over school breaks, but none of them has shown an interest. Lou is at his wits' end trying to get the next generation to take more responsibility for the business they one day will inherit.

The problem is that Lou already is doing too much of the work that belongs to the younger generation, as well as work that needs to be shared with his siblings. Lou had the right idea in creating a family council to educate and involve the younger generation in the family business. And he was being responsible in chairing the initial meetings, but it is not a good idea for him to continue doing so. For the meetings to succeed, everyone must feel an ownership in them, and this can't happen if Lou does all the work.

Lou needs to make some serious changes in the way the meetings operate. First, he needs to talk with his siblings and explain why his being the only chair is counterproductive. He should ask for their help in leading future meetings, which not only takes some burden off Lou but also sends a message that everyone shares responsibility for the family council.

After each sibling has chaired a meeting, the siblings need to introduce the younger generation to leadership responsibility. One person each from the older and younger generations can jointly chair subsequent meetings. Delegating some responsibility for the meetings to the younger generation will get them more involved and will increase the likelihood that they will come prepared.

One last piece of advice: The younger generation may or may not develop an interest in the business, and Lou cannot force it. Young adults are too old to have articles and reports read to them because they came ill-prepared. As young adults, they need to be treated as adults. If they don't learn about the business and the responsibility of shareholders, it will be unfortunate, but it will be their misfortune. Lou's generation has the responsibility to present an opportunity to the younger generation; the younger generation has the responsibility to take advantage of it.

My brother and I worked hard and earned the right to own and operate our father's business. Why do our children feel entitled to the company?

Stephen and his brother, Phil, literally grew up in the custom wood business that their parents started when they were babies. They learned to crawl on the plant floor; later, they did homework in the front office and spent summers working alongside their parents. They worked hard, knowing that if the business succeeded they would own it one day. Today they can proudly say that they own a profitable business.

When I saw Stephen for a consultation he was feeling guilty and confused. In his words, "Phil and I have tried to instill a strong work ethic in our children but somehow we've failed. When we were teenagers we sometimes worked without pay because the business couldn't afford to pay us; we never questioned the fairness of it. In contrast, our children wouldn't consider working without pay. In fact, my nephew complained that he should be paid more than other workers doing the same job because he's an owner's son! My own daughter let it be known that she thinks our policy of requiring family members to work outside the business before joining the business is unfair. She argues that my brother and I never had to find a job, and she shouldn't have to either. Is this a generational issue that we can ignore, or do we have a problem brewing?"

Stephen and Phil grew up in a family *aspiring* to wealth; their children, on the other hand, are growing up in a wealthy family. There is nothing intrinsically wrong with being wealthy, and all of us want our children to have more than we had. However, a problem develops when wealth creates a sense of entitlement in children, and this is the problem the brothers are facing.

Entitled children feel someone owes them whatever they want; they should not have to work for it. Stephen's nephew feels entitled to be paid more than a coworker doing the same job because of his last name, not because his work is superior. In fact, with his attitude I would bet that his work is mediocre.

The brothers need to talk with their children about the responsibility of business ownership. With ownership comes the responsibility to ensure both the current and the future success of the business. With ownership comes the responsibility to groom future leaders for the business. In addition to passing on knowledge and experience, responsible owners must instill their passion for the business in those who will one day run it. Running a business is hard work, very hard work, and you have to love it to stay with it.

Stephen and Phil should explain their hope that one day some of their children will be part of management. But they must emphasize that they place the highest value on having the best and most committed managers. Competence and commitment, not legacy, will determine who holds what positions in the company; to operate otherwise would cheat the business and the family.

They need to explain that working somewhere else before joining the family business is not a punishment but part of their early management training. While Stephen's daughter may think he is being harsh and unfair to insist she work elsewhere before working with him, it is the single best way for her to figure out what she wants to do, what she is good at (and not so good at), and whether she has something to offer the business. Choosing to work in the family business because it's the easiest thing to do is a terrible reason to work there and often dooms the child and the business. The brothers need to listen to their children's concerns but let them know that the policy is non-negotiable.

Entitled children rarely make good business leaders; the work is too difficult, the responsibilities too great. Stephen and Phil must stick to their guns on this issue. The business, and their children, will be better off if they do.

Epilogue

Nothing strengthens the judgment and quickens the conscience like individual responsibility.

—*Elizabeth Cady Stanton*

Women struggling to reach a decision about working in their family's business sometimes say to me, "You're the expert. What should I do?" Although I am no longer surprised by this request, I am ashamed to say that there was a time early in my career when I thought I knew how to answer such a question. After all, I was the consultant, the therapist, the expert on family relationships. I was the one who should know immediately and clearly what was best for my client and her family.

I know today how mistaken I was. After thousands of hours of private conversations, shared stories, and thoughtful consideration, I am now convinced that every individual and family is slightly different. Each possesses particular strengths and specific limitations, and only by listening carefully to my client's voice—the real expert on herself and her family—can I comprehend, and then help her understand, what is in her best interests.

Today I don't preemptively tell a young woman what she should decide about working in the family business. Instead, I tell her that I don't know what is best for her, and that *she* can't know until she better understands her unique circumstances. Together we can figure out if she has the ambition, skills, and courage that it will take for her to make an informed and wise decision. She will need to examine her family history and its implications on her life, understand her parents better as individuals, not only as parents, and become knowledgeable about the unspoken rules imbedded in the culture of her family and the business it operates.

Should she decide that she wants to work with her family, we will carefully assess her abilities, training, and commitment in order to determine her readiness to work in the business. When the assignments are completed, *she* will tell *me* what the best decision is for her.

I wrote this book for women who are conscientiously trying to find their way in their family's business. This process is very personal, it can be stressful, and it is time-consuming. It takes courage to question the inequities that may exist inside a business and to unravel the variety of unconscious prejudices that pervade a family. The inquiries and questions these women ask may at times create worry and anxiety for them and their families. They need patience and determination to stay the course, but through this process they discover their personal power and their business prowess. They ultimately become agents to control their own destiny. They learn where they belong—as a part of the business or out of it—and where they belong in their families.

Throughout this book, I have stressed the efficacy of women taking individual responsibility for their changes and decisions. Some may argue that this focus ignores the reality of an intractably bad family or work situation, or a family member who will unalterably oppose another's change efforts. I would counter that we all, at times, see certain situations as impossible, others as responsible for a problem, ourselves as victims of someone else's unreasonableness. These responses are simply ways of wishing and hoping for people and situations to change without our having to do anything differently.

In fact, there always will be situations and people that we can't change, but in spite of this we possess the power to change ourselves in response to other people or difficult situations. For example, a woman's older brother may treat her as his baby sister and deny her the respect she deserves in the family business, but she does not have to behave in a way that exemplifies that role. She can demonstrate her maturity and competence without her brother's permission. She can treat him with respect while she works to change his behavior, knowing that his willingness to change may be beyond her control. She can choose not to work with him. She can leave the company. Only by assuming responsibility and trying to solve the problem—and it is her problem since her brother is not uncomfortable with the situation—can she change it. The same can be said for each of us; that is, any problematic situation we face will change only when we decide to do something differently.

Working in or holding an ownership stake in a family business is not for everyone. In fact, I sometimes recommend against it. It is fraught with possibilities of failure. But when it works—when there is a good fit between a woman, her family, and the business—the rewards can be extraordinarily positive. I have consulted with women who have enjoyed the opportunity of being part of creating a family business legacy as well as with women who have had the courage to decide against a career in their family's enterprise. For each of these women, their sense of personal satisfaction and empowerment came from a profound understanding of their unique needs and as a result of daring to follow the course that they knew was best for them.

The most capable successors of tomorrow's family businesses are already among us—and some of them are women. It is imperative that every daughter find the daring to chart her own best course. It can benefit her for a lifetime, and the business for even longer.

Notes

Preface

1 Mass Mutual American Family Business Survey, 2007. http://www.
   massmutual.com/mmfg/pdf/afbs.pdf
2 Ibid.
3 Louis Barnes, "Incongruent Hierarchies: Daughters and Younger Sons in
   Company CEOs," *Family Business Review* 1(1), (1988): 9-11.

Chapter 1

1 David Herszenheim, "In a Family Business, the Beat Goes On," *The New
   York Times*, March 31, 1996.
2 U.S. Department of Labor Bureau of Labor Statistics, *Current Population
   Survey, Table 3: Employment Status of the Civilian Noninstitutional
   Population by Age, Sex, and Race, Annual Averages 2010* (Washington, D.C:
   GPO, 2011).
3 Jacqueline Scott, S. Dex, and H. Joshi (eds.), *Women and Employment:
   Changing Lives and New Challenges* (Cheltenham U.K.: Edward Elgar,
   2008).
4 Colette Dumas, "Integrating the Daughter into Family Business
   Management," *Entrepreneurship: Theory & Practice* 16(4), (1992): 41-56;
   C.F. Vera, and M.A. Dean, "An Examination of the Challenges Daughters
   Face in Family Business Succession," *Family Business Review* 18, (2005):
   321-346.

Chapter 2

1 Leon Danco, *Inside the Family Business* (Cleveland: Center for Family
   Business, 1980).
2 John Tagliabue, "Family Business Extended: In Italy New Generation of
   Leadership Looks Abroad," *The New York Times*, November 7, 1995.
3 Colette Dumas, "Understanding of the Father-Daughter and Father-Son
   Dyads in Family-Owned Business," *Family Business Review* 2(1), (Spring
   1989): 31-46.

Chapter 3

1 The sources drawn from in this discussion include: Helen B. Lewis and Judith L. Herman, "Anger in the Mother-Daughter Relationship," in T. Bernay and D.W. Cantor (eds.), *The Psychology of Today's Woman: New Psychoanalytic Visions* (Hillside, New Jersey.: Lawrence Erlbaum, 1986) 139-168; Carol Gilligan, *In a Different Voice* (Cambridge: Harvard University Press, 1982); Jean Baker Miller, *Toward a New Psychology of Women* (Boston: Beacon Press, 1976); Irene Stiver, *"Beyond the Oedipal Complex: Mothers and Daughters,"* in J. Jordan, A. Kaplan, J. Miller, I. Stiver, and J. Surrey (eds.), *Women's Growth in Connection* (New York: Guilford Press, 1991).

2 Chris Argyris, *Knowledge for Action* (San Francisco: Jossey Bass, 1993); Chris Argyris, *On Organizational Learning* (Cambridge, Mass.: Blackwell Publishers, 1992).

Chapter 4

1 The sources drawn from in this discussion include: Jerry Lewis, *How's Your Family?* (New York: Brunner/Mazel, 1989); Jerry Lewis, Robert Beavers, John Gossett, and Virginia Phillips, *No Single Thread: Psychological Health in Family Systems* (New York: Brunner/Mazel, 1976); Robert Beavers, "Healthy, Midrange, and Severely Dysfunctional Families," in F. Walsh (ed.), *Normal Family Processes* (New York: Guilford Press, 1982); Jules Riskin and M. McCorkle, "Non-Therapy Family Research and Change in Families: A Brief Clinical Research Communication," *Family Process*, 18 (1979): 161-62; Jules Riskin, "Research on Non-labeled Families: A Longitudinal Study," in F. Walsh (ed.), *Normal Family Process*, 3rd Edition (New York: Guilford Press, 2003); Peter Senge, *Fifth Disciple: The Art and Practice of the Learning Organization* (New York: Doubleday Currency, 1990).

Chapter 5

1 Mass Mutual American Family Business Survey, 2007. http://www.massmutual.com/mmfg/pdf/afbs.pdf

2 U.S. Department of Labor Bureau of Labor Statistics, *Women in the Labor Force: A Datebook* (Washington, DC: GPO, September, 2008).

3 Sally Helgesen, *The Female Advantage: Women's Ways of Leadership* (New York: Doubleday, 1990) 32.

4 Max Dupree, *Leadership Is an Art* (New York: Dell, 1989) 24.

5 Patricia Aburden and John Naisbitt, *Megatrends for Women; From Liberation to Leadership* (New York: Fawcett Columbine, 1992) 66.

6 David Packard, *The HP Way* (New York: Harper Business, 1995) 80.

7 Edgar Schein, "Leadership and Organizational Culture," in F. Hesselbein, M. Goldsmith, and R. Beckhard (eds.), *The Leader of the Future* (San Francisco: Jossey-Bass, 1996) 62.

Chapter 6

1 Schein, 69.

2 Helgesen, 145.

3 Rosabeth Kanter, "Collaborative Advantage: The Art of Alliances," *Harvard Business Review* (July-August 1994): 96-108.

4 "The Cow in the Ditch: How Anne Mulcahy Rescued Xerox," November 16, 2005. Knowledge@Wharton.com.

5 Judith Rosener, "Ways Women Lead," *Harvard Business Review* (November-December 1990): 121.

6 "America's Best Leaders," usnews.com 2010. http://politics.usnews.com/news/best-leaders/articles/2008/11/19/americas-best-leaders-in-america.

7 Warren Bennis, *On Becoming A Leader* (Reading, Mass.: Addison-Wesley, 1989).

8 Virginia Schein, "A Global Look at Psychological Barriers to Women's Progress in Management," *Journal of Social Issues* 57 (2001): 675-688.

9 Catalyst, *The Double-Bind Dilemma for Women in Leadership: Damned if You Do, Doomed if You Don't* (2007); Ashleigh Rosette, "Agentic Women and Communal Leadership: How Role Prescriptions Confer Advantage to Top Women Leaders," *Journal of Applied Psychology* 95(2), (March 2010): 221-235.

10 Catherine Copeland, James Driskell, and Edurdo Salas, "Gender and Reactions to Dominance," *Journal of Social Behavior and Personality* 10 (1995): 53-68.

11 Linda Carli, "Gender and Social Influence," *Journal of Social Issues* 57 (2001): 725-741; Susan Shackelford, W. Wood, and S.Worchel, "Behavioral Styles and the Influence of Women in Mixed-Sex Groups," *Social Psychology Quarterly* 59 (1996): 284-293.

12 Rochelle Sharpe, "As Leaders, Women Rule: New Studies Find that Female Managers Outshine Their Male Counterparts in Almost Every Measure," *Business Week* 74 (November 20, 2000). Retrieved from: http://www.businessweek.com/common_frames/ca.htm?/2000/00_47/b3708145.htm; M. Foschi, "Double Standards for Competence: Theory and Research," *Annual Review of Sociology* 26 (2000): 21-42.

13 Catalyst, *The Catalyst Census of Corporate Officers and Top Earners of the Fortune 500*, (December, 2008).

14 Ibid.

15 Ritch Sorenson, "The Contributions of Leadership Style and Practices to Family and Business Success," *Family Business Review* 13(3), (September 2000): 183-200.

16 Helgesen, 26.

17 Noel Tichy and Stratford Sherman, *Control Your Destiny or Someone Else Will* (New York: Doubleday, 1993).

18 Catalyst, *The Bottom Line: Connecting Corporate Performance and Gender Diversity* (2004).

19 Catalyst, *Advancing Women in Business: The Catalyst Guide* (San Francisco: Jossey-Bass, 1990) 31-35.

Chapter 7

1 U. S. Bureau of the Census, *Census Bureau Facts* (Washington, DC: GPO, February 23, 1999).

2 U. S. Department of Labor Statistics, *Current Population Survey, Employment Characteristics of Families, Table 5: Employment Status of the Population by Sex, Marital Status, and Presence and Age of Own Children under 18*, 2009-2010 *Annual Averages* (Washington DC: GPO, 2011).

3 Betty Carter, *Love, Honor, and Negotiate* (New York: Pocket Books, 1996) 55.

4 Shannon N. Davis and Theodore N. Greenstein, "Cross-National Variations in the Division of Household Labor," *Journal of Marriage and Family* 66(5), (December 2004): 1260-1271.

5 Suzanne Bianch, Melissa Milkie, Liana Sayer, and John Robisnon, "Is Anyone Doing the Housework? Trends in Gender Division of Household Labor," *Social Forces* 79(1), (September 2000): 191-228.

6 Jacqueline Scott, Shirley Dex, and Heather Joshi, "Women and Employment: Changing Lives and New Challenges," *British Journal of Industrial Relations* 49(1), (March 2011): 196-198.

7 Patricia Cole, "Women in Family Business," *Family Business Review* 10(4), (1997).

8 Jacqueline Scott, Rosemary Crompton and Clare Lyonette (eds.), *Gender Inequalities in the 21ˢᵗ Century* (Northampton, Mass: Edward Elgar, 2010).

9 David Allen, *Retaining Talent: A Guide to Analyzing and Managing Employee Turnover* (Society for Human Resource Management, 2008).

10 Dawn Carlson, "Health and Turnover of Working Mothers After Childbirth via the Work-Family Interface," *Journal of Applied Psychology* 96(5), (September 2011):1045-1054.

11 Carin Rubenstein, "The Joys of a 50/50 Marriage," *Working Woman* (April 1992): 60.

12 Carter, 66.

13 Geraldine Fabrikant, "Once Burned, the First Wife Is Twice Shy," *The New York Times*, October 27, 1996.

Chapter 9

1 Ellen Johnson-Sirleaf, interview with Margaret Warner, *MacNeil Lehrer Show*, PBS, April 2009.

2 Catalyst, *The Bottom Line: Connecting Corporate Performance and Gender Diversity* (2005).

3 Ibid.

4 Cole, 353-371.

5 Ernesto Poza & Messer, T., "Spousal Leadership and Continuity in the Family Firm," *Family Business Review* 14 (2001): 25-36.

6 Colette Dumas, "Women's Pathways to Participation and Leadership in the Family-owned Firm," *Family Business Review* 11(3), (1998): 219-228.

7 Matilde Salganicoff, "Women in Family Business: Challenges and Opportunities," *Family Business Review* 3(2), (1990b): 121-124.

8 Catalyst, *The Double-bind Dilemma for Women in Leadership: Damned if You Do, Doomed if You Don't* (2007).

9 Heather Haberman, and Sharon Danes, "Father-Daughter and Father-Son Family Business Management Transfer Comparison: Family FIRO Model Application," *Family Business Review* 20 (2007): 163-184.

10 Malcolm Gladwell, *The Outliers* (New York: Little, Brown and Company, 2008).

Suggested Reading

Aburden, Patricia, and Naisbitt, John. *Megatrends for Women*. New York: Fawcett Columbine, 1992.

Argyris, Chris. *Knowledge for Action: A Guide to Overcoming Barriers to Organizational Change*. San Francisco: Jossey-Bass, 1993.

Aronoff, Craig and Ward, John. *Family Meetings: How to Build a Stronger Family and a Stronger Business*. New York: Palgrave Macmillan, 2011.

Astrachan, Joseph and McMillan, Kristi. *Conflict and Communication in the Family Business*. Marietta, Georgia: Family Enterprise Publishers, 2003.

Bancroft, Nancy H. *The Feminine Quest for Success*. San Francisco: Berrett-Koehler, 1995.

Bennis, Warren. *On Becoming A Leader*. Reading, Mass.: Addison-Wesley, 1989.

Bennis, Warren, and Goldsmith, Joan. *Learning to Lead: A Workbook on Becoming a Leader*. London: Nicholas Brealey, 1997.

Carlock, Randel and Ward, John. *When Family Businesses are Best: The Parallel Planning Process for Family Harmony and Business Success*. New York: Palgrave Macmillan, 2010.

Carter, Elizabeth A., and . Peters, Joan K. *Love, Honor, and Negotiate*. New York: Pocket Books, 1996.

Danco, Leon. *Inside The Family Business*. Cleveland: The Center for Family Business, 1980.

Danco, Leon. *Outside Directors in the Family-Owned Business*. Cleveland: The Center for family Business, 1981.

DePree, Max. *Leadership Is An Art*. New York: Dell, 1989.

Fels, Anna. *Necessary Dreams*. New York: Anchor Books, 2002.

Gersick, Kelin. E., Davis, John A., McCollum Hampton, Marion, and Lansberg, Ivan. *Generation to Generation: Life Cycles of the Family Business*. Boston: Harvard Business School Press, 1997.

Gilligan, Carol. *In a Different Voice*. Cambridge, Mass.: Harvard University Press, 1982.

Fitzpatrick, John J. *The Human Side of Family Supermarket Succession: A Planning Guide*. Washington, D. C.: Food Marketing Institute, 1996.

Fitzpatrick, John J., and Francis, Anne E. *How Families Work: A Guide to Understanding Family Businesses.* Los Angeles: American College of Trust and Estate Counsel Foundation, 1993.

Handy, Charles. *The Age of Unreason.* Boston: Harvard Business School Press, 1990. .

———. *The Empty Raincoat, Making Sense of the Future.* London: Hutchinson, 1994.

Helgesen, Sally. *The Female Advantage: Women's Ways of Leadership.* New York: Doubleday Currency, 1990.

Hesselbein, Francis, Goldsmith, Marshall, Beckhard, Richard, eds. *The Leader of the Future.* San Francisco: Jossey-Bass, 1996.

———. *The Organization of the Future.* San Francisco: Jossey-Bass, 1997.

Jordan, Judith, Kaplan, Alexandra, Miller, Jean Baker, Stiver, Irene, and Surrey, Janet L. *Women's Growth in Connection.* New York: Guilford Press, 1991.

Kanter, Rosabeth. "Collaborative Advantage: The Art of Alliances," *Harvard Business Review* (July-August 1994) 96-108.

Kenyon-Rouvinez, Denise and Ward, John. *Family Business: Key Issues.* New York: Palgrave Macmillan, 2005.

Lansberg, Ivan. *Succeeding Generations: Realizing the Dream of Families in Business.* Boston: Harvard Business School Press,1999.

Lerner, Harriet Goldher. *The Dance of Anger.* New York: Harper and Row, 1985.

———. *Marriage Rules.* New York:Gotham, 2012.

Levinson, Daniel and Darrow, Charlotte. *The Seasons of a Man's Life.* New York: Knopf, 1988.

Levinson, Daniel, and Levinson, Judy. *The Seasons of a Woman's Life.* New York: Knopf, 1996.

Lewis, Jerry. *How's Your Family?* New York: Brunner/Mazel, 1989.

Lewis, Jerry M., Beavers, Robert W., Gossett, John, and Phillips, Virginia. *No Single Thread: Psychological Health in Family Systems.* New York: Brunner/Magel, 1976.

McGoldrick, Monica. *You Can Go Home Again.* New York: W. W. Norton and Co., 1995.

Mickel Brown, Lyn, and Gilligan, Carol. *Meeting at the Crossroads.* New York: Ballantine Books, 1992.

Miller, Jean Baker. *Toward a New Psychology of Women.* Boston: Beacon Press, 1976.

Packard, David, Kirby, David, and Lewis, Karen R. *The HP Way.* New York: Harper Business, 1995. Pipher, Mary Bray. *Reviving Ophelia.* New York: Putnam, 1994.

Schwartz, Felice N., and Zimmerman, Jean. *Breaking with Tradition.* New York: Warner Books, 1992.

Senge, Peter. *Fifth Disciple: The Art and Practice of the Learning Organization.* New York: Doubleday Currency, 1990.

Stiver, Irene. *Women's Growth in Connection.* New York: Guilford Press, 1991.

Ward, John. *Keeping the Family Business Healthy: How to Plan for Continuing Growth, Profitability, and Family Leadership.* San Francisco: Jossey-Bass, 1997.

Ward, John. *Perpetuating the Family Business: 50 Lessons Learned from Long-lasting, successful Families in Business.* NY: Palgrave Macmillan, 2004.

Wellington, Sheila, ed., *Advancing Women in Business: The Catalyst Guide.* San Francisco:Jossey-Bass, 1990.

Acknowledgments

Many people have contributed to the successful creation of *The Daughter Also Rises*, including some who helped before I knew there was going to be a book. I appreciate the many business families who shared their stories with me. Their willingness to share their business and private lives with me allowed this book to become a reality.

Leon Danco, founder of The Center for Family Businesses, and his wife, Katy, first convinced me that I had something important to say to young women in business families. I appreciate their encouragement and continued friendship.

I would not have started this project, and certainly not completed it, without the support of my business partner and husband, Jack Fitzpatrick. My primary editor, he read countless drafts, helped me focus my efforts, and lent me his humor when mine was gone. My daughter, Caitlin, an aspiring writer herself, took pride in what I was doing and never stopped bragging about her mother, the author. I liked that very much. My stepdaughters, Maia and Sarah, both mothers with careers, provided me examples of the struggles and satisfactions of combining work and family.

I am grateful to Bryan Welch, who had the confidence in my work to publish it, and to Janet Majure, my book editor, who suggested changes that made the book stronger. My book designer, Matthew Stallbaumer, was instrumental, as was my publicist, Marie Overfors. It is impossible to give credit to the countless friends and colleagues who contributed to this book. You know who you are. Thank you.

Endorsements

"*The Daughter Also Rises* provides indispensable, practical and timely advice for women working in both family-held and publicly owned organizations. I will strongly recommend this book to women who are beginning their business careers as well as those who are seeking to change or advance their careers."

Maxine Clark
Founder & Chief Executive Bear, Build-A-Bear Workshop,
ranked in the top 100 best companies to work for

"This is a wonderful book for all family business owners: It provides indispensable, timely and practical advice for integrating women into leadership positions. I am recommending it to all my family business owner friends and consultants to family businesses. While the book's primary audience is family businesses, there is a great deal of advice here that is applicable to all organizations."

Roger Greenberg
Chief Executive Officer, The Minto Group

"As a sibling in a family-owned business, *The Daughter Also Rises* taught me many lessons about the dynamics involved in generational and leadership change. My father and sister successfully navigated these waters, but mostly by trial and error—I can only imagine how much all of us would have benefited from Francis's insights. Most important to me, the book provides new ways of thinking about succession that apply to both small and large companies. As a President at Microsoft, succession was always a challenging topic at many levels of the organization, and Francis has plenty to teach those of us working in larger corporations. As a life-long learner, her examples of 'good enough fathering' and the relationship between mothers and daughters are valuable reading for their impact beyond the business. After all, if there's one thing I've learned, business is about relationships, and none are more important than those with family."

Robbie Bach
President, Entertainment and Devices Division (retired)
Microsoft Corporation

"Women have long been sources of family business success. Francis' book provides practical and illustrative case advice for those seeking a greater level of accomplishment. Through specific examples and experience-based wisdom, Dr. Francis provides a guidebook for women who are considering or currently engaged in family business roles. It is well organized so that one can go to parts of chapters for a valuable perspective on a specific matter, yet get drawn into reading well beyond a search topic. This is a must read for women in business families, yet also the parents, aunts and uncles, cousins, siblings and non-family managers who will be well served by advancing the development and careers of women in the family business."

Stephen McClure, Ph.D.
Principal, The Family Business Consulting Group

"This book is a must-read for daughters of business owners and for family business consultants. As a professor, global consultant to family-owned businesses and father of a successful 26-year-old businesswoman, I consider *The Daughter Also Rises* a very valuable resource. You will not find prescriptions and models here, but an honest collection of stories from courageous young women who have made the journey into the family's business. You will also find Anne Francis' insightful questions for reflection. By going inside, with the aid of Dr. Francis, you may very well find the maps most relevant to your own journey. The opportunity is great; many family business owners are finally realizing that their daughters are a most valuable resource in their efforts for family business continuity."

Ernesto Poza
Professor of Global Entrepreneurship and Family Enterprise,
Thunderbird School of Global Management
Owner, E.J. Poza Associates, Inc.

"During the time I was considering a mid-life career change, I read *The Daughter Also Rises*. It was instrumental in my making the decision to join my family's business. The exercises and thought-provoking questions that Francis asks throughout the book helped me to evaluate my strengths, weaknesses, and work style, as well as my relationships with family members already involved in the business. It is a wonderful resource for any woman interested in becoming a more active participant in business with family. I heartily recommend it!"

Becky Robb Dickinson
Vice-President, The Robb Company

"*The Daughter Also Rises* explores situations everyone will recognize and provides valuable ways for thinking about them with helpful ideas for navigating the myriad of family business relationships. The book raises a myriad of important questions every daughter and her family should ask themselves. Francis answers these questions with practical and sensitive advice."

Joseph H. Astrachan, Ph.D.
Cox Family Enterprise Center
Former Editor, Family Business Review

"*The Daughter Also Rises* is an insightful look at the challenges that daughters face in leadership and management of their family businesses. Untold benefits will accrue to family business colleagues that read this book."

Andrew Keyt
Executive Director, Loyola University Chicago Family Business Center
President, Family Business Network North America

"For all business collections."

—Library Journal

"Anne Francis probes an especially thorny phenomenon in *The Daughter Also Rises*. The author's language is refreshingly free of psychobabble, taking on daunting psychological subject matter with admirable clarity. For ambitious women and the people who love them, Francis offers a roadmap to uncharted territory."

—BookPage

Index

Childcare, 77, 139, 186, 188, 189,
190, 243, 278-279. *See also*
Motherhood; Working mothers
day-to-day, 275
outside, 78
provision for, 278-279
working mothers and, 189-191
Child rearing, 15-19, 70, 76-81, 139-
140, 171, 175, 199
Circular thinking, 127-128
Collaboration, 19, 39, 72, 106, 120, 143
157, 158, 159, 163, 256, 286
Commitment, 140, 149, 178, 197, 202,
253, 256, 289, 292
Communication, 38, 104, 105, 106,
114, 119, 123, 126, 154-155,
156, 284
problems, 37-39, 42-43, 47-56, 106,
281-283
style, 157-158, 166-167,169
triangles, 279-281
Comper Anthony, 174
Competence, 135, 136-152, 245, 250,
163, 164, 273, 176, 289
Competition, 13, 69, 73, 81, 82, 84,
141, 169, 189, 225
father and son, 40-41, 42
women and, 81-84, 141
Competitive, 138, 139, 167
edge, 139, 190
Conflict, 76, 108, 148, 149
family relationships and, 108-109,
112-117, 124-126, 128-132, 194-
199, 281-283
father and daughter, 37-38, 44-45,
47-55, 162, 164-165, 166-167
father and son, 119-126
mother and daughter, 69-70, 73-74,
85-89, 90-97
Consultant, 9, 10, 18, 37, 47, 50,
78-79, 92, 105, 122, 123, 202,
206-208, 256. *See also* Family
business consultants
Cooperation, 84, 141, 142, 165

D

Daughters. *See also* Mothers; Fathers
dependent, 44, 46-47, 48, 49, 50
fathers and, 12, 15, 33-34, 41-63,
119-124, 127, 162, 165, 166-
167, 172
mothers and, 65-101, 194-199
sons versus, 8-9, 17

E

Efficient problem solving, 117-119
Entrepreneurs, 25, 62, 103, 108-110,
111, 145, 147
assets of, 27
daughters of, 12, 41-61, 119-129,
165
fathers as, 16, 31-32, 35-36, 165
liabilities of, 27
loneliness of, 29-30
paternalism, 32-34
persistence of, 31-32, 34
self-confidence of, 30-31
self-reliance of, 26, 27-30, 34
sons of, 39-41, 119-124
Entitlement, 16, 125, 127, 288-289
Envy, 69, 83, 84
Expectations, 29, 33, 69, 177, 194, 221,
224

F

Family
assessment of, 21, 115, 118, 126,
223, 224, 227, 234
balancing business and, 17, 28, 35,
47-56, 76-81, 103-132, 181-
187, 189-191, 274-275, 278-279
beliefs of, 8, 9, 10, 11, 12, 13, 14,
15, 17, 19, 20, 104, 172, 223
boundaries between work and,
284-286
career and, 12-17, 33, 76-81, 171-
174
communication in, 76-81, 176-178,
279-281
competition in, 141, 258

About the Author

Anne Francis, Ph.D, is one of North America's leading family business consultants. She and her husband, Jack Fitzpatrick, are co- founders of the Family Business Resource Center, a consulting firm that provides long-term solutions to family businesses and the people behind them. Partners in business and marriage, Francis and Fitzpatrick understand firsthand the problems, pitfalls, and satisfactions of working and living together, and business families benefit from their unique perspective and consulting experience. They also provide executive and organizational consultations to publically traded companies.

Francis writes about business families from a dual perspective: She grew up in a large Midwest family with a business-founder father, and has worked professionally with families and businesses for over thirty years. She knows that in a family business, orderly and effective succession transition happens only by addressing the business needs and the needs of the family behind it. By cultivating the capabilities of daughters as well as sons, the likelihood significantly increases that the family will select the right leaders among its own best and the brightest to take the business into the next generation. Francis wrote—and revised— *The Daughter Also Rises* to help women take responsibility for their professional development and overcome potential roadblocks that might keep them out of the corner office.

Francis began her career working with families at crisis

points in their lives. She then joined the Menninger Clinic, where she provided employee assistance programs to businesses, consulted to public and private corporations, and provided executive consultations to senior managers and their spouses. She held a position with the Menninger Leadership Center, where she conducted seminars for family business leaders, their families and advisors, and lectured widely on how to thrive as a business and a business family. From business families she learned about the kind of person who turns a dream into a business reality and the kind of family that keeps the dream alive.

Francis is a Kansas native and she holds a master's degree from Kansas University and a doctoral degree from Kansas State University. She received postgraduate training at the Georgetown Family Center in Washington, D.C. She was a clinical supervisor in the Karl Menninger School of Psychiatry for ten years. She formerly directed Employee Assistance Programs through the Menninger Clinic. Francis is licensed as a clinical social worker and a marital and family therapist. She has a daughter, two stepdaughters, and three grandsons.

Reach her at: www.FamilyBusinessResourceCenter.org